200 Plays for GCSE and A-Level Performance

200 Plays for GCSE and A-Level Performance
A Drama Teacher's Guide

Jason Hanlan

methuen | drama
LONDON • NEW YORK • OXFORD • NEW DELHI • SYDNEY

METHUEN DRAMA
Bloomsbury Publishing Plc
50 Bedford Square, London, WC1B 3DP, UK
1385 Broadway, New York, NY 10018, USA
29 Earlsfort Terrace, Dublin 2, Ireland

BLOOMSBURY, METHUEN DRAMA and the Methuen Drama logo are trademarks of Bloomsbury Publishing Plc

First published in Great Britain 2021

Copyright © Jason Hanlan, 2021

Jason Hanlan has asserted his right under the Copyright, Designs and Patents Act, 1988, to be identified as author of this work.

For legal purposes the Acknowledgements on p. vi constitute an extension of this copyright page.

Cover design: Charlotte Daniels
Cover image: Backstage at the Dominion Theatre, London, 1986
(© Nobby Clark / ArenaPAL)

All rights reserved. No part of this publication may be reproduced or transmitted in any form or by any means, electronic or mechanical, including photocopying, recording, or any information storage or retrieval system, without prior permission in writing from the publishers.

Bloomsbury Publishing Plc does not have any control over, or responsibility for, any third-party websites referred to or in this book. All internet addresses given in this book were correct at the time of going to press. The author and publisher regret any inconvenience caused if addresses have changed or sites have ceased to exist, but can accept no responsibility for any such changes.

A catalogue record for this book is available from the British Library.

A catalog record for this book is available from the Library of Congress.

ISBN: HB: 978-1-3501-4661-7
PB: 978-1-3501-4662-4
ePDF: 978-1-3501-4663-1
eBook: 978-1-3501-4664-8

Typeset by RefineCatch Limited, Bungay, Suffolk

To find out more about our authors and books visit www.bloomsbury.com and sign up for our newsletters.

CONTENTS

Acknowledgements   vi

Part One

1   About this Book   3

2   Knowing Your Students and the Skills Audit   8

3   Which Play?   12

4   Design Options   15

5   Performance Exams (*The Bottom Line*)   30

6   Performance Spaces   34

7   Shakespeare   39

8   The Language of the Theatre   45

Part Two

Listing of 200 Plays   63
    Female-only Plays   63
    Male-only Plays   73
    Plays with Mixed Cast   83
    Plays with Flexible Casting   153
    The Ten Shakespeare Plays   158

Index of Plays   165
Index of Playwrights   169

ACKNOWLEDGEMENTS

Come, sit down every mother's son, and rehearse your parts.

I would like to acknowledge the 10,000 plus students and their splendid teachers from every part of the UK and beyond, who entertained me with vast helpings of excellent theatre as their visiting moderator. My own drama students, who for the last 25 years have inspired and proven to me that I was supposed to be a drama teacher.

My father, for whom 'making art' was everything.

Special thanks and love to my wife, Monica, who always believed I could write this book, even when I was convinced I could not.

PART ONE

1

About this Book

- 'Can you recommend a play for 21 keen girls and two timid boys that is fun yet serious as they're a mixed bunch?'
- 'I have a class of 14 boys and three very able girls.'
- 'Six girls.'
- '21 girls and one boy.'
- 'All boys. No girls.'
- 'Three boys only.'
- 'One lad who's a bit manic and three shy girls.'
- 'They're very keen, they all want to act, do costume, do lighting, do very little, do something physical, musical, lyrical, satirical.'
- 'Oh, but it needs to be challenging, yet simple, and preferably pre-19th century but engaging and relevant and topical, and popular and, available in print ... You see, my group always get an A* in everything they do because they're talented and theatrical, quite zany, yet oh so practical, their *Rosencrantz and Guildenstern* was really quite fantastical, all except for Billy who doesn't talk and does lights.'
- 'And the Head would like something non-political yet thought-provoking, and ... erm ... gender appropriate without any bad language, yet funny and dark but no violence, of course, and can we do it in the local woods?'

Does any of this sound familiar? These are just a few I've heard from drama teachers seeking advice on selecting the best material.

A Bit about Me

When I was lad of 15, Drama was about doing the school play. The Drama club that met on Tuesday lunchtimes was where kids with names like Tristan and Jason went to eat their sandwiches and avoid being beaten up. There was no O-level Drama, and in my school, 'Theatre' was a lesson once a week with an English teacher who got us to suspend disbelief while she marked essays. She never asked us to be trees and wouldn't have noticed if we had. That hour was by far the best of the long school week, and I decided that I too would like to be a Drama teacher. After leaving school, I got a bit sidetracked by the big wide world for 12 years or so, and by the time I got myself into university, Drama was taken far more seriously. My Bachelor of Education degree was actually intended for Drama teachers! Well, it was the late '80s by then! I qualified in 1994 and went on to teach in two large comprehensives in the UK, eventually becoming Head of Drama and, later, Performing Arts. Along the way I worked as an LEA advisor for Drama and a teacher trainer. I became a moderator fairly early on, solely as INSET for myself. Although I initially intended to be a moderator for just one year, I enjoyed it so much I did it for 14 more!

Going in to hundreds of other teachers' schools over the years to see thousands of students demonstrate their skills as performers and designers gave me a privileged insight into what works and why. I unashamedly took the best practices and materials I witnessed and shared them with my own students and staff. Now I've gone part-time, I reckon it's time to share with the wider Drama teaching community!

The first time a moderator/examiner walked into my studio to moderate my marking of my students' live performances, I was terrified. What if I'd got it all wrong? What if I believed them to be amazing, incredible, outstanding students and they were just mediocre or worse? What if, because they were hard-working and dedicated to my subject, I was blind to glaring faults? What if the weaker ones were in fact great and I'd failed to see it. What if I was wrong? The 21st time a moderator walked into my Drama studio to moderate my students, she had been trained by me and I was a senior moderator. I had conducted over 2000 moderations in schools throughout the UK and Channel Islands, led standardisation meetings for hundreds of Drama teachers, and I was still terrified.

Looking through my records of school visits for the Exam Board I found myself counting: 870 school visits to moderate 2344 performances; 1253 demonstrations of stage make up, set design and props; over a thousand costume designs drawn and realised; more than 10,000 students plus my own, performing, designing, lighting, singing, dancing and making art.

It is important to state that this book is *not* a collection of my 200 favourite plays with a brief critique! I'm no theatre critic! This is a record of what works for students, a list of plays that enable talent, ignite imagination, and challenge all abilities.

At the start of each exam season I armed myself with a large, crisp new A4 artist's notebook, into which I recorded every centre visit; marking and writing a justification for every mark I awarded against each performer; recording each performance seen, every design drawn, modelled and realised; making notes on how and why pieces worked and occasionally didn't. I noted early on that the best work I was seeing had been led by teachers who knew the play well and had an expertise/passion for playwright and practitioner. Teachers who knew their students and encouraged them to share the process of choosing from a range of challenging texts were consistently presenting work of excellence. It also became clear that teachers who had a good knowledge of the specification and shared the language of the marks criteria with their students were providing another vital element.

It is crucial that you, as a Drama teacher, know a play before sharing it with your students. It is equally important that you know your students before you present them with choices (see Chapter 2). The choosing of material should be a process in which students make selections from a pre-selected body of works, with whatever guidance each individual/group might require. My mantra is that there are three things a teacher of Drama must know: the *students*, the *material* and the *specification*!

It is essential that students understand their chosen extract(s) in the context of the whole play. They should be exposed to as wide a variety as possible, but within a carefully considered timeframe and always within the teacher's expertise.

This book is divided into two parts. Part 1 consists of eight chapters that link with the 200 plays listed in Part 2, exploring how teachers can enable students to succeed in performance exams – by having the best material and advice possible. Part 1 explores the thinking behind the performance exam, from finding the right material for your students to ensuring fruitful preparation and appreciation of a play. Coupled with a good working knowledge of theatrical language and an understanding of what the examiner will be looking for, we can guide students in their choices of the material best suited to their talents and passions.

In this book I will make no specific reference to any one of the main Exam Boards or their specifications. However, I will try to reflect the tone/language they use. OFQUAL requirements are referred to more directly as they inform the requirements of all the Boards. It is the responsibility of teachers to be completely familiar with their chosen specification. If you're not sure, check with the Board.

Each play in this book is one I have seen on a school visit or used with my own students. If I haven't included your favourite play, it's probably because I haven't seen it. I haven't, of course, seen everything, and not everything I've seen is included here. It is also entirely possible that I have omitted some best-loved pieces or failed to mention a great scene or two. Here, I'm suggesting material that works with 16- to 19-year-olds for the scripted performance element of their exam and *not* for the school play.

Part 2 is what this book is really about. It offers 200 plays I've seen work for performance/design students at GCSE and GCE levels. The list is the result of thirty years of teaching Drama, training Drama teachers and working as a visiting examiner/moderator. The list is not about studying the plays; rather, it is a tool to guide teachers through the challenges of selecting the right material for the right group/student.

Each play is presented in the following way:

	Title & publisher	*Title of the play*	Publisher of version I used (there may be others)
	Playwright/Date	Playwright/adaptor/translator	Date of first recorded performance
	Casting	Number of Male : Female parts plus observations on gender/casting	GCSE or GCE With a brief note on ability/challenge
	Notes, guidance and considerations for teachers/students	**Description:** What kind of play it is. **Summary:** A brief description of what happens in the play. **Where:** Where the action takes place. Country followed by a description of the location and setting. **When:** When the action takes place (not when it was written). **Themes:** The major driving themes of the play (and some less obvious ones). **Notes:** Observations, specific to this play, on what works well, as well as tips based on what I have seen in schools. **Design/tech notes:** Advice/suggestions for design students. Some plays may not present much of a design challenge whereas others are rich in opportunities. This is where I make such recommendations. **Warnings:** An important section. See notes below this chart. **Workshop/rehearsal/ideas/notes:** Based on my own experience of the piece on my visits, this section suggests some rehearsal/workshop ideas and at times a suitable practitioner. At times the suggestions may seem oddball or contradictory. Again, it's based on what I've seen work. **Research:** Any research that may be relevant. **Resources:** Any free online resources I have found with my students.	
	Section or scene(s)	A list of suggested sections of the text which produce good results. Scenes rich in dialogue/word-play or the best for physical work. **Monologues** or **Duologues** which provide opportunities will also be noted in this section.	

The book suggests enabling, trusted material, yet each play comes with a warning section. The warnings given are general and not restricted to 'Contains adult themes!' The comments may relate to casting, staging, age appropriateness, language or content. Sometimes it's a cautionary note based on a common mistake or misconception. It may carry a warning that the play is used by Exam Boards for a specific task, in which case you should check your current specification. The warnings 'Contains a car accident' or 'Refers to a suicide' may seem insignificant – until you have a student in the group who has experienced such an event. Unlike asking someone to watch a film containing a car crash, in a Drama production we're encouraging the students to get involved, empathise, enact, relive. You know your students, and you must check that the material you are working with is safe for them. Always bear in mind that schools differ on what they deem appropriate!

Exam Boards also differ, and this collection of materials is subject to the rules of your specification. If in any doubt, consult your support person at the Board. Some play combinations are not permitted due to clashes with set texts; again, you should check for this. In any case, you will be required to notify your board of your choice of performance texts, for which there is a deadline. Your exams officer should be aware of this.

Remember: exams are different, but if you want the students to perform publicly you *must* abide by all copyright rules and permissions. This also applies to any music that is used, whether recorded or played live.

Some of the plays listed in this book have much larger casts than an Exam Board will normally permit. They are included in order to give greater choices. However, do bear in mind the number of participants when making selections of scenes/extracts.

Where I suggest an exam entry level – GCSE or GCE – I am very aware that we all encounter GCSE groups that could easily take on GCE-style scripts. When deciding whether a piece is appropriate, we should always consider the maturity of the students and their ability to cope with some subjects/themes.

The sections or scenes I suggest are proposed on the basis of what I have seen working well. It is not intended as a list of the 'best bits'. All choices should ultimately be made by students under the teacher's guidance, having studied the *entire* play.

Many plays I mark as suitable for 'a range of abilities' or for a 'flexible cast' often refer to multi-role pieces. Such works are a very good way of enabling students to demonstrate a range of skills. However, in some cases the roles should be shared out in a way that allows the less able student to expand and demonstrate their abilities. Plays like *Adrian Mole* or *Animal Farm* lend themselves nicely to this, whereas plays like *Teechers* or *Our Country's Good* and *Two* should never have multi-roles split, as this is contrary to the express intentions of the playwright. When I say 'mixed ability', I mean there are a number of challenging roles and some less challenging.

When I refer to 'similar abilities', I am suggesting that the cast should be evenly matched and that the piece as a whole will suffer if one performer is obviously much more (or less) able than the other(s).

As you will see, the charts appearing in the following pages do not contain write-ups of the plays. Similarly, they do not offer literary critiques of the pieces treated. Instead, the charts supply a handy reference guide to 200 great plays, listing suggestions as to the needs of each piece and what it can offer your students. The pieces range from 480 BCE and the Western world's oldest surviving play, to material of the moment. I have sought to include theatre from all over the world, from many different cultures and religions. I believe that students should be just as well-prepared for their performance exams as they would be for their literature, maths or science exams. It is my hope that the materials gathered here inspire and help influence the choices you and your students make.

2

Knowing Your Students and the Skills Audit

Know Your Students

When I was a brand new, fresh-out-of-the-box Drama teacher I went into my first GCSE Drama class armed with the memory of my favourite plays from university and a scattering of tattered titles the last Drama teacher had obviously inherited from the English department. My 'uni plays' were fresh in my mind and of the moment. The inherited selection, although of a good pedigree, was rather less topical. As a class we discussed each of the available works and groups formed through a process of student reasoning: 'We're mates and this one has a fight in it', or 'No way I'm working with her' and 'I hate Shakespeare so I'm doing the one with the red cover'. I was passionate about 'my' plays and I knew them all (well most of them). But what I didn't know was the students, some of whom had their own ideas of what they should perform.

Allowing students to have free rein to pick a play to perform for their Drama exam is inviting calamity! There is so much out there, and without strong guidance and training many students are drawn to the over-dramatic, the sensational and the downright unsuitable. If you tell your students they can choose whatever they like and then you impose your choices, they will feel less guided and more 'Told what to do'. It is far better to foster a love for certain works, styles and genres (based on your own expertise and passion). In this way students feel they share the decision and will explore it as performers or technicians with genuine interest.

In order to achieve this, you must know your students. If you have taught them in KS3, you will know them enough to at least understand group dynamics and individual abilities. If they are new to you, as is often the case, it is vital in term 1 of the exam year that you get to know them as quickly as possible. Make sure you ask:

1. What have they done before?
2. Is there anyone in the group they work well with? (This will be their view.)

3 Do they have a knowledge of the techniques used for the making of Drama?
4 Can they use these techniques to communicate meaning to an audience?
5 Do they know why playwrights use the techniques they do?
6 Can they name any practitioners associated with these techniques?

At the beginning of 'getting-to-know you' process I typically choose a simple monologue and ask the students to work in directing pairs, with each student being responsible for the other person's performance. I find it useful that they all have the same monologue (common currency). Learning the monologue becomes the business of one lesson, where we all learn the script together in a shared circle. I have used, for example, PUCK's Epilogue to *A Midsummer Night's Dream* ('If we shadows have offended', Act 5 Scene 1) because it is genderless and has a rhyming pattern. You can, of course, choose anything you think the group will find accessible. With a script learned, the class can use the text as a basis for testing and improving their skills, returning to their common monologue to workshop anything from direct audience address to status games. Having a monologue in common allows you to make a point and/or give examples in role. You might perform the speech as a shy five-year-old, as an old woman, as a man awaiting execution, whilst putting your tie on, making a cup of tea, walking through a minefield. You might treat the monologue as a piece of pantomime, naturalism, physical theatre, surrealism. You might use alienation, high status, low status, using Brecht, Stanislavski, Artaud, Boal, Berkoff or DV8.

These workshops will enable you to begin thinking about the participants' abilities/skills, group dynamics and suitable materials. It also gets the students thinking about their preferences and strengths/weaknesses. Drama is an exam subject and performances are marked to a set of criteria. Students must be made aware of these criteria and begin preparations for their final performance pieces from day one, as they certainly would in any other subject.

'Students will be assessed on their ability to apply theatrical skills to realise artistic intentions in live performance (AO2)'.

The Skills Audit

One very useful exercise is to carry out what I call a 'skills audit' of the students. OK, they all want to 'do Drama', but what other skills do they have? Often a student's skill in another subject can lend itself to a piece of theatre and enhance both the piece as a whole and their individual grades. Students seldom volunteer what they do in other subjects. Why would they?

And, unless you are their form tutor or watch every celebration assembly, why would you know? Students have interests outside of school too, and the skills audit is an ideal way of uncovering those extra skills/interests that may contribute to a piece of theatre. So, what are these skills? Some more obviously lend themselves to theatre, others less so. Students with an identified skill or talent often possess confidence, and this in itself is transferable and enabling.

The skills audit explores the idea that students can bring other skills to Drama, ones which they may never otherwise reveal. During the audit it is important to explore how the various skills within the group can be sensitively exploited by a cast seeking to make their own artistic statement with their chosen piece. The acrobat, the ballet or street dancer, singer, musician, amateur magician, parkour runner, martial arts student, juggler, tightrope artist, or those with another language, sign language or mime. And that is not to mention the technical and design options for artists, carpenters, costume designers and makers, sound people, lighting people, DJs – they all have transferable skills. Sometimes the comfort students feel when using their own expertise in a performance context enables them to overcome nerves and become bolder artists and help others. The mantle of the expert!

Students are imaginative, creative, artistic, emotional, empathetic, generous, agile, adaptable and multi-talented. Sometimes they simply don't tell us! We must enable them to bring all their talents to the process of making art. Their artistic intent will be easier to demonstrate when they share as a group. To be clear, I'm not suggesting putting a karate scene in *A Midsummer Night's Dream* or force a dance sequence into *Blue Remembered Hills*, but there is always scope for skills to be transferred. I have, for instance, watched a ballet-trained, year 10 student portray abuse through dance in Sarah Daniels' *Beside Herself* in such a way that everyone in the room was moved to tears. 'Convey meaning to an audience, sensitive to the needs of the piece, artistic intent obvious.' A boy singing in *Grimm's Tales*; a banjo player as Feste in *Twelfth Night*; bokken swords in *Macbeth*; acrobats in *Bouncers*. The energy onstage can be electrifying when the skills of students are utilised, and the whole piece benefits from such expertise being sensitively incorporated from the start – though not as an added-on extra or as the means of covering a scene change.

It is important that the skills audit takes place at the start of term. Ask your students: What other things do you do? Sometimes they are reluctant to share, especially if it's a new group, but they will eventually really warm to it. Students also like to inform on or remind each other. One student's comment, 'What about your parkour stuff?', led to some jaw-dropping scenes in our sections from *The Curious Incident*. So, encourage students to show you and the class what they can do. They have chosen Drama, so they probably won't need too much encouragement! Some students, of course, will need the example of others.

I had a student in a Drama group who was really into tango. She went to classes every week, entered competitions, won trophies, but never told anyone at school. I only found out when a rehearsal clashed with one of her competitions. I suggested the play *Paper Flowers*, which features a number of tango sequences. She wanted to work on costume, but she choreographed and shared her knowledge/passion with those who went on to perform the tango scenes. The results were astounding – a true collaboration I could so easily have missed.

My point here is that getting to know your students will enable you to utilise the list of 200 plays in Part 2 more fully, and in new and creative ways.

3

Which Play?

Guiding Students in Choosing the Best Material

Half-way through my first year of teaching I inherited a year 11 class containing a group of three students with a real desire to perform Godber's *Teechers*. (Their original teacher had left them mid-January for a job in China.) They had 'done' *Julius Caesar* and *Antigone* and just wanted to laugh at something – anything! So, like thousands before, the class set about selecting a comedy, because comedies are fun and because it's easy to make people laugh, right? I recall we had by then acquired multiple copies of *Bouncers*, *Shakers*, *Stags and Hens*, *Teechers*, a sprinkling of Ayckbourn plays, and one copy of *Abigail's Party*. Selections were made (by the students) based on group size and gender (more than anything else), but the numbers worked and everyone was happy – for a while. Eventually it became apparent that comedy is not for everyone, and that comic timing is, well, all about timing. Some were delighted with their 'chosen' pieces, others less so. As a class, they learned the hard way that they needed to identify with the chosen material and engage with it, not just because it was 'funny'. As a teacher, I learned that for my students to have the best possible experience and to achieve the best possible grades it was essential that I, 'the expert', should guide them with their choice of performance pieces. It is, of course, wonderful when students really love a play or genre, but it may not be appropriate to their skill set. A work may be too demanding, not demanding enough, or simply a poor choice. This was still my first year. Later, OFQUAL would remind us that: 'Teachers must ensure all performance and design students have sufficient opportunity to demonstrate their chosen specialism fully, enabling them to access the full range of marks. This includes giving careful consideration not only to the choice of text, but to the size of groups and performance space.'

What works for one student may not, of course, work for another. Only you know your students, and in order to enable them to perform at their best, they must be guided toward the right material, the right group and the best design concepts. Students should be involved in the choice of material, but only from a selection made by you and guided by a number of factors. Each group will then be in a position to participate in workshops and rehearsals that enable their pieces to take shape.

Text and Extract Choices – *The Bottom Line!*

Exam Boards often make changes to the general rubric and individual specifications. What remains constant is that centres have a choice when selecting texts for performance – with some restrictions. You should build up a selection that you are familiar with and which conforms to the list below.

The selected plays must:

- be professionally commissioned/produced;
- be substantial and the required length for the level of exam;
- offer opportunities for performers and designers to demonstrate their interpretations of content, themes and characterisations;
- challenge theatrically, at the appropriate level;
- be age-appropriate for practical study (Head of Centre);
- not clash with or contravene any prohibited play combinations. (It is important that you check your specification on this latter point!)

Which Extract?

Once the choice of play(s) has been made, begin the task of selecting key extracts, as a group. Start by exploring the material practically. Try to focus on two or three key sections of the play which are significant to the play as a whole. Each section must be 'substantial', a term clearly defined in your chosen specification and dependent on group size. Students should study the sections in depth, taking time to thoroughly explore and interpret each one. Performers should read the play from the point of view of their character. Identify how much of each section needs to be performed to meet minimum performance times. The minimum performance time varies depending on the number of performers in a group. Large groups are likely to need to perform the whole section they have studied. If the performance is a monologue, the performer will only need to perform part of the section they have studied.

Text-Based Performance/Performance Texts. AO2

This component deals with developing knowledge, understanding and skills in exploring and performing from a chosen performance text. Students will interpret the text, rehearse and refine key extracts, leading to a final performance. They should demonstrate a wide range of acting and/or design skills to communicate their interpretation in performance.

What You Must Provide

As far as performance material is concerned, you must be able to provide guidance and assistance and make available everything that will enable your students to:

- investigate a range of play scripts suited to their skills and preferences (see Part 2 of this book for suggestions);
- research the script's context, historically and culturally, with a genre/style in mind;
- research professional practice for performance design;
- select extracts that will challenge appropriately (have examples to hand);
- decide upon a design specialism if they so desire (some pieces lend themselves to a particular design option, see Part 2 for suggestions);
- select a variety of appropriate rehearsal/workshop ideas (as shown in Part 2);
- use their research to refine chosen design ideas;
- rehearse and refine their character(s) (supported by guidance and feedback);
- develop an overall design concept for performance;
- develop and influence the group's artistic intention.

4

Design Options

- 'Oh, and this is Brian, he will be doing the lighting for the group.' (Brian didn't want to do the lighting for that or any other group. Brian wanted to be in *Bouncers* but there were no roles left, so we popped him into lighting for the group doing *Blood Brothers*. Brian actually hates *Blood Brothers*; he also hates his group.)
- 'Hannah is doing the costumes for *My Mother Said I Never Should*.' (All of them?!)
- 'Jo is doing make-up because she's not here much, and Tom doesn't like to talk so we hid him behind the sound desk.'
- 'This is Stephanie, she has a real interest in set design and has worked with her group, even over the initial choice of play.'

In the same way that you wouldn't cast Jack as Lord Capulet half-way through rehearsals and simply tell him to 'catch up', Brian, Hannah and the other non-performing students should be involved from the very start, be as interested and ready to learn about the skills and vocabulary of their 'chosen' option as the performers in the group. To put it another way, design options are not 'other' options – they involve important decisions and require levels of motivation that are fundamental to a successful production and, with that, examination achievement.

It is essential that you, as a Drama teacher, enable design option students to be a part of the artistic interpretation from the very outset. Groups should be empowered by involving everyone, with the contribution of the design candidate(s) being as obvious and powerful in the final piece as that of the performers. They should have equal say in decisions made about the selection of the piece, the artistic interpretation being obvious through technical aspects as well as performance.

This chapter covers each of the various design options for the scripted performance. Since these elements may vary across the different Exam Boards, I have included all of them. They are: set design and props; costume and make-up/hair; sound; lighting; puppets; and multimedia. (There is a directing option at GCE level with one Board.) Be aware of your specification's requirements regarding design students.

Designers are expected to work collaboratively with a group of performers and other designers, within their chosen area of design. Different Boards and exams have their own rules on the number of design students per group and the combinations of design/performance options a student can take within the performance exam. If a student is assessed in the role of a designer, it is their *design skill* and its success that is the focus of the assessment and not their technical competence in the operation of any equipment.

The performance texts should provide sufficient challenges for design students to enable them to meet the demands of the component. Design elements should be suitably theatrical and work in sympathy with other design features. Part 2 of this book gives suggestions (where appropriate) on how atmosphere, mood and tone can be influenced by technical decisions in each play.

Designers should learn to develop and articulate their design concepts and use information from their research to develop ideas for performance. They should be able to take creative design decisions about their own work in the context of a performance to an audience. Design students should also consider the era, style and genre of the piece throughout the process and above all contribute to the group realising their artistic intentions.

Bear in mind with technical options that you must provide a performance space which offers sufficient room for technicians as well as performers (and their audience). Teachers will need to offer guidance on working within any specified budgets.

All designs should also take into consideration health and safety implications as appropriate.

The Design Options

Lighting

Lighting has a variety of functions, which include indicating time, showing location and the communication of meaning, either abstract or symbolic. Lighting should direct the audience's focus towards or away from a particular character or piece of the action and create mood/atmosphere and enhance a performance. It doesn't simply illuminate a performance, it informs an audience.

Being able to see what is happening on stage is essential, but tone and mood can also be created by subtle use of light or shadow. It is an immensely technical area and therefore it's important to have a thorough working knowledge of what the different basic types of lights/lamps do. There are many pieces of lighting equipment and each one creates a different effect. The angles and distances at which lights are hung are as important as colour, tone and intensity. The creation of shadow on a character's face can change the whole meaning of a piece, just as a change of vocal pace or pitch by the performer can radically change the force and mood of the words being spoken.

Students who select lighting design as their specialism will be expected to:

1. learn how to design and realise lighting that creatively contributes to the overall effect of their group's performance;
2. communicate the group's intended meaning and artistic intent to its audience;
3. develop the ability to design and realise lighting which suggests, time, place, mood and atmosphere;
4. develop the ability to design and realise a variety of effects, such as angle, intensity, fades and cross fades, blackouts, gobos, gels and colour, filters, projections and gauze and the use of shadow and projections;
5. understand and select the right equipment for each situation and know how to position it in order to realise their intended outcome;
6. build a working knowledge of the types of equipment available, including the range of lanterns and lamps;
7. develop an understanding of rigging, positioning, angling and focusing the different types of equipment;
8. adhere to the latest safe working practices.

If you offer your students the lighting design option you must ensure they have the appropriate equipment needed to realise their designs. This should include access to a minimum of three different types of lantern, lighting bars or stands with T bars from which to hang lanterns, a minimum of twelve independently controllable channels and a lighting console. This may be manual or programmable, but should allow for cross fading and facilitate two-pre-set operation.

Lighting design candidates should become familiar with some of the language of their chosen option:

Accent Lighting. Lighting on a particular area or item on stage to highlight it for aesthetic reasons, rather than to illuminate an actor.

Back Projection. The use of projected slides of images on a cyclorama, screen or stage. In *The Beauty Manifesto* the set should be simple and uncluttered, using projections and other multimedia. (Katie Mitchell.)

Backlight. Light that comes from upstage (behind the scenery or actors) in order to sculpt and separate them from the background. *The Collected Grimm's Tales* offers great opportunities for working with mask/puppet and eerie backlighting.

Bar. The horizontal steel bar or bars hung above the stage from which lighting equipment/scenery is hung.

Barndoors. An attachment that is fitted to the front of a lantern to restrict the beam in a particular direction.

Blackout. The act of turning off (or fading out) all stage lighting. This can be highly significant and dramatic, with a snap blackout or a slow fade having different results. *The Birthday Party* is divided by a series of blackouts and fades.

Board. Refers to the main control unit for the stage lighting rig.

Bounce. Light that is reflected/diffused from the stage walls or the cyclorama. Usually light bounced off a white cloth in order to light another area.

Burnt Out. A burnt-out gel will need replacing as it will have lost its colour or melted due to excessive heat and/or prolonged use.

CMY. Cyan/Magenta/Yellow – the three secondary (additive) colours of light used in moving lights for colour mixing.

Colour Scroller/Changer. Remotely controlled strings of coloured gels that scroll in front of a lamp to rapidly change lighting. These can be noisy but are effective. (See also colour wheels and LED colour changers.)

Control room/box. In a theatre, a room usually high up, towards the back of the auditorium and often shared with lighting technicians where the equipment for running the sound/lights are housed.

Cross Fade. When lighting levels are gradually altered from one setting to another, bringing another lamp up to completely replace the existing light. This term also applies to sound effects/music. Sometimes the abbreviations Xfade or XF are used. In *Bedroom Farce* the quick cross fades between the action in the three bedrooms adds to the pace and comedy of the piece.

Cue. Just like an actor's cue, a lighting cue (either visual or scripted/programmed), tells/warns the lighting technician when to change a lighting state.

Dimmer Rack. A dimmer rack is made up of a number of individual lighting dimmer circuits (packs) built into a single case. Such racks consist of a single power input, a lighting control (DMX) input and sockets to connect lanterns. A dimmer rack can be set to respond to any control channel by setting its start address (known as 'addressing' the rack).

DMX or Digital Multiplex. This is the standard digital communication protocol used in modern remotely controlled lighting systems.

Dress Lighting (also known as PRESET). This is the lighting state that bathes the stage in a low-level light from the time the audience enters the house until the point at which the performance starts.

Fade. A fade is a change to the lighting level. This can be either an increase or decrease. Fade also applies to sound. (See also cross fade and fade to black out.) In *Bouncers* the lighting and music/sounds quickly fade in and out to signify the club doors opening and closing.

Flood. A lantern without a lens that produces a broad, non-focusable spread of light. Flood lighting covers a large surface area of the stage.

Floor can. This refers to a par can (see below) that has been designed to sit on a short stand on the floor.

Focus. All lighting equipment on the rig will need to be focussed before a production. This involves ensuring the correct angles, directions and beam sizes being adjusted to the director's satisfaction.

Follow Spot. Usually, a follow spot is a powerful profile lantern that is manually operated to highlight a featured actor or location. In *The 39 Steps* the clever use of follow spots and cross fades lends great atmosphere to the train scene.

Fresnel. This a kind of lantern that produces an even, soft-edged beam of light. The lens is the important part of this lamp. Fresnel lamps are a very common part of a school's lighting kit.

FOH or *Front of House Lights.* This term refers to every lamp position in front of the Proscenium arch, including the audience area.

General Cover. This lighting is created by (wash) lanterns that are rigged specifically to illuminate the acting areas. The stage is normally split into a number of areas for this purpose. Once the areas are defined, they can then be isolated or blended together as required by the director. The stage for *Mother Courage* is lit by a general cover of bright, white light.

Gobo. A thin stencilled metal plate placed inside or in front of a profile to project images onto a stage or backdrop. There are many gobo designs available, and they are used widely in the theatre. The city skyline in *Kvetch*, the leafy foliage in *DNA* and the church window in *Four Nights in Knaresborough* can all be produced using a gobo.

Going Dark. This is a warning given, whilst working on the set/lighting, to everyone onstage that the lights are all going out. Safe working practices dictate everyone stops until light is restored.

Lantern. The general term for a piece of lighting equipment, including spotlights, floods etc.

Lighting Plot. This is recorded information about each lighting state. The plot can be noted on paper or entered into the memory of a computerised lighting board that is used to run the lighting throughout a play. Some editions of *Chatroom* carry very detailed lighting plots. However, more recent interpretations have allowed for creative freedom.

LX. This is the generally accepted script shorthand for lighting. Lighting instructions in a script typically take the form LX BO (DBO), meaning go to Lighting: Black Out.

Par Can. One of the most widely used lighting elements. Par cans can be LED, which are particularly light and versatile.

Costume, Make-up and Masks

Costume can denote the character, historical era and style of a production. Candidates should carefully consider the type of costume that best suits their work. It is important that costumes are accurate, believable and easy to wear/change safely during performances. Often it is decided to keep things uncomplicated and minimal to avoid slowing the pace of a piece, but when chosen as an option, costumes must assist the actor in achieving a role and an audience believing in it.

Naturalistic pieces demand costumes that are both authentic and appropriate. They should signify a character's status and the setting of the play.

Costume students will need to research the garments, styles, colours and fabrics of the time and location of the play. More abstract, surreal/impressionist pieces need to be costumed in a manner that demonstrates the group's artistic intentions. Costumes can be symbolic, in that they can be used to show a character's personality.

As with other design options, costume should be considered right from the start and, if possible, performers should be able to rehearse in costumes or part costumes to help develop character. Costume changes the way we feel and move on a stage and can be a vital part of the process of developing a character.

Students who select costume design as their specialism will be expected to:

1. learn to design and realise costumes and/or make up/masks that creatively contribute to the overall effect of the group's performance;
2. communicate the group's intended meaning and artistic intent to its audience;
3. develop the ability to design and realise costumes that establish character, period and location and contribute to the style/mood and genre of the piece;
4. be able to select appropriate materials and create costumes, demonstrating an understanding of fabric, texture and accessories;
5. create costumes with an appreciation of colour, shape, fit, period detail and ethnic authenticity;
6. be aware of and make allowances/adjustments for movement and comfort on stage;

7 develop and create costumes with an understanding of the intentions of the piece and the individual character's requirements;
8 understand and appreciate the effects of stage lighting upon their designs;
9 adhere to the latest safe working practices.

Costume designs may also include masks, hair and make-up. Where students take the hair and make-up option they are expected to:

1 develop the ability to select appropriate materials for their make-up design and demonstrate an understanding of different types of make-up;
2 develop the skills required to apply stage make-up paints/powders, eyelashes and facial hair gum, as well as putty, prosthetics, stage blood and scar tissue as the character/text requires;
3 understand the effects stage lighting may have upon their designs;
4 appreciate how their make-up contributes as a part of any costume;
5 develop the ability to alter a character through the application of make-up;
6 develop the ability to create appropriate hairstyles for their chosen character/text.

With masks it should be remembered that a partial or complete covering of the performer's face should be considered when deciding upon how to incorporate them. Some pieces call for the use of a mask, but consider for how much of the performance it is worn and for what purpose – for example, disguise or comedic effect, Greek or commedia dell'arte. When using a mask, performance candidates must be aware that their facial expressions can't be seen and therefore body language has to be adjusted appropriately and in the correct style, bringing the whole body into a more physical performance.

If you offer your students costume/make-up/hair design as an option you must ensure that they have the resources and appropriate equipment needed to realise their designs and meet the demands of the exam. Provide access to an appropriate range of materials and, if required, the equipment needed to manufacture costumes. The ability to make the costume is not a requirement, but candidates have to be involved in the execution of the design. Students may source some parts of their costume design, but complete costumes cannot be sourced.

Costume design (including make-up and hair) candidates should become familiar with some of the language of their chosen option:

Blacks. This term refers to the black clothing worn by stage crew and management during productions. Blacks can also be worn by cast members when a plain or working outfit is called for. In *Walking with Shadows* members of the chorus wear blacks with masks.

Greasepaint. A make-up in stick form, for application to the face or body. Greasepaint requires special cream for its removal. (As with all make-up, an allergy test should be carried out before application.)

Masks. These can be full or partial face coverings that can represent a character or emotion. Neutral masks allow the actor to express feeling through physical work while the face remains hidden. For example, the use of blank white masks is found in Berkoff ensemble work or Greek Chorus; Trestle theatre masks are used in *Grimm's Tales* and worn by FESTE in *Twelfth Night*.

Quick Change. This is a costume change that needs to happen quickly, either just offstage or sometimes on stage. If a character has a Quick Change the costume designer must take this into consideration when assembling the costumes involved. For example, Velcro can be used instead of buttons, allowing for rapid underdressing. One costume can be worn under another.

Stock Costumes. These are standard, assorted costume items that can be used in a number of different productions. They can be reused and adjusted from past productions. For instance, an officer costume from *Our Country's Good* could be kept and used in other productions which called for an officer's (redcoat) costume, for example, *The Recruiting Officer*.

Wardrobe. This is the general name given to the costume department and anyone who works in it.

Set and Props

The scenery and furniture onstage and the items held or used by the performers can range from very minimal to highly elaborate and detailed. In performance exams I have always found that unless there is a set/prop candidate it is better for the performers to err toward a minimalist effective set using light and projections.

However, many naturalistic plays offer fantastic opportunities for set and prop design students.

As with costume, if you use props in a performance, it's a good idea to enable performers to work with them at an early stage in rehearsals. This has implications for prop designers.

Students who select set and/or prop design as their specialism will be expected to:

1 learn how to design and make sets/props that creatively contribute to the overall effect of the group's performance;

2 communicate the group's intended meaning and artistic intent to its audience;
3 develop the ability to design and realise sets/props that establish the character, period and location and contribute to the style/mood and genre of the piece;
4 develop the ability to identify the appropriate materials and equipment to realise their set design, as well as a working knowledge of the most efficient and safe uses of flats, cyclorama, floor coverings, drapes, furnishings, levels, projections and media;
5 develop the ability to construct sets showing an understanding of stage configurations, rake, levels, steps and wings;
6 appreciate the performer–audience relationship, and what will be happening on the set/with the props;
7 be thoroughly aware of the plotting of any scene changes;
8 develop the ability to design and realise sets, selecting appropriate dressings, furnishings, material, colour, texture and props;
9 adhere to the latest safe working practices.

If you offer your students set/prop design as an option you must ensure that they have the resources and appropriate equipment needed to realise their designs. They should have access to an appropriate range of construction materials and, if needed, the equipment required to manufacture the set. While ability to manufacture the set is not a requirement, students need to be involved in the execution of the design. Set and construction materials may come from the school's stock or can be hired/purchased.

Set/Prop design candidates should become familiar with some of the language of their chosen option:

Box Set. (Also known as a 'Room set'.) Box sets are made of three walls, often built from flats open to the audience (fourth wall) in order to represent a space like a room.

Braces. These are angled (often weighted) timber joists used to support a flat.

Cloth. A cloth is an element of backdrop scenery painted on fabric. These can be flown, hung or rolled usually at the back of the scene.

Cyclorama. (Also known as the Cyc.) This is a very large white fabric or plastered wall at the back of the stage, filling the whole space. It can be lit in various colours or projected onto with multimedia slides or gobos.

Entrances/Exits. Either a part of the set through which an actor can enter or exit or the act of entering or exiting the stage.

Flats. These are flexible, oblong, light timber frames that have a stretched canvas or a wooden board affixed to them. Flats are typically painted to form elements of the set. Some flats include doors or windows.

Fly. To fly is to raise and lower into place (on stage) scenery/lights, or even people, via a system of pulleys and ropes from a fly tower.

Fourth Wall. This is the imaginary wall that closes the box in which actors perform, unaware of the audience (Naturalism). So, to break the fourth wall is to break this convention and involve/address the audience (Non-Naturalism).

Gauze. This is a coarse, loosely woven cloth with multiple uses in the theatre. Gauze can be used to diffuse light, helping to create an entire scene/backdrop. When lit from behind, gauze becomes transparent.

House. This refers to the auditorium or the audience: house lights, house tabs/curtains, front of house, etc.

Model Box. This is a wooden box/shoe box representing the walls of a theatre space in which scale models can be placed. The model box can help set designers plan the set layout before finally realising it.

Props. These are items on stage that can't be called scenery or costume. Props handled by actors are known as hand props, which may include such things as a sword or a briefcase. Those items kept on the actor's person or in their costume, such as a handkerchief or a lighter, are referred to as personal props.

Rake. The rake is the angle at which a stage is slanted for perspective and audience viewing. The rake is generally higher at the back than the front. Seating is also often raked.

Set. This refers to the scenery for a particular show or scene. 'Set' can also be used to refer to the act of preparing the stage for action.

Strike. To strike is take down, disassemble the set after a show: 'Strike the set'.

Tabs. These are curtains that open and close. House tabs are the curtains that close across a proscenium arch.

Truck. A truck is a rostrum or platform on wheels that allows for scenery to be easily moved about the stage before being locked into place.

Wings. The wings are the sides of the stage that are out of audience sight lines. Actors and scenery props all wait in the wings before entering the stage.

Sound Design

Sound effects (SFX) and music – live or recorded – can add much to a performance. Sound can create mood and atmosphere, build tension, help set the scene/location/time and even strengthen an emotion or focus attention on to a particular character. Underscored music is desirable in some of the plays noted in this book, but take care not to detract from performances. Scripts that encourage students to select music will often add that this should be sensitive to the needs of the piece. Whether it's disco music in Godber's *Bouncers*, the Blues used in Tennessee Williams' *The Glass Menagerie* or the compositions by Schubert in Dorfman's *Death and the Maiden*, music should enhance not detract.

Physical theatre often uses a lot of music to accompany the movement work onstage. As it's often closely related to dance, this is important in giving work energy, pace and rhythm. Specific sound effects should be subtle and entirely in keeping with the piece and the group's artistic intent. Timing is critical when using SFX.

Students who select sound design as their specialism will be expected to:

1 learn how to design and realise sounds that creatively contribute to the overall effect of the group's performance;
2 communicate the group's intended meaning and artistic intent to its audience;
3 develop the ability to design and realise sounds that help establish the period and location and contribute to the style/mood and genre of the piece;
4 develop the ability to select sounds that enhance the mood or atmosphere;
5 acquire a working knowledge of the available equipment and be able to select appropriately to realise the intended sound design by the skilful use of different types of microphones, amplifiers, software, musical or percussion instruments and SFX recordings;
6 develop the ability to use a range of SFX to realise the intended sound design;
7 be able to manipulate sound/music through audio effects, edited and/or mixed sound, distortion, reverb, echo, volume/amplification, fades and soundscapes;
8 adhere to the latest safe working practices.

If you offer your students sound design as an option you must ensure that they have the resources and appropriate equipment needed to realise their designs, such as access to a sound reproduction system, sound-processing devices, at least two different types of microphone and access to pre-recorded sound sources.

Sound design candidates should become familiar with some of the language of their chosen option:

Acoustics. This is an important consideration. The acoustics of a space depend on its size and shape and the level of sound-absorbing and reflecting material. A full house will often surprise performers by absorbing/dampening the acoustics. Some spaces, such as large empty halls, have naturally good acoustics, while the black box Drama studio with tabs may deaden sound.

Ambient Noise. This is background noise over which you may have little or no control.

Control Room/Box. In a theatre, a control room/box is usually high up, towards the back of the auditorium, and often shared with lighting technicians where the equipment for running the sound/lights are housed.

Microphone/Mike. These are used for picking up sound and either amplifying or recording it. Microphones can either be hand-held or worn. Microphones can be mobile (radio mike) or fixed around the stage (boom, telescope, hemispherical).

Mixer Desk. A mixer desk is a device for mixing and modifying sounds from microphones, musical instruments or recorded sounds and special effects. Mixer desks are usually housed in the control room.

Soundscape. This is created by using sounds or words to create an environment for a scene. For example, other cast members echo Caliban's lines in *The Tempest* to create a magical, haunting soundscape.

Puppets *(Not all boards offer this option)*

Puppets can be used within productions as a dramatic device to represent a character. A well-realised puppet should allow the audience to invest in that character and enhance the storytelling within a performance.

Puppets can help support the overall style of the production by reflecting its design ideas. For example, if a puppet is used in a naturalistic piece, then it would be considered a prop rather than a dramatic device used to represent a character. On the other hand, if a puppet is used in a non-naturalistic/surreal piece it could be considered in any number of ways. Puppets may be used for more practical reasons, too, perhaps in a piece that needs a dog or a baby. Puppets should be designed with careful consideration of the needs of the piece and this may well influence the type of puppet chosen. For example, when designing puppets, there are several types to consider (see the list in vocabulary section below).

Selecting the appropriate puppet is crucial and must take into consideration the puppeteer, whether they are to be seen or unseen, and how this fits with the overall style of the piece. Puppet designers need to consider the puppeteer and what exactly they will be asked to do and for how long, the scale and realism required. These considerations should inform decisions concerning the materials used and are an important part of the process.

Students who select puppets as their specialism will be expected to:

1 learn how to design and realise puppets that contribute positively to the overall effect of the performance piece;
2 communicate the group's intended meaning and artistic intent to its audience;
3 develop the ability to select the appropriate materials to realise a puppet, demonstrating an understanding of materials, colour, texture, shape and costume;
4 understand characterisation possibilities for their creation;
5 develop the ability to assemble a puppet with an understanding of structure, size, shape and scale;
6 appreciate the functionality of the puppet and its operation onstage to realise the intentions of the piece;
7 develop the ability to realise a suitable puppet which takes into consideration a variety of puppet types;
8 adhere to the latest safe working practices.

It is the student's puppet design that is assessed. Although students are expected to construct and/or operate the puppet(s) when possible, this will not form part of the assessment. The puppet designed must be a part of the live performance, but the designer need not be the puppet's operator during the performance. A different puppet should be created for each extract or be adapted specifically for each extract.

If you offer your students the puppet design option you must ensure that they have the resources and appropriate equipment needed to realise their designs. They should have access to an appropriate range of materials and, if needed, the equipment required to manufacture the puppet. Although the ability to manufacture the puppet is not normally a requirement, students need to be involved in the execution of the design.

Puppet design candidates should become familiar with some of the language of their chosen option (note that the following list is not exhaustive):

Hand Puppets. These are usually worn on one hand, which operates the mouth and arms.

Marionettes. These puppets are controlled by strings from above.

Rod Puppets. Rods are used to make elements of the puppets move, usually from below.

Shadow Puppets. These are typically cut-out paper/card figures that are placed between a light source and usually a white screen or sheet (that is front or back projected). I have seen shadow puppets used very successfully in the *Grimm's Tales*.

Full-body Puppets. These are large puppets worn over the puppeteer's head and body like a costume.

Manipulation. This is the way in which a puppeteer moves or works their puppet.

Lip sync. This is the synchronizing movement of the puppet's mouth with the spoken words.

Puppeteer. This is the person giving the puppet movement and life (via manipulation).

Multimedia

The use of image, sound, text and/or video follows the same basics/requirements as sound or lighting. It is only offered as an option by one Board.

Directing

At GCE some Boards offer direction as an option.

A director has overall responsibility for the creative vision of a play. A director will need to bring the different elements of the piece together and create a final production. This will entail meetings and research with the performers and other designers. It is also the director's responsibility to direct performers during rehearsals and assist them in the creation of believable characters.

Students who select directing as a specialism will be expected to:

1   develop appropriate strategies that contribute to the overall effectiveness of the group's performance and respect their dramatic intentions as a whole;
2   develop the skill of communicating a script's meaning to an audience through accurate and sensitive interpretation of the chosen extract;
3   work imaginatively and with a clear directorial vision;
4   develop the ability to explore texts with the cast using a variety of rehearsal methods;

5   develop the ability to select and exploit performance spaces that enable good performer/audience communication;
6   develop the knowledge and skills required in rehearsals and use various techniques to direct movement, such as proxemics, use of space, status, set/props etc. in order to achieve the dramatic intentions of the piece/group;
7   develop the ability to create pace, tempo and rhythm with the cast in ways that are appropriate to the needs of the piece;
8   develop a vocabulary of theatrical terms and practices applicable to the chosen piece;
9   adhere to the latest safe working practices.

Directing candidates should become familiar with some of the language of their chosen option.

This includes the vocabulary of all the other options and the basics of the literal use of directing terminology. Knowing the five basic areas of the stage is fundamental. Directors will also need to be familiar with the requisites of their chosen form/practitioner. For example, if they were to choose Stanislavski for a piece of work by Ibsen, they would need to become familiar with 'The System' and the development of characters, to be able to rehearse the cast effectively. Or if the chosen piece was *Kvetch*, they would need to be aware not only of the artistic needs of the piece but also have familiarity with Berkoff's highly stylised movement, notably his use of slow motion and exaggerated facial expressions, stylised mime, direct address, exaggerated vocal work, tableaux, mask, ensemble, minimalism and Lecoq.

* * *

Each Exam Board differs slightly and some offer options that others do not. Options also differ from GCSE to GCE and each Board uses its own terminology. With this in mind, please remember to check the specification for your Exam Board's exact requirements, paying particular attention to restrictions on the number of designers and the permitted combinations.

5

Performance Exams (The Bottom Line)

Maybe it's because it's a non-exam assessed (NEA) component, or perhaps it is because art is open to too much interpretation, too subjective, the eye of the beholder and all that, but one thing is for sure, the scripted performance exam has many names. At GCSE it has six: Texts in practice, Scripted performance, Performance from text, Performing theatre or Presenting and performing texts, and OFQUAL call it Text-based performance. GCE mixes it up again for us with: Exploring and performing texts, Text in performance, Performance, Making theatre or Realising, and this time OFQUAL call it Interpretation of performance texts. Even the visitor on the day comes in many guises: Examiner, Assessor, Moderator. But what's in a name? In a nutshell, you are going to prepare your students to perform in/design for a scripted piece of theatre for which they will be awarded a grade ... by a visitor ... from the Board, who, for mercy's sake, I will refer to as 'an examiner'.

The scripted performance part of the exam is just that, *part* of an exam. Whichever Board or exam you are using, the performance of a text is supported by study of scripts, playwrights and practitioners, and by live theatre visits, improvisation, devising and workshops. All of the Boards offer a broad, coherent and rigorous course of study intended to inspire creativity in students. They all provide opportunities for making and understanding Drama. Each Board recognises Drama as a practical art form in which ideas and meaning are communicated to an audience through choices of form, style and convention. They all lead students to a written exam and NEA performances.

Preparing Your Students

AO2 assessed. The Application of theatrical skills to realise artistic intentions in live performance.

Supervision

During the rehearsal process teachers are expected to support students through workshops/lessons to develop skills and understanding. Guidance should be provided for students so that they understand the requirements of any task they undertake. They should also be aware of the marking criteria used.

You should give guidance to your students on the suitability of their work whilst ensuring that they meet the requirements of the specification. You are required to follow all instructions regarding the provision of advice and feedback to students as outlined in your specification.

In addition to conducting workshops, you should 'regularly monitor' students' rehearsals and planning sessions, observing their work at each developmental stage in order to authenticate it when required. You are not expected to directly supervise your students during all rehearsals and meetings, but there should be adequate supervision to ensure that work can be authenticated. With my classes, I film a workshop/rehearsal session each month and highlight in advance the areas in which I am looking for development/improvement from each piece. The students know the purpose of these sessions and prepare to demonstrate their individual contributions and development.

You are obviously not permitted to offer any guidance during the assessed performances. All rehearsals/preparations and the final live performance must take place in appropriate, risk-assessed, safe environments. Performances must take place in live performance conditions and (where possible) with stage lighting. Performers are not required to present their chosen pieces within the context of a full production, that is, with full set and costume.

The eventual space in which your students perform should enable them to fulfil their chosen specialism as much as is possible (see Chapter 6, 'The Performance Space'). They should be made aware of any health and safety factors relating to their chosen specialism and the piece as a whole.

Remember to supply the examiner with directions to the venue, along with clear instructions about how to access the actual performance space. This last piece of information is vitally important for evening visits, as wandering around a semi-closed site in the dark is not a good way for your examiner to start! Include a contact name and mobile number too.

It is the teacher's responsibility to ensure students are aware of the criteria against which they will be assessed. When doing this, it is a good idea to demystify some of the terms used in the specification (see Chapter 8, 'The Language of the Theatre').

Assessment Evidence

The performances/designs presented for assessment must be the student's own work, and students and teachers will be required to authenticate all work. It must be clear and obvious to the visiting examiner when each performance begins and ends.

Programme Notes

Teachers must provide programme notes for the examiner at the start of the performance, and these notes must include photographs of each student to enable clear identification for the examiner. The programme notes must also state each student's chosen specialism, chosen play and, if they are performing, the character(s) they are playing. Each individual student's dramatic intentions should be clearly stated, since assessment cannot take place without reference to these. Justification of context and an explanation of the theatrical choices made should also be given.

Recording

Assessed performances must be recorded with a single video camera from an unobstructed, audience perspective. The recording must be complete and unedited. It is essential that you check your sound levels before recording!

Every assessed student must clearly identify themselves at the start of the recording. Name and candidate number need to be given. Students should also state their chosen specialism and the name of the play. If they are performing, they should name the character(s) they are playing. Any set designs, costumes etc. must be shown at the start of the recording, accompanied by a clear statement of who was responsible for those elements. Recording medium requirements and possible differences/amendments should be checked with your individual Board.

Performances must be carried out in live performance conditions and ideally under stage lighting, all of which must have been formally risk-assessed and safe.

Group Sizes

It is important to be aware that some Boards do not permit performances to consist solely of monologues. However, all Boards permit monologues within a piece of Drama.

At GCSE, most Boards have a limit on the group size to a maximum of six, with one designer per design discipline. Other Boards, however, allow a maximum of four performers and a limit of two different design options per group. What this reminds us is that we must check our specification for the details!

At GCE, Boards are more complex in their requirements and differ far more on maximum/minimum number requirements. It would be prudent to check your specification at each stage.

Non-Examinee Students

While it is acceptable to have non-examined students performing alongside performance candidates, this should be done only when absolutely necessary in order to comply with minimum group size requirements. Staff are not permitted to perform. However, design candidates are allowed to receive technical support from non-examinee students and staff.

Performance Timings

For students (performance and design) who do not meet the regulatory minimum performance requirements, examiners will use their professional judgement and a proportional time penalty will normally be applied. For students who exceed the maximum performance time, examiners will be required to stop marking after the maximum point has passed. Some boards do not apply penalties for exceeding the maximum time. However, it is always unlikely that students will demonstrate any further skills if they do go over the allotted time, and less able students in particular are often exposed by overlong pieces. Bear in mind that 'on the day' nerves can speed up a performance and unforeseen circumstances may prolong it. However, examiners know this and are understanding. The main thing is that students are comfortable and not worrying about their timings.

	At GCSE (rough guide)	At GCE
Monologues	2–5 minutes	2–3 minutes
Duologues	3–10 minutes	5–6 minutes
Group	4–20 minutes	20–45 minutes (depending on group size)

Assessment Objectives

Assessment objectives (AOs) are set by OFQUAL and are the same across all Drama specifications and all Exam Boards. The non-exam performance assessment will measure how students have achieved the assessment objectives in AO2: Apply theatrical skills to realise artistic intentions in live performance.

Make sure that you have a copy of the specification open on the assessment page and that you refer to it when discussing marks/grades.

6

Performance Spaces

The notion that, 'all the world's a stage' does not apply to performance exams! Performances must be carried out in live performance conditions and ideally under stage lighting. Furthermore, the space should enable students to fulfil their chosen specialism as much as possible and have been formally risk-assessed and deemed safe.

For many of us there is little or no choice regarding performance spaces, so the question never really arises. The space set aside for Drama in schools can vary greatly depending on budget, build, the status of the subject in your school, and even the day of the week.

I have seen performances marred by disturbance or lack of atmosphere, but also by issues related to venue. (A lack of facilities is much less common.) A performance taking place in a shared dining hall that a few short minutes earlier saw 400 dinners dispensed may hold problems for the suspension of disbelief – we are all familiar with the lingering aroma of boiled cabbage! – but these problems are not insurmountable. The main issue is not with the space itself, but what is going on in and around it. We have all probably experienced kitchen staff, clattering and chatting as they clear up during a performance. It happens! So, before we look at where a performance should take place, let us look at when.

Schools can be noisy places, and school days are punctuated by the movement of classes every hour or so, break times and lunchtimes, with each event often heralded by bells, buzzers, beepers or hooters. While my school has a no bell policy, I cannot honestly say that it makes it a much quieter place. Certainly, while there is no ringing, buzzing, beeping and hooting, there is still the thunderous sound of a thousand chairs scraping backwards, teacher instructions and goodbyes being shouted, and then the reverse, as the classes take up their place in the next classroom. Even strategically placed signs outside your performance space and any number of well-meaning shhhhhhhes from staff and prefects cannot drown out the din of 2000 feet on the move!

So, it is important to consider in advance what else will be happening in your school at your chosen performance time. Sports events, written examinations (resulting in 200 desks being placed in your performance space!) and evening classes might all be factors you need to think about. I once moderated extracts from *The Crucible* whilst a surprisingly loud yoga lesson took place across the corridor.

Most Exam Boards offer day, twilight and evening slots for their visits, and some will also come in on a Saturday. Make sure you give lots of consideration to the time of day, the week and the month before making your selection of preferred dates. Then, get your booking in as soon as possible to maximise your chances of securing your preferred slot.

Now about that space?

Many plays can be performed in any number of locations. The theatre should be adaptable and accommodating, but remember that this is a performance that will be graded. As such, the choice of space is an important consideration both artistically and in terms of more down-to-Earth logistics. Does it have a lighting rig? Is it appropriate to the needs of the piece and allow for the students' stated artistic intentions? Your guidance here is crucial, whether it be to advise against a location or to explain how the students can make the most of/adapt the space available. For some, it's the Drama studio or nothing! After all, this is a space the students are familiar with, and one that is (hopefully) also relatively quiet and undisturbed. Drama studios normally have sound equipment, levels and lights. Other students opt for the main school stage, with its Proscenium arch and (sometimes) raked seating! Having said this, I should note that I've visited schools that possess neither a studio nor a stage.

It is important to bear in mind that the shape and nature of different performance spaces can affect the way that plays are staged, performed and seen.

The following are some of the most popular types of performance spaces:

Proscenium Stage. Many schools – especially older ones – have this kind of stage. This is a stage that has the audience position directly in front. This kind of configuration is also referred to as 'end-on staging', and it sees the audience sitting slightly below the level of the stage. If you are lucky there might be tiered seating that affords the audience a better view of the stage. In many traditional, older schools, the stage is framed by a proscenium arch that can help define the imaginary fourth wall needed for realistic theatre. The area in front of the arch is the proscenium; the majority of the scenery appears behind the proscenium arch. Plays like *The Resistible Rise of Arturo Ui* lend themselves well to such staging. From a proscenium stage we can build a 'thrust stage' that projects into the audience area. This results in the audience sitting on three sides of the action of the play, allowing for a more immersive effect.

In-the-Round Stage. This kind of stage has the audience sitting on all sides of the performance space. While in-the-round staging creates a more intimate experience for both the performers and the audience, it often presents logistical problems, typically related to entrances and exits. Although in-the-round is good for Drama that requires audience involvement, it is possible to perform on elevated platforms or to have the seating tiered up and away from the performance area. When choosing this option you should be aware of where your examiner is going to be seated. Not turning your back on your audience is not an option with this type of staging and performers will need to keep all of the audience involved through careful consideration when directing/blocking. Also known as 'arena theatre', plays such as *That Face*, *Equus* and *Dancing at Lughnasa* work well with in-the-round staging.

Traverse Stage. With traverse staging the audience sits on two sides of what is essentially a thrust (without the main stage), rather like at a fashion show. This type of stage is great for creating an intimate atmosphere with the audience positioned close to the action. Depending on which side they sit, audience members often get a quite different experience, so it is important to consider where your examiner will be seated. The audience members can see each other with this set up, which serves to remind them that they are in the theatre. Traverse staging is a feature of *Kabuki* dance-based theatre but I've also seen it used for scenes from *Bouncers*.

Raked Stage. This kind of staging has the rear of the stage higher than the front. It helps with visibility and was common in older theatres. A raked stage can have an impact on perspective because it isn't level. Raked staging has to be considered carefully when planning the design for a production. Some plays use the altered perspective of a raked stage to great effect (e.g. the street in *Blood Brothers*).

Black Box Studio. Many schools have or can accommodate black box staging in their Drama studio. This kind of stage can be either purpose-built or adapted from a classroom or sectioned-off multi-purpose space. Ideally, the space inside is empty, with storage areas for mini sets, props, costumes and blocks or staging. Black tabs are an important part of a well-equipped studio, as is a lighting rig. Black box studios are ideal for intimate rehearsals and plays that benefit from a confined space and small, up-close audiences. Plays such as *Death and Dancing*, *Death and The Maiden*, *School Play* and *Jane Eyre* work particularly well in such stages.

Promenade. This kind of staging has audience members moving from space to space during a performance, often at the request of the performers. Promenade can be immersive and challenging! It is important to remember that your examiner will need to write notes. As such, it is a good idea to seat examiners in a place where they can observe the piece as a whole, including how the audience is managed. Good examples of works featuring promenade would be *The Mysteries*, *At the Black Pig's Dyke* or *The Cheviot, the Stag and the Black, Black Oil*.

Amphitheatre. I add amphitheatre stages here because I have visited two schools that had one. In fact, my own school had a grass amphitheatre!

Amphitheatres are typically circular, open-air settings with raked, semi-circular seating areas that slope down towards the stage. They were used in ancient Greece and are still popular today. The use of amphitheatres should not be limited solely to ancient Greek theatre – *Julius Caesar* or *Mother Courage* would work very well in this kind of staging.

Open-Air (Street Theatre). This is informal theatre that often sees the actors simply choosing an open space, although a small stage platform can be used. Street theatre usually involves some level of interaction with the audience. Beware of the public and again think of your examiner and the weather! I once moderated *A Midsummer Night's Dream* in a woodland at the back of a school's football field. The performance was beautiful and immersive – until it began to rain!

Site-Specific Theatre. This kind of staging is usually a unique site specifically adapted for the performance (often far removed from a theatre space). The choice of such staging can be linked to some kind of architectural feature or simply selected because of its everyday purpose. Some locations tie in very well with the piece being performed – *Titus Andronicus* in an abattoir, or *As You Like It* in a woodland (weather permitting!). The works of Eddie Ladd or Punchdrunk lend themselves well to site specific theatre.

Some schools are able to take their groups to alternative professional venues/theatres if they specifically require the space/equipment on offer there.

Your eventual decision must take into consideration how effectively the space will be used. Proxemics is an important issue here. The audience's perception and sight lines are vital considerations. Remember your examiner too! It is important that they should be seated (ideally) in a location that affords them the best possible, unrestricted view of the performance as a whole, in order to appreciate the artistic intentions of the whole group.

The Use of Levels. Using different levels (heights) on your stage will create visual interest and ensure that the audience sees everything they need to. Levels can be used to denote different things; for example, in *Adrian Mole* or *The Government Inspector* levels can show the different locations, or in *Female Transport* they indicate events taking place above and below deck. In plays like *A Memory of Lizzie* or *Find Me*, levels can be used to signify changes in time (flashbacks). Levels can also signify status, for example placing the king's throne set on a higher level in *Macbeth*.

Lighting the Space. Most of the requirements for lighting are covered in Chapter 4 ('Design Options'). Remember that lighting requirements and what is available will vary greatly depending on your chosen space/venue.

A knowledge and understanding of the stage (including its terminology and conventions). In addition to a knowledge of the configurations/venues of the stage, it is also important that students are familiar with the terminology used when working on any stage.

In order to take and give directions, for example, performers have to be familiar with basic stage positioning: upstage (left, right, centre), downstage (left, right, centre) and centre stage; staging concepts, including entrances, exits, proxemics and spatial awareness; the relationship between actor and audience and the convention of the fourth wall; scale and perspective on stage as well as their interaction with set, props, lights and acoustics.

7

Shakespeare

The day I introduced my GCSE Drama class to Shakespeare has left a vivid scar upon my memory. 'I thought this was a Drama lesson sir, why are we doing English?' I informed my visibly disappointed class that I was not in some way betraying the theatre and that Shakespeare had actually written some pretty good plays. They were sceptical to say the least, but I persevered.

So much has been written about Shakespeare already, and I don't intend to add to that here. My purpose here is to address two reasons I often encounter for not using his works for Drama performance exams.

The arguments against are usually quite simple, citing complex/archaic language and overcomplicated stories. I have come to encapsulate this view with the phrase 'The Bard is tward [i.e. too hard]'. 'Sir it's tward, what's he on about?' Like Shakespeare's 'cut-throat' or 'lack-luster' too-hard found its way into the school vocabulary.

I include ten works of Shakespeare in my list of 200 because I have seen them passionately performed in schools or by my own students at GCSE and GCE. My only warning to a teacher considering providing students with Shakespearian texts is this: if *you* think it's irrelevant, confusing, archaic or simply 'tward', don't ask your students to perform it. Students need their teacher to be passionate about *all* of their chosen texts and to have a good working knowledge of them.

Two of the most common objections to Shakespeare:

1 The stories are old and unnecessarily complex!
2 The language is old and unnecessarily complex!

The Stories

It is not fair to expect students to get to grips with the language of Shakespeare if they are not stimulated by the stories. I would like here to explain how I bring a plot to life, using a simple 'page to stage' exercise for any Drama space.

Before the lesson, divide the play up into sections (depending on group size). Working in pairs, give each couple a section and ask them to discover three facts about their scene:

1 Where is it?
2 Who is there?
3 What are they doing?

Keep each pair numbered to ensure they respect the correct order. Each fact should be written down on a piece of card in one sentence only. Depending on the group, allow sufficient time for the task to be completed, providing help where needed. Some pairs will finish quicker than others. Ask these students to write out a name label for every character and others labels for the locations. Position the location labels around the Drama area. For example, the castle, the moor, the forest etc. Use levels if you wish.

When everyone is ready, each pair in turn should lay out their facts on the floor so that the story reads from left to right. Then the pair with the first section of the play should select the character labels they need for their piece and place them on willing players. These should remain constant. They should go to the places in which their characters are placed. So, for example, the scene in which Macbeth returns to his castle to meet with Lady Macbeth would have Lady Macbeth already in the castle and Macbeth walking from the moors across the space to his castle. As you move through the play and meet new characters, assign the character labels to the other students as they are mentioned. If you have to double cast, try to ensure the main protagonists only have one label. It may be an idea for the teacher to read the students' work out loud, having the whole class moving like chess pieces around the space. Students should be encouraged to act out or form a tableau for each scene. The results of the first attempt may seem like absolute pandemonium, but the basic story will become apparent, as will the play's main protagonists and their motivations. A second run (or more, if needed) should be filmed and watched back and discussed as a class.

The purpose of this exercise is to help students better understand the complex plots and sub-plots of, for example, *A Midsummer Night's Dream* with the four lovers or *Twelfth Night* with mistaken identities and sub-plot after sub-plot. Breaking down the various elements of the play, having the students move from location to location, helps them to see the plays as moving pieces of theatre and helps them become familiar with the key characters and components.

Even at A level, the above process can be a fun exercise that allows students to get right into the story from the start. Particularly at KS5, by which time students will be familiar with some of Shakespeare's plays, this is still a very useful exercise. Importantly, the process I have just outlined can also be used with any complex text, not just Shakespeare. The point is that it helps students to break down the storyline, showing that it's not, in fact, 'tward'. Students come to see that what's actually going on in the play is not such a mystery and that the themes involved are eternal. All this leaves is the problem of Shakespeare's language!

The Language

We are all familiar with the words and phrases Shakespeare added to our language. He introduced over 1700 words by changing nouns into verbs, connecting words never before joined, making verbs into adjectives, adding suffixes and prefixes, and so on. In addition to all this, Shakespeare also invented totally new words.

It is believed that Shakespeare had a vocabulary of over 60,000 words, as opposed to between 10,000 and 20,000 most of us use. When reading Shakespeare, students will discover words they have never used before or see familiar words used in unusual ways. Yet even the most unfamiliar words take on a familiar sound when they are performed and heard. Their meaning will be uncovered. The key to Shakespeare is to *do* it. Word patterns and their meanings become apparent in performance.

Shakespeare's works are almost completely void of stage direction (save a few famous exceptions). What this means is that a performer must hear the clues within the lines they speak. This is not as complicated as it sounds. Often the sound of the words will inform the actor how to perform them, both vocally and physically. A good example would be the dialogue between LADY MACBETH and MACBETH after the murder of DUNCAN. Let us demystify the text by *doing* it.

Divide the students into pairs and try this simple exercise:

LADY MACBETH	*My husband!*
MACBETH	*I have done the deed. Didst thou not hear a noise?*
LADY MACBETH	*I heard the owl scream and the crickets cry. Did not you speak?*
MACBETH	*When?*
LADY MACBETH	*Now.*
MACBETH	*As I descended?*
LADY MACBETH	*Ay.*
MACBETH	*Hark! Who lies i' the second chamber?*
LADY MACBETH	*Donalbain.*
MACBETH	*This is a sorry sight.*
LADY MACBETH	*A foolish thought, to say a sorry sight.*

In pairs, the students should first simply read the lines. At first, they are only lines of text. Next, have the students imagine themselves at the bottom of the dark castle steps down which MACBETH has just descended. Have the students go to a corner, a dark space, and have them imagine the bloody crime just upstairs, the body of a murdered King. Have the students now read the description of the night: *'I heard the owl <u>scream</u> and the crickets <u>cry</u>'*. Remind the students that it is dark and that the castle sleeps. Remind them too that discovery of LADY MACBETH and MACBETH would mean death to them both. In such a context the students will see that the lines need to be whispered yet urgent, fearful. Having the students think about the words and their setting will help them see how they are to be spoken. They will realise that a lack of stage directions isn't too bad, as the setting gives the clue. In the case of the above scene from *Macbeth*, it will become clear that the words *'A foolish thought, to say a sorry sight'* are best said in a whisper, and that the lines *'When, Now, As I descended? Ay'* are urgently spoken. Couple these together and the students will see that we have here an urgent, furtive conversation. The students can now consider the proxemics of the whispered scene.

It is important that the students understand that the text gives us the *where* and the *how* to speak the lines, but that the *why* is for the actor to interpret. In the above example from *Macbeth*, is it fear of discovery or fear of failure? Each interpretation will change how we see the murderous couple/victims of prophesy. The actor's interpretation (artistic intent) is an important aspect of the marking criteria.

Basic Terms

The following are some important basic terms:

Blank Verse. Blank verse is so called because it doesn't rhyme line-by-line. This is everyday speech made up of ten syllables (five iambic feet).

Experience has taught me that we can easily get over-technical, making things unnecessarily confusing by using the dreaded terms 'iambic pentameter' or 'decasyllabic verse', and by talking about stress and unstress. It is better, I think, to avoid this.

I always ask actors to feel their heartbeat: di-DUM di-DUM di-DUM di-DUM di-DUM, *'His name is Jason and he likes Drama'*, or *'If music be the food of love play on'*. It *sounds* like natural, everyday speech. However if we alter the natural rhythm by adding or removing a syllable, listen again: di-DUM di-DUM di-DUM di-DUM di, *'His name is Abraham and he likes acting'*, or *'If music be the food of love play'*. In Shakespeare, when the pattern is unbalanced, the words sound 'wrong'. But there is always a good reason for this: a lack of balance changes the natural rhythm, so the line is spoken with a changed emphasis. For example, the well-known line *'To be or not to be that is the question'* contains eleven beats. The irregular extra syllable at the end of the sentence highlights that last word. In fact, if you continue with the next four lines of the famous soliloquy, they too have an extra syllable. As I just mentioned, if a line of Shakespearean text doesn't scan there is always a reason for it. In this case, the imbalance leads the actor into the emotional turbulence of HAMLET's mind.

Prose. This term refers to lines that are not in verse, with no consistent rhythm. Prose is less formal than blank verse but every bit as important. For example, in *Romeo and Juliet,* ROMEO uses prose when he is teasing the NURSE, but blank verse when wooing JULIET. In *Macbeth*, LADY MACBETH reads MACBETH's letter, which is written in prose, yet speaks to her husband in blank verse. Prose is often, though certainly not always, the language of the lower status characters. It is also used in comedic word play. As such, in *A Midsummer Night's Dream,* NICK BOTTOM responds in prose to TITANIA's poetic declarations of love:

> TITANIA   *Thou art as wise as thou art beautiful.*
> BOTTOM   *Not so, neither: but if I had wit enough to get out of this wood, I have enough to serve mine own turn.*

Monosyllables. With the words *'In sooth I know not why I am so sad'*, which appear in *The Merchant of Venice*, we know *that* ANTONIO is sad and depressed, but we don't know *why*. What the actor knows is that the line is delivered slowly, deliberately – it can't be delivered any other way. If you try, you trip on the words. So, Shakespeare tells the actor to speak slowly here, but why he is speaking slowly is for the actor to interpret emotionally.

Rhyme. Rhyming text conjures beauty in the eyes of the audience, and the beauty of *'The grey eyed morn smiles on the frowning night Chequ'ring the eastern clouds with streaks of light'*, from *Romeo and Juliet*, is undeniable. Rhyme can be used to end a scene:

> OBERON   *And look thou meet me ere the first cock crow*
> PUCK   *Fear not, my lord, your servant shall do so.*

Rhyme can also be used to whet the audience's appetite for the next scene:

> HAMLET   *The play's the thing*
>   *Wherein I'll catch the conscience of the King.*

Rhyme tells the actor how to deliver the line and tells the audience something is afoot.

Onomatopoeia. Related to rhyme, use of onomatopoeia helps to create soundscapes. We need only think of *'Double, double . . . cauldron bubble'* and *'Hurly-burly's done'* in *Macbeth,* or LEAR's calling upon the storm to *'Blow, winds, and crack your cheeks! Rage! Blow!'* in *King Lear*.

Assonance. The use of repeated vowel sounds, known as assonance, helps to add rhythm to a line, reminding the actor of the richness and import of the words being spoken. Consider ROMEO's line: *'To twinkle in their spheres till they return'*.

Alliteration. Like assonance, the use of alliteration, which uses repeated consonantal sounds, serves to highlight vital moments. Alliteration appears in *Romeo and Juliet*'s prologue, *'From forth the fatal loins of these foes'*, and in the comedic lines from *A Midsummer Night's Dream*: *'Whereat, with blade, with bloody blameful blade, He Bravely broach'd his boiling, bloody breast'*. And, of course, alliteration appears alongside assonance in the famous line from *Macbeth*: *'Fair is foul and foul is fair'*.

Personification. Shakespeare made use of personification when he wrote of *'the rosy fingered dawn'* in *Hamlet,* and when he spoke of ROMEO's sad moon *'Sick and pale with grief'* compared to the beauty of his JULIET.

Soliloquy. These monologues, which have the characters speaking out loud to themselves, revealing their inner thoughts, are ideal for students needing a good monologue piece. It's worth remembering that Shakespeare wrote some rather memorable soliloquys that are open to interpretation and imaginative dalliance.

'Ok, enough!', I hear you cry. And yes, I'm going to stop now! The point I want to make is that the language is *not* archaic, boring or irrelevant, but rich, beautiful and full of meaning, which when understood and sensitively exploited enables students to achieve the top marks available. My hope is that I have given you some useful ideas for helping your students see this.

8

The Language of the Theatre

The first section of this chapter looks at the vocabulary used to describe the skills examiners will be looking for on the day of their visit. The second section is a guide to the language used when researching and selecting material, as well as in the performance of the selected scripts.

The Language of the Performance Exam

I was once told that you could grade a student's performance by what was referred to in hushed whispers as 'The school play scale'. This rather dubious system judged young performers on the single criterion, 'Would I give them a part in the school play?' The possible grades ranged from 'Lead in *Grease*', to 'Perhaps one of the Pink Ladies', to, sadly, 'Maybe in the crowd scene at the dance'. The idea of 'accomplished' or 'limited and ineffective' being replaces by DANNY ZUKO or JIMMY's understudy, seemed rather crude. And then there's the fact *Grease* is a musical! Fortunately, there are more precise grading criteria, though at times the language leaves you yearning for the simplicity of casting *Grease*.

Teachers who find the terminology confusing or ambiguous should bear in mind that it is their responsibility to ensure students are aware of the criteria against which they will be assessed. I believe it's a good idea to demystify the terms used in the specification. This can be done through wall displays or in student Drama journals. The terms can and should be reinforced throughout the course by frequently referring to them in rehearsals/workshops. The following section looks in more depth at those skills and what the examiner will be looking for. I have made the tone as generic as possible to reflect the language used by the various boards and OFQUAL.

There are six basic areas to the assessment and students will be graded on:

1 their *overall contribution* to the performance, by performance or design;
2 the *range of theatrical skills* they demonstrate in their performance or design;

3 how *effectively* they use their performance or design skills;
4 how *appropriate* their interpretation of the play is as a whole, as demonstrated by their performance or design;
5 how *sensitive* to the context of the play they are in their performance or design;
6 how successful they are in *achieving their artistic intent*, as demonstrated by their performance or design.

Students who are performing chosen extracts from a text should, through study and teacher-led workshops, develop the following 'Theatrical Skills'.

Learn How to Commit Dialogue to Memory for Performance

Students need to be able to recall and perform without the use of prompt or written text.

Develop Interpretative Skills

The skill of interpretation can be developed through investigating and experimentation with the themes, issues, performance conventions, genre, structure, form, style and language. It can also be enhanced by studying stage directions and the relationships between characters onstage.

Be Able to Interpret and Perform a Character, Appropriate to the Demands of the Script and Communicate this to an Audience

This can be achieved through the use of voice, physical and non-verbal techniques, such as facial expression and gesture, as well as the considered use of space and proxemics. A student's interpretation and performance will be improved when they have an understanding of their character and the relationships between performer and audience.

Develop a Range of Vocal Skills

Vocal skills can include diction, inflection, accent, intonation and phrasing; pace, pause and timing; projection, pitch; emotional range; song and choral work.

Develop a Range of Physical Skills

Physical skills can be movement, body language, posture, gesture, gait, co-ordination, stillness, timing, control, facial expression, eye contact, listening, expression of mood, spatial awareness, interaction with other performers, as well as dance and choral movement.

Develop an Appropriate Performer–Audience Relationship

This can be achieved by ensuring sustained engagement throughout the performance.

Marking your Students

At GCSE level, the various Boards divide into four or five levels of assessment, with 1 being the lowest and 4 (or 5) being the highest awarded. Since the marks vary numerically between each board, I shall focus broadly on the descriptive language used for each level.

For the realisation of artistic intent in a live performance, the theatrical skills marked are broadly as follows:

- the application of a range of vocal skills (pitch, pace/tempo, pause, accent, volume and clarity);
- the application and sustaining of a range of physical skills (gesture, stillness, fluency, expression, posture, facial expressions, movement and proxemics);
- characterisation;
- communication.

Level 0. All Boards agree a zero will be awarded to work that is not worthy of a mark.

Level 1. Key words for this grade will be: Underdeveloped, Limited, Ineffective, Inconsistent, Lacking, Inappropriate, Restricted.

So, in this mark range you might see the following phrases: *'Vocal skills were underdeveloped/limited/lacked effectiveness/range'*, or *'Physical skills were ineffective/limited'*, or *'Did not always take account of the audience'*, or *'Lacked variation and/or range'*.

Level 2. Key words for this grade will be: Satisfactory, Uneven, Limitations, Generally, Adequate, Mostly.

So, in this mark range you might see the following phrases: *'Accent was mostly consistent'*, or *'Generally sound understanding'*, or *'Demonstrated a fair range of vocal techniques'*, or *'Intent was mostly apparent'*.

Level 3. Key words for this grade will be: Good, Wide, Confident, Mostly, Consistent, Effective, Competent, Secure, Reasonable, Sustained.

So, in this mark range you might see the following phrases: *'Some sensitive interaction where appropriate'*, or *'A wide range of vocal skills'*, or *'A competent individual contribution to the performance'*, or *'Characterisation is consistent and secure, demonstrating effective focus and confidence'*.

Levels 4/5. Key words for this grade will be: Excellent, Extensive, Entirely, Highly, Comprehensive, Accomplished, Skilful, Sophisticated, Thoughtful, Fully, Engaging.

So, in this mark range you might see the following phrases: *'Highly effective application of physical skills throughout the performance'*, or *'Personal interpretation is entirely appropriate to the play as a whole'*, or *'An extensive range of vocal skills'*, or *'A comprehensive understanding of the role'*, or *'Assured rapport and communication with audience/other performers'*.

At GCE level, the levels use very similar terminology, though obviously with higher expectations:

Level 1. Limited, Ineffective.

Level 2. General, Reasonable, Basic.

Level 3. Competent, Appropriate, Adequate.

Level 4. Assured, Excellent, Highly appropriate, Confident.

Level 5. Sophisticated, Exceptional, Highly developed, Consistent.

So that's the language of the exam. Now let's take a look at the language of the theatre.

The Language of the Theatre

Students who refer to a scene as 'The bit when' or 'Good bloke, bad bloke' instead of 'protagonist' and 'antagonist' will be at a disadvantage when researching and selecting their performance texts.

The language of the theatre is one with which both teacher and student need to become very familiar. This will help demystify the assessment criteria, enable research and foster an appreciation of the creative process of page to stage.

In order to provide a context, I tried to give examples for each term from the list of 200 suggested plays in Part 2.

When researching, selecting and studying the chosen performance texts, teacher and students should make use of the following terms:

Acts and Scenes. In most plays 'Acts' divide the sections of a play, with further subdivision referred to as 'Scenes'. Some texts (notably works by Shakespeare) are also given 'line numbers'.

Antagonists and Protagonists. A protagonist is a leading character/hero of a play who usually opposes the villain/anti-hero or antagonist. So, ROMEO would be a protagonist and TYBALT would be an antagonist. Or, in *The Crucible*, JOHN PROCTOR is protagonist and ABIGAIL the antagonist. Not all plays have such obvious distinctions; indeed, some have none at all.

Anti-climax and Climax. An anti-climax is usually incomplete and disappointing or unsatisfying, solving nothing, whereas the climax is the significant moment in the plot when things change, reach a crisis point or a conclusion. A good climactic moment can be found in *Entertaining Mr Sloane*, when KEMP is kicked to death by SLOANE. The moments after this are anticlimactic.

Character. A character is an individual, usually named, within a play. For example, there are many characters with the name 'Mary' in *Once a Catholic*.

Chorus. In Greek theatre, the chorus was a character or group who represented an element in the play that commented on the action and advanced the plot (the words being either spoken or sung). However, the term is not restricted to Greek theatre. A chorus appears in *Dr Faustus*, for example.

Comedy and Comic Relief. Humour can be used to make an audience laugh, often for a variety of reasons. Brecht's *Tickle and Slap*, for example, encourages frivolity before considering something terrible or frightening, whilst *That Face* uses dark humour and realism to uncover a family in turmoil. Comic relief is a scene (or line) included in an otherwise serious play to provide a relief from tension for the audience.

Dialogue. This is the 'spoken' text of a play. Conversations between two or more characters. *People, Places and Things* contains many pithy dialogues.

Dramatic Irony. In theatre, dramatic irony refers to that moment when an audience knows (or thinks they know) more about a situation on stage than one or more of the characters. There are many examples of this in *An Inspector Calls*. Plays with a prologue often rely on dramatic irony, allowing the audience to know what is going to happen. This alters their perspective as events unfold on stage. For example, in the prologue to *Romeo and Juliet* the audience is given foreknowledge of the fates of the title characters.

Dramatic Tension. This refers to the moment(s) in a play when the audience feels a heightened sense of anticipation/fear about what is going to happen next. For example, significant dramatic tension can be felt when ARTHUR KIPPS reaches out to the door handle in *The Woman in Black*.

Duologue and Monologue (see also Dialogue). These terms refer to those sections scripted as a conversation between only *two* of the characters. The dialogues between the LANDLORD and the LANDLADY in *Two* can be both uplifting and very sad. A monologue is when only one person is speaking, either to another or to the audience or themselves, often expressing their thoughts (see Soliloquy).

Epilogues and Prologues. The scenes or speeches at the end and start of the main action of a play are known as epilogues and prologues, respectively. A prologue often sets the scene, as in *Romeo and Juliet*: 'Two households both alike in dignity'. An epilogue comes after the main action of a play and offers a summing up or insight into events. The epilogue of *The Rover* is written in rhyming couplets and is thought to mock the audience.

Exposition. This is the section of plot at the beginning of the play which allows the audience to gain important information about the characters, their situation, and their relationships. In Act 1 of *Macbeth*, for instance, we are introduced to the main protagonists and the problem.

Flashback. A flashback is a device whereby the natural flow of time is interrupted so that a moment from the past can be presented. (Plays can also flash forward, either to return from the past or indeed jump into a future situation.) The play *100* is set in the present with flashbacks into each character's past. *A Memory of Lizzie* flashes forward from the 1890s.

Genre. The categorising of different types of Drama sees the works being classified into genres. For example, *Hamlet* is a tragedy, *Groping for Words* is a comedy and Pinter's *The Birthday Party* is a tragi-comedy. Plays are often categorised using more than one genre type.

Monologue (see Duologue).

Narration. This term refers to a dialogue that tells a story within a play or gives the audience information. Narration can accompany on-stage action, as in *Blood Brothers*, or it can be presented in its own right, as for example at the start of *Find Me*.

Plot/Sub-Plot. The plot is the basic story line of a play, a sequence of events that gives the reason(s) for the characters' actions. Generally speaking, every plot has these five elements, in this order:

1 Exposition/introduction
2 Rising action
3 Climax/turning point
4 Falling action
5 Resolution/denouement

A sub-plot is a secondary story/plotline taking place within the main plot. So, in *Twelfth Night* the plot is that VIOLA disguises herself to find her brother SEBASTIAN. The feud between SIR TOBY and MALVOLIO, on the other hand, is a sub-plot. There can be many sub-plots within a play, and they often impact upon the main plot and vice versa.

Rising Action. Rising action is the name given to events that build up the pace/tension or excitement in a play. These events follow the exposition and precede the climax of a play. Rising action can clearly be seen in *A Doll's House* during NORA's first conversation with KROGSTAD when he threatens to tell TORVALD of her loan.

Script. The script is the written text of a play (musical or film). Typically, a script also contains notes/stage directions and other important information from the playwright. The script of *An Inspector Calls* opens with a long and very specific series of notes on the set and stage directions.

Setting (Set). This is the place in which the action of the scene or play is set. *Waiting for Godot* works well with a minimal set, meaning it needs very little onstage. *Abigail's Party* requires a complex naturalistic set.

Soliloquy. This term refers to the lines spoken by a performer on stage to themselves, often when they are alone or believe themselves to be alone. A soliloquy allows characters to speak their thoughts, sharing them with the audience. Act 3 Scene 1 of *Hamlet*, *'To be or not to be'*, is one of Shakespeare's most famous soliloquys.

Stage Directions. These are the instructions given by the playwright regarding how a play should be performed and staged. Usually printed in a different font, stage directions tell actors when, where and how they should make their entrances and exits. Stage directions also often indicate how lines should be delivered. The stage direction 'Pause' is very important in the works of Harold Pinter. Sarah Kane's *4.48 Psychosis*, however, can be confusing for actors as it is almost completely without stage directions.

Stereotype. A stereotype refers to a role with set characteristics, easily recognisable and often exaggerated so as to be very obvious. The DRUM MAJOR who beats up *Woyzeck* is a stereotypical bully.

Stock Character. This is a role with set characteristics that frequently occurs in certain types of Drama. For example, the FOOL or DRUNKARD are stock characters in Shakespeare's plays, the VILLAIN features in melodrama, while the DISHONEST SERVANT often appears in Commedia dell'arte. Stock characters are often stereotypes.

Structure. The structure is the way a play is put together – its connections, plots, episodes, acts and scenes. The structure is the very framework of a play. *My Mother Said I Never Should* uses a kaleidoscopic time structure to examine four generations of a single family.

Subtext. In theatre and when analysing characters, subtext refers to other meanings hidden below the surface of what is actually said and done. In *Dealer's Choice*, the men talk about cards but the subtext is a commentary on how small and meaningless their lives are.

The following terms are important for performers of the chosen performance texts:

Accent. The accent is the vocal inflection given to the words spoken by a character and it should be best suited to the character. For example, a 'thick accent' can be used for the woman in *The 39 Steps* to suggest a spy from Eastern Europe. A more specific South Wales 'Valleys' accent can be used for *Bruised*. (If an accent is attempted, apart from being appropriate it should be sustained throughout the performance.)

Ad Lib. This refers to improvisation by an actor when another performer fails to enter on cue, the natural progress of the play is disturbed or when lines are forgotten. Ad libbing should be avoided in performance exams unless absolutely necessary!

Aside. An aside is the name given to lines spoken by an actor to the audience with the appearance of not being overheard by other characters on stage. *Kvetch* uses frozen moments to speak in frantic asides to the audience.

Blocking. This is the precise arranging of an actor's movements during a play. These will be recorded by stage management in the prompt script.

Characterisation. This is the art of creating a character. In a play, characters may be presented through description within stage directions or character descriptions which actors have to show through actions, speech, or spoken thoughts within the text. Stanislavski focussed on how to build a character using his system.

Corpsing. Corpsing is when an actor drops out of character during performance. Laughing when unscripted is an example of this. (Waving to a parent in the audience counts as corpsing too!)

Diction. This is the quality or style of speaking of a character within the play, consisting of components such as accent, inflection, intonation and enunciation. Good diction means every word spoken is heard and understood by the audience. In order to give the GERMAN OFFICER in *Fear and Misery* a stereotypical flavour, a candidate might decide to speak the lines with a clipped diction.

Gesture. The movements of the body or face of a character during a play are known as gestures. Playwrights often suggest certain gestures in their stage directions in order to create a certain mood or disposition. Directors will often ask actors to adopt certain gestures to give a character more depth or to signify a particular trait. In *What Are they Like*, for example, the actor needs to show changes through altered speech and gesture.

Inflection. This refers to the way in which a word is pronounced. A change of inflection can stress and even change the meaning of spoken words. Different accents can also alter the inflection of a word. A change of inflection can turn the word 'sorry' from an apology into a request.

Mime. Mime in itself is a performance art. Mime within a play also communicates emotion, meaning or an idea without words, using only gesture, expression and movement. Often, but not exclusively, mime is used as a comedic device. *Metamorphosis* by Berkoff works well with no props, where everything is mimed.

On/Off Book. When an actor has to refer to their script during a scene, she/he is said to be 'on book'. Rehearsals, blocking and so on progress much faster when a performer is 'off book'.

Pace. The speed an actor delivers their lines and reacts with others on stage. For example, *Teechers* uses a fast pace and multi-role to keep its audience entertained.

Pause. A pause is a moment on stage when a performer stops speaking. They may be doing something else but for one reason or another they stop speaking. Often during a pause there is a heightening of tension or focus. Pauses are given as a stage direction, the 'Pinter pause' being a famous example of a weighted silence.

Pitch. Pitch is the vocal quality where the tone of voice is high, low or mid-ranged. Usually male voices are lower pitched and female voices are higher pitched. *Under Milk Wood* is often described as 'A play for voices using pace, *pitch*, power and pause'.

Projection. This is a vital tool of the actor. Using the voice deliberately and clearly means the audience can hear every word (spoken or sung). It is not simply a matter of being loud!

Proxemics. This refers to the distances between characters, signifying relationships and their feelings toward each other.

Read-Through. A read-through is a full-cast meeting, one including performers *and* design option candidates too, at which the entire play/script is 'read through'. Ideally, the read-through will take place at the start of the rehearsal process, to enable the cast to get to know their characters, relationships and the text, including cues, entrances and exits.

Stillness. Stillness is the art of acting without movement, and it can have a strong impact upon an audience. It needn't be total, simply using a quiet tone and subtle body language will cause a change of atmosphere on stage. Stillness can say a lot about a character. The use of stillness and silence in *The Caretaker* is as powerful as any spoken word.

Tone. This is the way in which an actor's words are spoken to demonstrate the emotion behind them. For example, a sad or miserable tone, an angry tone, and so on. *Billy Liar's* tone changes depending on who BILLY is telling his 'story' to. *King Lear's* tone changes as LEAR sinks further into madness.

The language specific to the *design options* is given in Chapter 4.

In Part 2, many of the plays suggest a specific practitioner or company as an approach to working with and rehearsing the material. These should be taken as suggestions only. They are based on what I have used with my KS4/5 students or otherwise have seen when visiting schools as a moderator/examiner. Below is a list of these practitioners and companies, along with cursory notes about some of the techniques associated with them. I will also indicate plays that work well using the practitioner's techniques. While some of these may be surprising, I have seen them work!

Practitioners

Artaud, Antonin. Early 20th century. Theatre of cruelty, movement, gesture and dance, masks and puppets, shocking the audience, attack on the emotions, shocking action and images, striking costumes, minimal dialogue, symbolic objects. *Monsters, 4:48 Psychosis, Metamorphosis* (Berkoff), *Pool No Water, The Pillowman.*

Berkoff, Steven. Contemporary. Highly stylised movement (slow motion), exaggerated facial expressions, stylised mime, direct address, exaggerated vocal work, tableaux, mask, ensemble, minimalism, Lecoq. *Metamorphosis, Sink the Belgrano, Kvetch, The Persians, Antigone, Equus.*

Berry, Cicely. Contemporary. Vocal work (predominantly Shakespeare), sound and rhythm, finding language beneath the words, vocalising from the stomach or chest, diction work, the fluidity and fabric of speech, the potential of sound. Resistance exercises. *Romeo and Juliet, Julius Caesar, A Midsummer Night's Dream* (and potentially any other piece by Shakespeare).

Boal, Augusto. Late 20th century. Theatre of the Oppressed, social and political change, Interactive Theatre, Forum Theatre, Image Theatre, Invisible Theatre, short scenes with a strong image that the audience can easily understand and identify with. *The Joker, The Importance of Being Earnest, La Chunga, Paper Flowers, Of Mice and Men.*

Brecht, Bertolt. Early 20th century. Direct address, narration, episodic structure, political message, multi-role, 'gestus', placards, spass/'tickle and slap', music and songs, alienation, montage, didactic, gestic, epic theatre, no fourth wall. *The 39 Steps, Find Me, Andorra, Ghetto, Woyzeck*, in addition to all of Brecht's own works.

Chitty, Alison. Contemporary. Costume and set designer, minimalist set. *The Winter's Tale, Macbeth, Andorra, Woyzeck.*

Donnellan, Declan. Contemporary. Psychological depth of a character, the process of creating realistic, believable characters, influenced by Stanislavski. *Cheek by Jowl, The Winter's Tale, King Lear, Hamlet, Macbeth, Shades, Bully Boy.*

Elliot, Marianne. Contemporary. Directs using all aspects of theatre making, Brechtian techniques, physical theatre, puppetry, music and song. *At the Black Pig's Dyke, The Collected Grimm's Tales, The Cheviot, the Stag and the Black, Black Oil.*

Fry, Gareth. Contemporary. Sound designer (collaborations with Complicité), sound and how it alters emotions, 'immersive multimedia', binaural sound and storytelling, sound manipulation. *Too Much Punch for Judy, Jerusalem, Death and Dancing.*

Godber, John. Contemporary. Political comedy (Hull Truck Theatre), Action theatre, 'imagination, elliptical language, character and transitions', multi-role, stylised realism, comedy. *Bouncers, Shakers, Teechers, Advice for the Young at Heart.*

Grotowski, Jerzy. Mid-20th century. Poor Theatre, not encumbered by lavish set or costume, little or no props, focus on the physical skills of the actor, the bare space, non-traditional space, paratheatre, non-commercial, Experimental Theatre. *Find Me, Road, 100, Playhouse Creatures.*

Ladd, Eddie. Contemporary. Dance and physical theatre, Welsh and English texts, political, technology lead pieces, sometimes site specific. *Bruised, Tonypandemonium, Death and Dancing.*

Lecoq, Jacques. Mid-20th century. Physical Theatre, movement and mime, seven levels of tension, gesture, masks, uncomplicating, mimodynamics. *Metamorphosis, Sink the Belgrano, Kvetch, The Persians, Antigone, Equus.*

Littlewood, Joan. Late 20th century. British Proletariat Theatre. Movement and Laban, physicality in performance, music hall, stand up, voice, movement and improvisation, 'the Working-class voice', music and rhythm, Children's and community theatre. *A Taste of Honey, Billy Liar, Look Back in Anger.*

Mitchell, Katie. Contemporary. Naturalism/multimedia, Deconstruction of text, Stanislavskian methods of character creation, use of technology to enhance the performance, projections, re-interpretation of classic texts, stage imagery. *Top Girls, Black Watch, The Beauty Manifesto, Pool No Water.*

Meyerhold, Vsevolod. Early 20th century. Constructivism, anti-illusionistic, non-naturalistic, stylisation, use of rhythm and music, mask, the grotesque, robotics, biomechanics, symbolism movement. *The Government Inspector, The Caucasian Chalk Circle.*

Pilbrow, Richard. Mid-20th century. Lighting designer, projections, lighting the theatre space, traditional theatre space, musical theatre. *Blood Brothers, Rosencrantz and Guildenstern Are Dead.*

Rice, Emma. Contemporary. Improvisation, music and song, ensemble, Shakespeare, storytelling, socially relevant, Kneehigh, no fear. *Collected Grimm's Tales, A Midsummer Night's Dream, The Mysteries.*

Rees, Marc. Contemporary. Performance, installations, sense of place, physical theatre, interdisciplinary, multi-media, Welsh and English texts, work rooted in history, culture. *Lord of the Flies, Boudica.*

Stafford-Clark, Max. Contemporary. Political/ensemble theatre, improvisation, research, workshop process, flashcards, Out of Joint. *Our Country's Good, Top Girls.*

Stanislavski, Konstantin. (Also spelled Stanislavsky.) 19th–20th century naturalism, the fourth wall, feeling of truth, the magic 'if', emotional memory, muscle memory, circles of attention, intonation and pauses, naturalistic movement, the three-dimensional character. Stanislavski's 'System/Method'. *Agnes of God, The Maids, A View from the Bridge, Of Mice and Men, The Crucible, Julius Caesar, A Doll's House.*

Teal, Polly. Contemporary. Mix of physical theatre and text work, narrative very rarely linear, feminist theatre, adapts texts for Shared Experience. *Grimm's Collected Tales, Dancing at Lughnasa.*

Companies

Cheek by Jowl (Declan Donnellan). Hands-on Shakespeare, re-visiting classical works, character motivation, realistic believable characters, using 'the space', language in performance. Texts in English, Italian, French and Russian.

Complicité. Contemporary. Physical theatre, extreme movement, surreal imagery, Lecoq, storytelling, experimental approach to subject, space, form, sound and the actor. *The Caucasian Chalk Circle.*

DV8. Contemporary. Physical Theatre, dance, a collaboration of art forms using physical/dance, dialogue, soundscape and music to build an emotional story for a character, the clear communication of ideas and feelings without pretention, 'taking risks', visual media. *Observe the Sons of Ulster, Lord of the Flies, Black Watch, Death and Dancing, Virgins, The Static.*

Forkbeard Fantasy. Contemporary. Multimedia, projections and lighting, strong visual elements, elaborate and intricate sets. *The Curious Incident of the Dog in the Night Time, Disco Pigs.*

Frantic Assembly. Contemporary. Physical Theatre, Theatre of the absurd, cross-artform multimedia, humour, spatial awareness, focus and observation, non-naturalistic, music, 'Round by through' and 'Chair duets'. A leading contemporary practitioner/company, studied at A level and beyond. Popular at GCSE too. *Lovesong, Things I Know to Be True, Hymns, The Madness of Esme and Shaz, Burning Bridges, Hamlet, Games and After Liverpool, Beautiful Burnout.*

Gecko. Contemporary. Stylised/physical theatre, epic, the complexity of human nature, 'athletic, honest and emotional'. *Too Much Punch for Judy, Boudica.*

Imaginary Body. Contemporary. Visual style, magical realism, reality and fiction. *100, Paper Flowers, The Guffin, La Chunga.*

Kneehigh. Contemporary. Broad eclectic approach, storytelling and adaptation, honour the story, comedy, live music onstage, audience interaction, song and dance, multi-role, puppetry, inventive use of props. See the work of Emma Rice. Shakespeare.

Out of Joint. Contemporary. (Max Stafford Clark.) Political, humane theatre. Some revival of classic works. *Top Girls, Our County's Good, Macbeth.*

Punchdrunk. Contemporary. Immersive, interactive theatre, promenade theatre, non-traditional, site sympathetic. *Death and Dancing, Disco Pigs, Risk.*

Shared Experience. Contemporary. Expressionism, 'inside out', the conflict between the inner and outer self, physicalisation of emotions, the hidden subtext, conveying meaning/feelings without words. *A Doll's House, Kindertransport, Jane Eyre.*

Tamasha. Contemporary. Multiculturalism in Britain, British Asian influences, new writing, multiple narratives of Britain's changing culture, crossover of Asian culture and British mainstream. *Blood, The Usual Auntijies, True Brits.*

Performance Styles *(Referred to within the 'Description' section in the list of 200 plays)*

Absurd. European, using multiple features to express a tragic theme through comedy, the universe is irrational and meaningless, anti-literary, anti-theatre, human beings trapped in an incomprehensible world. *Waiting for Godot, Rosencrantz and Guildenstern are Dead.*

Comedy. Intended to make an audience laugh, funny, amusing and satirical in tone, usually with a happy ending. *Abigail's Party, School Play, The History Boys.* However, comedy can be used to relieve tension or make an audience laugh before shocking them. Brecht's *Tickle and Slap, (Spass) Fear and Misery of the Third Reich.* Comedy can also be used to cover a more subtle message. *That Face, The Memory of Water.*

Commedia dell'arte. Usually improvised comedy, stock characters like the lovers, the servant, stylised and recognisable costumes and characters, mask and exaggerated gesture, panto/slapstick, 'lazzi', originated in 15th-century Italy. *The Servant of Two Masters, Black Comedy, Volpone.*

Epic. Didactic Drama avoiding illusion. Using 'gestus', alienation effect, to distance the audience from emotional involvement, Brechtian, the absence of realism, political. *Mother Courage, Fear and Misery.*

Expressionism. A modernist movement. European and later USA, the depiction of emotional experience rather than physical reality. Berkoff's *Metamorphosis, Kvetch, Sink the Belgrano.*

Forum. Boal. Theatre of the Oppressed. Using theatre to achieve socio-political aims. Audience interaction exploring different options to deal with a presented problem or issue. *Blackout.*

Immersive. Theatre which relies on audience immersion such as promenade or performance art, audiences become part of the performance itself. *The Mysteries, Female Transport.* Punchdrunk.

Melodrama. Usually a sensational plot, highly emotional and dialogue led, over sentimental, using music and exaggerated love, revenge and lust, plot over character. *The Importance of being Earnest.* A play may also contain melodramatic moments or elements. For example, *Romeo and Juliet.*

Metatheatre (Metadrama). Theatre which draws attention to the fact it is unreal by the use of a play within a play for example, or reflecting comedy and tragedy together. *Hamlet's* play within the play or a tragicomedy like *The Birthday Party.* The term 'metatheatre' is much debated.

Naturalism. Late 19th and early 20th century European movement. The creation of a perfect illusion of reality on stage, given circumstance, Stanislavski. *A Doll's House.* A heightened form of 'Realism'.

Physical. Making use of the body over the spoken word, the body being the primary communication with the audience, dance, mime, body props. Physical theatre companies like DV8 could be used in a production like *Virgins* or *Pink Mist.* Other Physical theatre companies like Frantic Assembly co-produce plays like *Lovesong, Beautiful Burnout* or *Hymns.*

Political. Theatre that comments on political and social issues. Political playwrights would include Sean O'Casey, Caryl Churchill, Arthur Miller, Dario Fo or Grotowski and even Shakespeare. Political plays would include, *Accidental Death of an Anarchist*, *The Crucible*, *Top Girls*, *The Resistible Rise of Arturo Ui*, *Julius Caesar*.

Realism. Late 19th and 20th century. Everyday people and everyday problems. Believable dialogues spoken by believable characters in common settings. Ibsen is widely regarded to be the father of realism. Stanislavski was a firm believer. (See also Naturalism.) Theatre of the fourth wall removed. Examples of such plays include, *Look Back in Anger*, *A Doll's House*, *Britannia Waves the Rules*.

Stylised. The method of showing personality or mood by a character's movement onstage. There are specific techniques such as mime, dance, gesture and movement. Practitioners like Berkoff use stylised movement in their works, including robotic movement, slow motion with an ensemble, exaggerated movements and facial expressions and the use of asides. Plays like Berkoff's *Kvetch* or Godber's *Bouncers* are two very different examples of stylised theatre. Elements of Greek theatre were also stylised.

Symbolism. In the theatre, symbolism may be achieved through costume, colour, props, character and even that character's movement. The symbol stands for or represents another thing. Props and set often have symbolic significance which audiences identify quickly. Symbolism can be obvious, like red robes for LADY MACBETH or a large throne for HAMLET'S UNCLE, or more subtle, like MARILYN MONROE in *Blood Brothers*.

T.I.E. Theatre in Education. Usually highly interactive, an aid to learning, uses forum techniques.

Tragedy. Terrible events, death/downfall of heroic characters, an individual's fate decided due to a moral weakness or flaw. MACBETH brings about his own downfall through greed and ambition. In *A View from the Bridge*, EDDIE's downfall is due to his jealousy and impotency. Enables an audience to reflect upon what might have been.

Verbatim. Documentary theatre (although documentary theatre is less about people's testimony and more about events). Using pre-existing documentary material as the source of a play about real people and events. Could be TV documentary, newspaper or even a diary. Voice, movement, interviewing and storytelling. *Too Much Punch for Judy* or *Monsters* are examples of Verbatim theatre. Often much of the text is unaltered from the original source.

* * *

Well, that's it. Enjoy the list of 200 plays that follows. Remember that I have tried to include something for every student – they just need your expert guidance to discover what is best for them and their group.

PART TWO

Listing of 200 Plays

Female-only Plays

Play 1

	Title & publisher	*Hannah and Hanna* Oberon Modern Plays
	Playwright/Date	John Retallack 2001
	Casting	2F **GCSE or GCE** Able performers, singer/dancer
	Notes, guidance and considerations for teachers/students	**Description:** Theatre for teenage audience. Two-hander/comedy. **Summary:** Hannah is 16. She loves karaoke and her boyfriend; she hates her home town of Margate and the Kosovan asylum seekers who have come to live there. Hanna is also 16. She loves karaoke, loves Margate – and is one of the asylum seekers. **Where:** Margate (could be any seaside town), various locations and Kosovo. **When:** 1990s. **Themes:** Karaoke; asylum seekers; prejudice; racism; friendship. **Notes:** This play for two young women addresses important issues through comedy, personal drama and the uniting power of music. The songs are important! **Design/tech notes:** Minimalist works best. Various interior and exterior settings on a bare stage. Great opportunities for technical candidates, projections and sound. **Warnings:** Mild adult themes. Racism, ethnic hatred. **Workshop/rehearsal/ideas/notes:** Physical theatre. DV8 song and dance. **Research:** Kosovo War 1998–99. Margate 2000. Refugees from Kosovo.
	Section or scene(s)	The whole play is 70 minutes. HANNAH's monologue in Scene 3 followed by HANNA'S. HANNA as her MOTHER, monologue about England. HANNAH as NAN/JOE. Excellent opportunity for multi-role.

Play 2

🎭	Title & publisher	*Cuttin' it*	Faber & Faber
✏️	Playwright/Date	Charlene James	2016
👥	Casting	2F	Able GCE
📋	Notes, guidance and considerations for teachers/students	**Description:** Women's theatre. **Summary:** Teenagers Muna and Iqra catch the same school bus. They were both born in Somalia, but their backgrounds are different. They share a painful secret. **Where:** Various settings. Inner city flats/school/bus. **When:** Contemporary. **Themes:** Female genital mutilation; war; pain; secrets. **Notes:** Mainly told as a series of connected monologues. **Design/tech notes:** Minimalist set. Few props. Projections/SFX. **Warnings:** Very disturbing. Check your students and study the play before introducing this very important material. **Workshop/rehearsal/ideas/notes:** Finding the humour within the heartbreak and pain. Tickle and slap. Monologues. Verbatim. **Research:** Female genital mutilation (under careful, sensitive supervision and guidance).	
🎬	Section or scene(s)	MUNA'S visit to IQRA'S flat and the ensuing conversation. Monologues: IQRA'S 'I do not know the answer...' MUNA'S 'I get to the school gates...' IQRA'S 'I was 6 years old'.	

Play 3

🎭	Title & publisher	*A Memory of Lizzie*	Nelson (Part of the Anthology *Sepia and Song*)
✏️	Playwright/Date	David Foxton	1987
👥	Casting	2F (Lizzie and Rachel) plus 12 characters who can be M/F	GCSE Mixed ability
📋	Notes, guidance and considerations for teachers/students	**Description:** Historical drama. **Summary:** A fictional look at the childhood years of the infamous murderess Lizzie Borden. Uses flashforward. **Where:** An average suburban school, Massachusetts, USA. **When:** 1871. **Themes:** Murder; guilt and innocence; bullying; social rejection; the cruelty children are capable of. **Notes:** Try to point the commentaries and flashforwards using spotlight/freeze frame etc. Cast sings 'Oranges and Lemons'. **Design/tech notes:** Works well in the round. Minimal with levels. Good opportunities for lighting for flashforward and reality. Costume: period apron and pinafore. **Warnings:** References to violent murder. **Workshop/rehearsal/ideas/notes:** Look at children's games of the era (1870s). Observe 12-year olds at play (perhaps younger!). **Research:** Lizzie Borden, 4th August 1892 axe murders.	
🎬	Section or scene(s)	Can be performed as a whole. 15–25 minutes.	

Play 4

🎭	Title & publisher	*Agnes of God*	Samuel French
✏️	Playwright/Date	John Pielmeier	1979
👥	Casting	3F	GCE or able GCSE
📋	Notes, guidance and considerations for teachers/students	**Description:** Tragedy. **Summary:** A court-appointed psychiatrist is charged with assessing the sanity of a novice nun accused of murdering her new-born. The Mother Superior determinedly keeps young Agnes from the doctor, further arousing suspicion. Who killed the infant, and who fathered the tiny victim? **Where:** A Roman Catholic convent near Montreal, Quebec, Canada. **When:** 1970s. **Themes:** Faith and the power of love; Christianity; miracles; child abuse; sin. **Notes:** If Agnes can sing so much the better! **Design/tech notes:** Light and dark with good lighting effects opportunities. Absolutely bare minimum on stage. Two chairs. Blood effects. No clutter. Two Nun's costumes. **Warnings:** Child abuse discussed, death of a new-born. Hypnosis. The doctor smokes throughout most of the first act! **Workshop/rehearsal/ideas/notes:** Research the role of Mother Superior, Novice and Psychiatrist. Role on wall. Stanislavski. Emotion memory.	
🎬	Section or scene(s)	Two hours of excellent duologues/monologues to choose from. Three very strong and different female roles. Act 1 Scene 1 DOCTOR'S monologue. First meeting of DOCTOR and MOTHER SUPERIOR. Encourage students to read the play and choose scenes. Sensitive students always find the parts that make an audience sit up a listen!	

Play 5

🎭	Title & publisher	*Di and Viv and Rose*	Methuen Drama
✏️	Playwright/Date	Amelia Bullmore	2011
👥	Casting	3F	GCE Similar abilities
📋	Notes, guidance and considerations for teachers/students	**Description:** Tragi-comedy. **Summary:** A powerful three-hander about a female friendship that spans three decades. **Where:** Manchester/London/New York. **When:** Three decades starting in the 1980s. **Themes:** Female friendship and enduring bonds and the toll life's journeys take on each of us; sharing. **Notes:** The wit and pace of the piece is relentless. **Design/tech notes:** There is quite a complex set needed for the first act in particular. Good opportunities for design students. Props too. Costume is important to the plot. Lighting and projections. Music/SFX all needed for this one. The script is quite specific. **Warnings:** Some strong sexual language. Reference to a rape. **Workshop/rehearsal/ideas/notes:** Strong character work. Wide range of intense emotions. The actors should not try to get older over the generations, rather start at the age they are in the final scenes.	
🎬	Section or scene(s)	Act 1 Scenes 5, 6, 7, 8. Act 2 Scenes 1, 2, 3, 4, 5, 6, 7, 8 and projections for 9. Monologues: Act 1 Scene 2 VIV *'Clothes are signifiers'*. Scene 4 VIV *'Can it be argued?'* VIV *'Society!'* Scene 5 ROSE *'Well it's partly the pills'* Scene 7 DI *'I always thought. . .'* and *'She's really easy to talk to'*. VIV *'My mother was top of her class'*. Act 2 Scene 2 ROSE *'Oh. I'm. I'm okay'*. Scene 5 DI *'When Rose asked me'*.	

Play 6

	Title & publisher	*Girls*	Methuen Drama
	Playwright/Date	Theresa Ikoko	2015
	Casting	3F	GCE or able GCSE
	Notes, guidance and considerations for teachers/students	**Description:** Tragi-comedy. **Summary:** Three ordinary girls, best friends forever, are kidnapped from their hometown in Northern Nigeria and their world is turned upside down. **Where:** Nigeria. Various locations. Mainly inside. **When:** Contemporary. **Themes:** Enduring friendship; girlhood; the stories behind the headlines that too soon become yesterday's news; hope and despair; religion; terrorism. **Notes:** Casting should respect the ethnicity of the three girls. The humour is necessary and should not be played down. **Design/tech notes:** Minimal set to give the feeling of a small, confined interior. Dark and light changes, sound effects. Costume becomes increasingly grimy and dishevelled. **Warnings:** Very harrowing in places. A miscarriage and death. Beware of the tickle and slap! **Workshop/rehearsal/ideas/notes:** Use a small, intimate place to rehearse. Tension, fear, confinement. **Research:** Giving a voice to the abducted women/girls of the world. Boko Haram/kidnap.	
	Section or scene(s)	Scenes 1, 2, 3, 4, 6, (HALEEMA's monologues) 8, 9, 11, 12, 15, 16, 18, (RUHAB's monologue) 20, 25, 26 and 27.	

Play 7

	Title & publisher	*The Maids*	Faber & Faber
	Playwright/Date	Jean Genet	1947
	Casting	3F	GCE or able GCSE
	Notes, guidance and considerations for teachers/students	**Description:** Absurdist French theatre. **Summary:** Two sisters, maids to a wealthy society woman, play out their dreams of wealth, love and revenge while their mistress is out on a romantic rendez-vous. Their playing becomes more real and violent as they await madame's return. **Where:** The bedroom of a wealthy madame. Paris, France. **When:** Can be played at any time. **Themes:** Illusion; otherness; authority; betrayal; death. **Notes:** Although given as present time, the play is now over 80 years old and works well in 1940s France (original language French). **Design/tech notes:** Good set design opportunities. Costume also offers great opportunities, as do props (flowers). Lighting can play an important part in the show. **Warnings:** Mild adult themes. Some Boards use this as a prescribed text. Check your specification! **Workshop/rehearsal/ideas/notes:** Stanislavski role work. 'Magic if' status. **Research:** The real life (Papin) murder case of 1933.	
	Section or scene(s)	Some really excellent dialogues. Select any of the work with the two sisters and follow the rising tension. Monologues: CLAIRE's opening scene. MADAME SOLANGE's final monologue *'Madame is dead . . .'*	

Play 8

	Title & publisher	Notes to Future Self	Faber & Faber
	Playwright/Date	Lucy Caldwell	2011
	Casting	4F	GCE or very able GCSE
	Notes, guidance and considerations for teachers/students	**Description:** One-act family drama. **Summary:** When 13-year-old Sophie develops bone cancer, the family go to her Grandmother's home for her to die. Three generations of women begin as strangers under one roof as Sophie comes to terms with her mortality. **Where:** Sophie's world and the literal. A small two-bedroomed terrace in Birmingham, UK. **When:** Present day. Early autumn to early winter. **Themes:** Parenting/family; courage; illness, growing up; death. **Notes:** Establishing who/which/where Sophie and is challenging. **Design/tech notes:** The author states that the play should be done with a minimal set: 'The less there is, the better'. Costume offers great design opportunities. There must be clearly defined separate spaces for each character, perhaps pools of light or levels. Kitchen, attic, shed and Sophie's bedroom. Music is an important part of the whole piece. **Warnings:** Death of a child from cancer. Adult language. **Workshop/rehearsal/ideas/notes:** Kneehigh Theatre. Allow the script to challenge students to explore and experiment with the characters, how they navigate the emotions of each moment and how they move in and out of reality/view.	
	Section or scene(s)	Cast should select pieces of dialogue between their characters, then select powerful monologues: 1: SOPHIE's opening *'True story'*. JUDY's story of her man. 2: SOPHIE's description of death. Two: CALLIOPE's *'I want you to stop praying'*. 3: JUDY. Final piece by SOPHIE to future self.	

Play 9

	Title & publisher	Shakers Re-Stirred	Methuen Drama
	Playwright/Date	Godber and Thornton	Original 1985
	Casting	4F Multi-role	GCSE Suits a range of matching abilities
	Notes, guidance and considerations for teachers/students	**Description:** Stylised social comedy. **Summary:** Four waitresses, each under pressure in different ways, describe a typical night at a bar called Shakers. **Where:** A trendy cocktail bar in the North of England, UK. **When:** Maggie Thatcher's yuppie '80s. **Themes:** Thatcher's Britain; high unemployment; aspiration; gender stereotyping; the sexualisation of women in the workplace. **Notes:** The actresses play all the characters in the bar, including the customers the four waitresses have to deal with. **Design/tech notes:** Set should be simple and uncluttered. Four stools/chairs and a bar. Props are best mimed. **Warnings:** Some strong language. Adult themes. **Workshop/rehearsal/ideas/notes:** Hot seating for character work, mime workshops and group work. Stylised ensemble movement.	
	Section or scene(s)	A sequence of quick-fire humour interspersed with serious monologues; encourage students to make choices. Monologues: Act 1 MEL *'Bleeding cocktails'* CAROL *'I can't help it'*. ADEL *'I want to get out'*. Act 2 NICKY *'I know they're jealous of me'*. MEL *'This job's not bad'*. ADEL *'You know at times like these'*.	

Play 10

	Title & publisher	*My Mother Said I Never Should*	Methuen Drama
	Playwright/Date	Charlotte Keatley	1988
	Casting	4F	GCSE Fairly able group of similar abilities
	Notes, guidance and considerations for teachers/students	**Description:** A feminist play about life! **Summary:** A sharp focus on the lives of four women through the immense social changes of the 20th century. Using a kaleidoscopic time structure, we examine four generations of one family as they confront the most significant moments of their lives. **Where:** Various locations in and around Manchester, UK. **When:** The 20th century. **Themes:** Mother–daughter relationships; social change over the 20th century; love; jealousy; the price of freedom; the desire to love and be loved. **Notes:** A very popular play with students and drama teachers. With four very strong female characters the play is non-naturalistic with a minimalist set. Fantastic opportunities for performers to display many strong emotions. **Design/tech notes:** The 'Empty Space' filled with the children as they grow into their adult characters is very important. Costume should represent the generations through which the play moves back and forth. The non-linear chronology demands an adaptable set as well as performers. **Warnings:** Adult language in some scenes. **Workshop/rehearsal/ideas/notes:** Objective and Super objective. Emotion memory. Character work. Stanislavski.	
	Section or scene(s)	Act 1 Scene 1, 2, 7, 9 and 10. Act 2 (whole act) Act 3 scenes 5 to 7. It is best to allow the cast to show sections of scenes which follow the chronology of the play. Monologues: Act 1 Scene 10 ROSIE *'It's my birthday today and. . .'* Act 2 DORIS *'If you like. . .'* Act 3 Scene 4 MARGARET *'I know the door is. . .'* Act 3 Scene 5 JACKIE *'How dare you. . .'* Act 3 Scene 8 DORIS *'Mother! Mother!'* to end.	

Play 11

	Title & publisher	*Playhouse Creatures*	Samuel French
	Playwright/Date	April De Angelis	1994
	Casting	5F	GCE Able, singing/dancing
	Notes, guidance and considerations for teachers/students	**Description:** Feminist theatre. **Summary:** Five actresses (real women) who pioneered women on stage after the re-opening of the theatres. Centres on Nell Gwyn and her seven-year struggle from prostitute and fruit seller to one of the greatest stars of the stage. **Where:** London, UK. Five locations, interior and exterior. **When:** 1669. **Themes:** Sexual harassment/exploitation; wage discrimination; ageism; women in the workplace; maternity rights. All themes are as relevant today as they were in the 1600s. **Notes:** Five huge/challenging female roles. Should be able to sing and dance. **Design/tech notes:** Fantastic opportunities for design students, with period costume and a fast-moving plot through five different locations. Research costume of the period but also consider what the actresses themselves say about their costumes. The Samuel French edition has set and prop lists and a lighting plot. **Warnings:** Mild adult themes. **Workshop/rehearsal/ideas/notes:** Character work. Grotowski. History and objectives. Comic timing.	
	Section or scene(s)	Act 1 Scenes 1, 2, 4, 5, 6, 8, 10, Act 2 Scenes 1, 4, 5, 6, 7, 8. Some scenes are highly comedic, others are dramatic. DOLL has good monologues. Witches scene/Macbeth. Consider the role of the play within the play.	

Play 12

	Title & publisher	*Dreamjobs*	Samuel French
	Playwright/Date	Graham Jones	1979
	Casting	5F	GCSE Various abilities
	Notes, guidance and considerations for teachers/students	**Description:** Comedy. **Summary:** Five teenage girls waiting for interviews with an employment service dream of the romantic, exciting jobs they would like before reality hits. **Where:** A waiting room. **When:** Scripted as 'The present'. The 1970s but relevant any time. **Themes:** Ambition; youth employment; self-image. **Notes:** Samuel French copy has lighting and effects plot. **Design/tech notes:** Calls for a bare stage with six simple chairs. Lighting/projections to suggest the different dream locations/events. SFX and music technical opportunities. A nail file. Five costumes which differ according to character as scripted. **Warnings:** Dated references but still works. I've seen it with up to the minute references and music and it worked very well. **Workshop/rehearsal/ideas/notes:** Five very different people requiring detailed subtle character work and some great physical theatre opportunities.	
	Section or scene(s)	A 20-minute short play. Possible to perform as a whole piece for five.	

Play 13

	Title & publisher	*Be my Baby*	NHB
	Playwright/Date	Amanda Whittington	1998
	Casting	6F	GCSE Range of abilities
	Notes, guidance and considerations for teachers/students	**Description:** Tragi-comedy. **Summary:** Mary Adams: 19-years-old, unmarried and pregnant is sent in secrecy and shame to St. Saviours, a Church of England mother-and-baby home. **Where:** A mother and baby home in the North of England, UK. **When:** Two months in 1964. **Themes:** Teenage pregnancy (outside of marriage); hope; friendship; adoption and grief; secrecy and shame. **Notes:** The NHB revised edition carries an appendix of three added scenes for productions in 2002 and 2004, titled Five A, Six A and Six B to indicate their place within the text. **Design/tech notes:** Minimal set to reflect the austere setting. Two single beds and a functioning door. A small desk and two chairs. A dormitory and a study. The revised NHB edition carries notes on featured music which is important to the '60s feel of the piece. Costume, simple uniform, aprons for the girls and a Matron's uniform if desired. Mum dressed according to the period. **Warnings:** Adoption issues. **Workshop/rehearsal/ideas/notes:** Build up good portraits of each character/role on wall. Stanislavski. Status games.	
	Section or scene(s)	The duologues of MATRON & NORMA and MATRON & QUEENIE, or three in the laundry scene with MUM, MATRON and MARY. MATRON & MARY telephone scene.	

Play 14

	Title & publisher	*Bazaar and Rummage*	Methuen Drama
	Playwright/Date	Sue Townsend	1982
	Casting	6F	GCSE A range of abilities
	Notes, guidance and considerations for teachers/students	**Description:** Comedy. **Summary:** Three agoraphobic women have left their homes for the first time to go to a jumble sale organised by their social workers. **Where:** A Church Hall, UK. **When:** 1980s. **Themes:** Agoraphobia; the nature of caring; suffering; fear; courage. **Notes:** Do not play for laughs. *'Play it for the truth in the lines. The laughs will come'*. S. Townsend. **Design/tech notes:** A simple set cluttered gradually by lots of Bric á Brac (Jumble) Props/Costume/rails etc.! It's a church hall set up with tables for a jumble sale. Basic lighting. Some call for sound effects/music. A working piano (if a member of cast can play). Other props are specific and named in the text (this also applies to costume in some cases). **Warnings:** Sexual references and bad language. Some racist remarks. **Workshop/rehearsal/ideas/notes:** Very character based. Each woman has her story to tell and should be driven by it right from the start. Stanislavski. **Research:** Has been made into a movie (1983).	
	Section or scene(s)	Act 1 Opening sequence. GWENDA's monologue *'looking after Daddy'* with interruptions. MARGARET's entrance. The women dress their tables and the rules! *'Rummage sale opera'* End of Act. Act 2 The women discuss GWENDA. Then all of the Women's stories in order.	

Remember to check the maximum performers being assessed in each piece is in line with your specification.

Play 15

	Title & publisher	*Girls Like That*	NHB
	Playwright/Date	Evan Placey	2013
	Casting	6F +	GCSE An able group with good physical skills
	Notes, guidance and considerations for teachers/students	**Description:** Social drama/Ensemble. **Summary:** Uses shifts in time to explore feminist consciousness. The play focuses on adolescent female friendship now and its fragility in the face of social and cultural pressures. A very relevant and powerful piece. **Where:** In and around any school (girls initially). **When:** Contemporary. **Themes:** The pressures on young people; technology; peer pressure; cyber bullying; reputation and why isn't it the same for boys? **Notes:** Great opportunities for music and dance sequences. **Design/tech notes:** Minimalist; however, changes in time/the ages of the girls calls for clever lighting/sound or use of costume and props. **Warnings:** The language is appropriate to the subject matter. Some sexual references. **Workshop/rehearsal/ideas/notes:** Brainstorm ideas as a company. Change time rapidly by light, sound or actors changing position. Stylised, physical works well. Ensemble rehearsals where appropriate.	
	Section or scene(s)	Great for monologues/duologues or as a larger group of 6–20. Excellent multi-role (age) opportunities.	

Play 16

	Title & publisher	*The Madness of Esme and Shaz* Methuen Drama
	Playwright/Date	Sarah Daniels 1994
	Casting	8F GCSE Some multi-role Able
	Notes, guidance and considerations for teachers/students	**Description:** Black comedy. **Summary:** Shaz is recently released on probation and haunted by the crimes that put her in prison. The probation office has put her in touch with an elderly maiden aunt who takes her in and helps her find peace. **Where:** Various, a day ward in a secure unit, a park, a living room and a train, UK. **When:** Contemporary. **Themes:** Women's mental health; redemption; family; friendship; love; crime. **Notes:** Various settings call for minimalist approach for exam/performances. **Design/tech notes:** Minimal with clever use of lighting/versatile set. SFX and the idea of motion. **Warnings:** Contains a description of killing a baby. Strong language at times. Mental health issues. Child abuse in families. **Workshop/rehearsal/ideas/notes:** Stanislavski to study the characters/emotions. Nice opportunities for physical duet work with PAT & SHAZ/ESME & SHAZ. Frantic Assembly.
	Section or scene(s)	All of the duologues are powerful. Strong, often very differing characters. Allow cast to study and make guided choices. Monologues: Scene 6 DENA. Scene 7 SHAZ. Scene 11 ESME. Scene 15 ESME.

Play 17

	Title & publisher	*The Cagebirds* Samuel French
	Playwright/Date	David Campton 1971
	Casting	8F GCSE/GCE A range of abilities
	Notes, guidance and considerations for teachers/students	**Description:** Theatre of the absurd/fantasy. **Summary:** Six women live in a locked room, each absorbed in her own petty life and pleasing the mistress. Then the 'Wild One' joins them in their 'cage' and talks of breaking out and seeking freedom. The others want to remain secure in their cage, and unite against her! **Where:** A room with a large locked door. **When:** Now. **Themes:** Oppression; human behaviour; individual vs. society; violence. **Notes:** One set. A single room with a large door. A one-act allegory. **Design/tech notes:** The Samuel French copy carries furniture/prop/lighting and effects requirements/suggestions. Minimalist. Lighting calls for sinister shadows. Works well in the round with set made to resemble a cage. **Warnings:** The piece carries many stage directions. Movement is crucial and benefits from a choreographic approach. **Workshop/rehearsal/ideas/notes:** Physicalising of bird-like qualities/movements challenging but very rewarding. Each woman reflects a bird like quality both in movement and vocally. Berkoff. Well-considered costume or props can also extend the illusion.
	Section or scene(s)	55 minutes in total. Many long monologues. Encourage cast to select characters and identify the physical qualities of their choice. In rehearsal they should consider movement and props which might highlight these qualities. Some of the monologues are challenging but each character should have one where provided.

Play 18

Title & publisher	*Daisy Pulls it off*	Samuel French
Playwright/Date	Denise Deegan	1983
Casting	16F 2M but not necessary	GCSE A range of abilities

Notes, guidance and considerations for teachers/students	**Description:** Naturalistic comedy/parody. **Summary:** Daisy Meredith gets a scholarship to a private girls' school. The plucky heroine faces many tribulations, some very dangerous, before she is accepted. **Where:** Grangewood School for Young Ladies, UK. **When:** 1920s. **Themes:** School; privilege; class; friendship; perseverance; inclusion. **Notes:** Often chosen by all-girls' schools. Can easily be performed without the two male characters actually appearing. Cast can be reduced. **Design/tech notes:** Great minimalist set, chairs, blackboard and body props (physical theatre). Lighting and costume opportunities. Use stage and other areas of the theatre. **Warnings:** Don't lose sight of the tongue-in-cheek, parody. **Workshop/rehearsal/ideas/notes:** Remember it's a parody. Audience address. Character work for each of the girls. Vocal work/accent. History and objectives. Status games. **Research:** Angela Brazil's schoolgirl novels. Photos of the period. What else was happening in the world (1920s)?
Section or scene(s)	Opening sequence Act 1 Miss GIBSON's audience address. DAISY's narrative/journey from home and first impressions of Grangewood. Any of the classroom and dorm scenes. The hockey match!

Play 19

Title & publisher	*Top Girls*	Methuen Drama
Playwright/Date	Caryl Churchill	1982
Casting	16F But can be multi-role and reduced to 4–6	GCSE A fairly able group

Notes, guidance and considerations for teachers/students	**Description:** Historical feminist. **Summary:** The play focusses on the character of Marlene, the head of a London employment agency, and explores the compromises that she has had to make to achieve a successful career. **Where:** Restaurant in London. Act 1 Scene 1. An office, a garden and one room in a house, UK. **When:** Early years of Thatcher (1980s). **Themes:** 1980s' Britain; being a successful woman and whether it is possible for women in society to combine a successful career with family life; bourgeois feminism during the Thatcher era. **Notes:** A real favourite with schools. The all-girl cast is appealing to girls' schools or classes with mainly girls. The play is nonlinear and usually for examination purposes schools focus on the play after Act 1 Scene 1, which reduces the cast to 4–6 characters depending on the chosen scene. Great opportunities for a series of short, intense pieces which stand alone. **Design/tech notes:** Minimal set. Use levels for locations. Costume in Act 1 important. **Warnings:** Very strong language in some scenes. **Workshop/rehearsal/ideas/notes:** Character study and intense emotions. Emotion memory. Status. Multi-role if required. Katie Mitchell/Stanislavski/Max Stafford Clarke.
Section or scene(s)	Act 1 in the restaurant can stand alone with a strong cast of 6, Act 2 Scene 2 KIT and ANGIE then later JOYCE. Act 2 Scene 3 MARLENE & ANGIE. Main office. All of Act 3 ANGIE, MARLENE & JOYCE. Monologues: Act 1 JOAN. GRET; ISABELLA Act 2 Scene 3 LOUISE 'There you are,' SHONA 'My job at present'. WIN 'Oh yes, all of that'.

Play 20

	Title & publisher	*The House of Bernarda Alba* *Le casa de Bernarda Alba*	Methuen Drama
	Playwright/Date	Federico García Lorca	1945
	Casting	17F	GCSE/GCE Able
	Notes, guidance and considerations for teachers/students	\multicolumn{2}{l	}{**Description:** Tragedy. **Summary:** Five daughters live together in one house with their tyrannical mother. **Where:** A rural village near Granada, Andalucía, Spain. **When:** A hot summer in 1936. **Themes:** Love; sex; class; repression; death; gossip; religion; depression; desire. **Notes:** I have seen the play done in a very stylised manner using stark Brechtian sets. 'A drama of the women in the villages of Spain'. **Design/tech notes:** Costume and set both present good design opportunities. A good, simple, naturalistic yet flexible representation of Bernarda's home. Lighting to set atmosphere more than scene. **Warnings:** Lewd in places. **Workshop/rehearsal/ideas/notes:** As much as possible rehearse with full company, sharing all aspects. Use the space and set from as early as possible; include costume. Music and dance should be authentic and choreographed. **Research:** Spanish Civil War.}
	Section or scene(s)	\multicolumn{2}{l	}{ACT 1 up to where the mourners leave the house. Act 2 PONCIA & MAGDELENA- Chorus. AMELIA & MARTIRIO. Act 3 from final entrance of PONCIA to end. Monologues/Duologues: Act 2 BERNARDA/PONCIA. Act 3 MARIA JOSEFA.}

Male-only Plays

Play 21

	Title & publisher	*True Brits*	Methuen Drama
	Playwright/Date	Vinay Patel	2014
	Casting	1M	GCSE/GCE
	Notes, guidance and considerations for teachers/students	\multicolumn{2}{l	}{**Description:** British Asian monologues. **Summary:** Rahul struggles to remain part of a post-7/7 British society that now distrusts him on sight. Moves between paranoid London of 2005 and the euphoric city of the 2012 Olympics. **Where:** London, UK. **When:** 2005 and 2012. **Themes:** British identity; racism; fitting in; relationships and love. **Notes:** The part of Rahul is written for one actor but can be shared between more (for example, the 18-year-old and the 25-year-old). **Design/tech notes:** Minimal set, good opportunities for light/projections. Set as a 'stand up' in a club. Costume as per script, reflecting the year and the age of Rahul. **Warnings:** Some adult themes. Racist chants. **Workshop/rehearsal/ideas/notes:** Audience address. Delivery and timing. Physical work with others in the company. Katie Mitchell. **Research:** 7th July 2005 London Bombings. 2012 London Summer Olympics.}
	Section or scene(s)	\multicolumn{2}{l	}{Monologues: Opening monologue (2012) *'Do you feel British?'* Mid-March 2005. Late April 2005. Mid-June. Early June RHYS *'I'll go'*. 2012 *'Everyone's just been. . .'* Early August 2005 Early September 2012, NERVY. Mid-September 2005. Mid-August 2012–end.}

Play 22

	Title & publisher	*Blackout*	Methuen Drama
	Playwright/Date	Davey Anderson	2012
	Casting	1M and ensemble 2M 2F	GCE Physically demanding
	Notes, guidance and considerations for teachers/students	**Description:** Storytelling, monologue. **Summary:** The true story of a boy charged with attempted murder at 15 and how he tries to piece together the moments in his life that sent him to a secure unit. **Where:** Glasgow, Scotland. **When:** Now. **Themes:** Crime; growing up; being bullied and fighting back. **Notes:** The part of James can be shared carefully with the ensemble sharing all parts. The whole piece is 30 minutes long, if uncut. **Design/tech notes:** Minimalist, works well on a series of stage blocks/levels in stark lighting. Intimate studio. **Warnings:** It's important that the Scots accent is respected throughout. Strong language and reference to violent acts. **Workshop/rehearsal/ideas/notes:** Needs a strong physical performance that includes the ensemble right from the start. DV8 highly choreographed/stylised. Use forum theatre to explore how different events affected James. **Research:** Interviews with young offenders. Lyric Theatre.	
	Section or scene(s)	Scenes 1, 2, 4, 5, 7, 8, 10, 11, 12, 13, 14, 15, 16, 17, 18, 19, 20. This could be a series of monologues and shared ensemble work to give more than one performer an opportunity.	

Play 23

	Title & publisher	*Private Peaceful*	Oberon plays
	Playwright/Date	Morpurgo and Reade	2004
	Casting	1M and supporting multi-role characters	GCSE/GCE Demanding
	Notes, guidance and considerations for teachers/students	**Description:** Storytelling/history **Summary:** Tommo (who tells the story) remembers his childhood, life, love and family. He recalls with the help of a supporting cast a story he retells that leads to his execution by firing squad for cowardice in wartime. **Where:** A barn/prison, Ypres. Various locations in UK/France. **When:** 1916. **Themes:** Love; family; class; duty; bravery; war and its effects on the lives of young men. **Notes:** The storytelling is done by one actor interspersed by a chorus of multi-role performers. **Design/tech notes:** Minimal set/props and costume. A single bed. The creation of Tommo's imagination could be assisted by projections. SFX and lighting. **Warnings:** Very demanding. Death of a young boy's father. **Workshop/rehearsal/ideas/notes:** Extreme naturalism combined with extensive use of multimedia/projects. Physical theatre. **Research:** 'The Last Laugh' by Wilfred Owen. The 2012 movie *Private Peaceful* and the book by M. Morpurgo of the same name.	
	Section or scene(s)	Monologues with interspersed lines from multi-role others. After reading as a group, discuss and choose the parts you wish to work with. Respect the order. Key moments should be included.	

Play 24

	Title & publisher	*The Duck Variations*	Samuel French
	Playwright/Date	David Mamet	1972
	Casting	2M	GCSE Should be of matching ability
	Notes, guidance and considerations for teachers/students	Description: Comedy. Summary: Two elderly men on a bench discuss life, amongst other things! Where: A park bench by a lake on the edge of a big city. When: Contemporary. An afternoon around Easter. Themes: Natural law; friendship; death; ducks! Notes: Comic timing and delivery awareness essential. Design/tech notes: Minimal. A bench and a rubbish bin. Back drop/projections. Warnings: The occasional mild adult phrase. Workshop/rehearsal/ideas/notes: Research comedy duos. Two Ronnies' scenes. Relationships in duologues. Observational comedy and stand-up. Looking for the punch line. What makes us laugh. Timing and facial expression and vocal tone. Making meaning. Improv conversations about people, places and things.	
	Section or scene(s)	40-minute duologue divided into 14 variations. Select according to the ability of the pair. The 6th, 7th, 9th, 10th, 13th and 14th variations are personal favourites.	

Play 25

	Title & publisher	*The Dumb Waiter*	Faber & Faber
	Playwright/Date	Harold Pinter	1959
	Casting	2M	GCSE Can be a great piece for weaker boys right up to the most able. However, the pair should be evenly matched
	Notes, guidance and considerations for teachers/students	Description: Dark comedy. Summary: Two 'hit men' wait to kill a third party, before we realise one has to assassinate the other. Where: A basement room in a hotel (anywhere). When: 1960s (any time). Themes: The unspoken threat of violence; social class and power; obedience and authority. Notes: If it says pause, pause! Every stage direction matters in this short piece. Design/tech notes: Good set design option. Fairly prescribed. Two beds, two doors, a table and chairs and a serving hatch. Newspapers, two guns. Sound effects. Warnings: Many references to violence and violent crime. Workshop/rehearsal/ideas/notes: A tension must be built up between the two performers, both implied and later physically. Explore the seven levels of tension. The use of pause is the key to this tension in many places and what is not said must be explored by the actor. Looking at newspaper coverage of violent crime. Stanislavski explorative strategies, research character and life outside of the script. Explore motivation behind lines and 'thought tracking' during the many pauses. Improvisation.	
	Section or scene(s)	All parts of this excellent one-act duologue are pacey and accessible. Keep to the order of the play. Scene in which GUS & BEN go over the instructions before GUS exits is great for fast-paced interchange which begins to expose the raw tension. The final moments are a must!	

Play 26

	Title & publisher	*The Train Driver*	Faber & Faber
	Playwright/Date	Athol Fugard	2010
	Casting	2M	GCSE/GCE
	Notes, guidance and considerations for teachers/students	**Description:** South African theatre. **Summary:** Roelf is seeking the identity of a mother and child who stepped deliberately in front of his train. His quest leads him to an eye-opening encounter with an old grave digger. **Where:** Eastern Cape graveyard outside Motherwell, South Africa. **When:** Post-Apartheid, February 2001. **Themes:** Guilt; bonds between strangers; redemption in post-Apartheid South Africa; ghosts. **Notes:** Very powerful monologues. Quite static, try to physicalise the pain in the lines. **Design/tech notes:** A simple set. The graveyard and inside Simon's shack. A tarpaulin covered with sand/dirt. Few props. Lighting should play an important role. **Warnings:** Some strong language. Suicide and a murder alluded to. **Workshop/rehearsal/ideas/notes:** Both characters are powerful in their own way. Research Apartheid in South Africa. Explore the distance between the two men and how it closes. Deliver monologues to each other.	
	Section or scene(s)	End of Scene 3 SIMON and the fish. Scene 4 SIMON sings to the dead. Monologues. SIMON's prologue. Scene 1 ROELF's *'No I give up. . . . That's the one. . .'* Scene 5 ROELF speaks to Red Doek. SIMON's Epilogue.	

Play 27

	Title & publisher	*Stones in His Pockets*	NHB
	Playwright/Date	Marie Jones	1996
	Casting	2M Playing 15 parts, male and female	GCE Able
	Notes, guidance and considerations for teachers/students	**Description:** Tragi comedy. **Summary:** A small town where the inhabitants are all extras in a Hollywood movie. **Where:** County Kerry, rural Ireland. **When:** Contemporary ('90s) with flashbacks. **Themes:** Brotherhood; rural decline; the seduction and exploitation of people by big industry. **Notes:** The Irish accent is an important aspect of the story. **Design/tech notes:** Simple, little to no set. Minimalist works well with this. A costume rail fully stocked for the performers to adapt/adopt the various characters. Plenty of SFX scene changes. Projections might be an option fitting in with the movie idea. **Warnings:** A suicide. Adult language. References to drugs. **Workshop/rehearsal/ideas/notes:** Character study, physical differences, gestures, posture and vocal quality to define the many rich characters.	
	Section or scene(s)	Act 2 is a two-hander. Most scenes involve a degree of multi-role. An able pair should choose just how much they want to do this. Great opportunities for quick comic interchanges. Monologues: Act 1 CHARLIE *'Aye . . . . I says to myself. . .'* End of Act 1 FIN *'M Da has brought terrible news. . .'* Act 2 FIN *'Jake everything he wanted. . .'* to *'He saw your woman talking to you'*.	

Play 28

	Title & publisher	*Bully Boy*	NHB
	Playwright/Date	Sandi Toksvig	2011
	Casting	2M	GCE Very able physical performers
	Notes, guidance and considerations for teachers/students	**Description:** Naturalistic/dance/political. **Summary:** Falklands War veteran Major Oscar Hadley, now confined to a wheelchair, is sent to a Middle East combat zone to investigate allegations that private Edward Clark threw an eight-year-old boy down a well during a military raid. As the interrogation develops, Oscar begins to discover that 'truth' in modern war can be a point of view rather than a fact. **Where:** Army interrogation room (Middle East) and various UK locations. **When:** Iraq war, Tony Blair years. **Themes:** Military occupation and its effect on the mental health of serving soldiers. **Notes:** The relationship between the two men is the power of the piece. The physicality of the wheelchair and how Eddie lifts and dances/carries Oscar needs careful consideration/choreography. **Design/tech notes:** Bare set. A table and a chair. The various locations can be achieved on a simple set with SFX and LX/projections. A wheelchair and a mobile phone, iPod and music as described in script. **Warnings:** Mental illness, war and suicide. Strong language. **Workshop/rehearsal/ideas/notes:** Some very powerful physical work. DV8. Character work, Declan Donnellan. Hot seating.	
	Section or scene(s)	14 scenes plus Epilogue and Prologue. Scenes 1, 2, 3, 6, 9, but choices should be made by students once the whole play has been studied. Monologues: Scene 4b OSCAR & EDDIE Scene 5 EDDIE *'People talk about explosions,'* but really full of very powerful monologue/soliloquy throughout.	

Play 29

	Title & publisher	*Blue Orange*	Methuen Drama
	Playwright/Date	Joe Penhall	2000
	Casting	3M	GCE Able
	Notes, guidance and considerations for teachers/students	**Description:** Comedy. **Summary:** Christopher is a young Black Londoner who has reached day 28 of his detention at a psychiatric hospital and just wants to go home. His bags are packed but there is a problem: he thinks oranges are blue and that Ugandan dictator Idi Amin is his father. **Where:** A modern NHS Psychiatric hospital. London, UK. **When:** Contemporary. **Themes:** Race, mental illness, care in the community and 21st-century British life. **Notes:** The script calls for a black actor. **Design/tech notes:** Bare set. Table and two chairs. A door. Bowl of oranges. **Warnings:** Some strong language/sexual reference and racist comments. Smoking. **Workshop/rehearsal/ideas/notes:** Role on wall, character work. Stanislavski.	
	Section or scene(s)	Act 1 BRUCE & CHRISTOPHER/BRUCE & ROBERT. ROBERT'S monologue on schizophrenia. Act 2 ROBERT & CHRISTOPHER. ROBERT, BRUCE & CHRISTOPHER. Many opportunities for fast-paced dialogue.	

Play 30

	Title & publisher	*The Caretaker*	Faber & Faber
	Playwright/Date	Harold Pinter	1960
	Casting	3M	GCE Able GCSE
	Notes, guidance and considerations for teachers/students	**Description:** Realist, dark comedy. **Summary:** A tramp is offered lodgings by a man decorating an apartment. The man, it transpires, was a patient in a mental hospital. His elder brother owns the flat. The tramp sees an opportunity to establish himself and a three-way battle of wills ensues. **Where:** One room. An apartment within a West London house, UK. **When:** A night in winter and a fortnight later. 1950s. **Themes:** Identity; family; loneliness/isolation; social class; absurdity; communication; violence and menace; mental illness. **Notes:** The pause is vital. Don't be afraid of silence and stillness. It's meant to be awkward! **Design/tech notes:** A basic box of a room. A bed. A vast array of props/junk (see script). Some are essential to the plot – the heater and the hanging bucket, for example. **Warnings:** Racist language. Mental illness and treatment. Smoking. **Workshop/rehearsal/ideas/notes:** The importance of movement to set a scene. Mick in the opening scene. Pay particular attention to stage directions. Look at Aston's long monologue and the wiring of the toaster plug. Intense character work. Look at the silence of the bag-passing scene in Act 2. **Research:** Dan Leno monologues. **Resources:** Old Vic teaching resources.	
	Section or scene(s)	Opening scene, MICK alone then DAVIES & ASTON to DAVIES' shoe monologue. MICK's entrance at end of Act 1. Act 2 MICK & DAVIES. MICK's monologues and the bag sequence. DAVIES & MICK when the lights go off. ASTON's large monologue at end of Act 2. Act 3 The pair of shoes.	

Play 31

	Title & publisher	*Bouncers*	Methuen Drama
	Playwright/Date	John Godber	1990s' remix
	Casting	4M Multi-role	GCSE A range of abilities. Requires lots of energy
	Notes, guidance and considerations for teachers/students	**Description:** Stylised social comedy. **Summary:** A night on the booze from the point of view of the men on the door. **Where:** On the doors outside a nightclub and various other locations, UK. **When:** Could be now, with a few changed references (contemporary). **Themes:** The drinking culture of the working classes; violence; power play. **Notes:** An absolute timeless classic. A favourite with students, teachers and examiners! If you choose to use music (I do) make sure it's of the moment and relevant. A fast pace is essential with the energy sustained from start to finish. **Design/tech notes:** Good opportunities for sound and lighting candidates. Minimalist set works best. **Warnings:** Adult themes throughout. **Workshop/rehearsal/ideas/notes:** The use of multi-role playing and the actors directly addressing the audience plus the use of monologue show the influence of practitioners such as Brecht. Ensemble stylised realism. **Resources:** There are a number of excellent education packs available online (Hull Truck).	
	Section or scene(s)	Total run time (very approx.) 120 minutes. The opening scene with its audience interaction and address is a must! Literally any section from Act 1 or 2 works. However, the more complex multi-role sections require more focus and pace. Monologues: LUCKY ERIC's first and second speeches. Act 1 and 3rd and 4th Final in Act 2.	

Play 32

	Title & publisher	*Neville's Island*	Samuel French
	Playwright/Date	Tim Firth	1992
	Casting	4M	GCSE/GCE Mixed/high ability
	Notes, guidance and considerations for teachers/students	**Description:** Comedy. **Summary:** Four out-of-condition businessmen on a team-building exercise get themselves shipwrecked in the Lake District. **Where:** Rampsholme Island, Derwent water in the Lake District, UK. **When:** November. Contemporary. **Themes:** Being a man; survival; class; competing; cooperation; fear. **Notes:** It is worth paying attention to the fairly specific physical descriptions of the four characters. According to ability some scenes have great rapid interrupted and over-spoken arguments. (Interrupted lines are obvious and well indicated on the script.) **Design/tech notes:** Very detailed set and props directions given but it is possible to make a far more minimal set for exam purposes. However, fantastic opportunities for design students. Varied lighting states to indicate time of day and weather. A smoke machine (a comedy in thick fog!), a dead bird of prey and a rucksack with very specific contents offer some interesting opportunities. **Warnings:** A demanding piece with all four characters on stage for most of the play. Refers to suicide. **Workshop/rehearsal/ideas/notes:** Character work to clearly define the four very different men. Stanislavski.		
	Section or scene(s)	90 minutes, two Acts. Act 1 Scene 1 to set scene. Then choose through agreement of cast. Keep the order and sense. Monologues: Scene 3 ROY. *'Steady, stead-y'*. Scene 5 ANGUS *'I watched you do that'*.		

Play 33

	Title & publisher	*Hymns*	Oberon Modern Plays
	Playwright/Date	Chris O'Connell	1999
	Casting	4M	GCE Able. Very physical
	Notes, guidance and considerations for teachers/students	**Description:** Physical theatre. **Summary:** Four friends are reunited for the funeral of a friend. As they drink it becomes evident that they were never what they seemed to be and one of them had a secret. **Where:** A funeral. Various locations. **When:** Contemporary. **Themes:** Male responses to death and suicide amongst young men; death. **Notes:** There are no dance/choreographic notes in the script. With the script and practitioner in mind, students should be challenged to create their own movement. **Design/tech notes:** Levels and ladders/scaffolding. But see Notes. **Warnings:** Do not copy Frantic's show. Encourage students to do their own thing whilst sticking to the script. Beware of working at heights – take all precautions or don't do it! **Workshop/rehearsal/ideas/notes:** Using the script and with the practitioner in mind, students should work on their own safe routines where a routine is indicated. Highly choreographed. Frantic Assembly. **Research:** *The Frantic Assembly Book of Devising Theatre* (Routledge). **Resources:** Frantic have produced an excellent resource pack for *Hymns*. They have many excellent resources including masterclasses on YouTube and will come to your school for a practitioner workshop.		
	Section or scene(s)	Explore the relationship between movement and the text. Scene 1, Funeral (joke sequence). Talking about death. Monologue: SCOTT Scene 4 *'Where were you on 9/11?'* STEVEN Scene 5 *'It's not anything'*. SCOTT Scene 5 *'This is what you wanted'*. KARL'S final monologue to end.		

Play 34

	Title & publisher	*Waiting for Godot*	Methuen Drama
	Playwright/Date	Samuel Beckett	1953
	Casting	5M	GCE Or able GCSE
	Notes, guidance and considerations for teachers/students	**Description:** Tragi-comedy (absurd) **Summary:** Estragon and Vladimir (two wandering tramps) are waiting for Godot. He never shows up. **Where:** A country road by a tree and a rock. **When:** Beginning on the evening of one day and ending on the evening of the next. **Themes:** The absurd; humour; modernism; existentialism; freedom and confinement; the devaluation of language; religion; time; truth; choices; the futility of man's hopes. . . I could go on! **Notes:** Beckett was notoriously particular about his stage directions. A useful exercise is to challenge students to perform a section without them and discuss how/if the meaning of the scene changed. **Design/tech notes:** Minimalist set. Lighting important (shadows/moonlight). Research Charlie Chaplin's tramp and costume. **Warnings:** Demands a great deal of focus and energy. Select sections with great care. Some Boards use this as a prescribed text. Check your specification! **Workshop/rehearsal/ideas/notes:** Rehearse and workshop in a small, safe place. From early on try to establish the essential concerns of the play. Understanding the characters, what motivates them, how they walk, talk, move and why. Stanislavski, history, objectives, circumstances and memory. **Resources:** West Yorkshire Playhouse and Talawa Theatre Company have produced an excellent teacher resource pack.	
	Section or scene(s)	Act 1 VLADIMIR & ESTRAGON alone. Arrival of POZZO & LUCKY. LUCKY'S speech. The BOY MESSENGER. Departure of BOY leaving VLADIMIR & ESTRAGON alone. Act 2 as above. Allow students to select if they are able.	

Play 35

	Title & publisher	*Dealer's Choice*	Methuen Drama
	Playwright/Date	Patrick Marber	1995
	Casting	6M	GCE Or able GCSE
	Notes, guidance and considerations for teachers/students	**Description:** Tragi-comedy. **Summary:** Stephen, a restaurateur, has a weekly poker game in the basement. The stakes are high and the waiters often lose their paycheques. Stephen's son, Carl, is an obsessive gambler who has run up debts, and when Ash, a professional gambler, threatens to kill Carl if he doesn't pay the £4000 he owes, Carl arranges for him to play in the weekly game. **Where:** Kitchens and restaurant and the cellar of the same building. London, UK. **When:** A Sunday night and Monday morning in 1996. **Themes:** Poker; personal achievement; father–son relationships. **Notes:** Comic timing is important. Stage directions matter. London accents! **Design/tech notes:** Tables/tablecloth and chairs. A bar. Cards. Good lighting opportunities. **Warnings:** Some adult language. **Workshop/rehearsal/ideas/notes:** Detailed character studies. Improv work, tension/men playing poker. Watch card scenes in the film *Cincinnati Kid*.	
	Section or scene(s)	Act 1 great duologues, Act 2 MUGSY, CARL & ASH Act 3 Scene 2. The poker game in the basement. Monologues: ASH Act 2 *'Listen fuckbrain'* through to *'You want me to go in there?'* ACT 3 Scene 2 SWEENEY *'They're your rules. . .'*	

Remember to check the maximum performers being assessed in each piece is in line with your specification.

Play 36

	Title & publisher	*Observe the Sons of Ulster*	Faber & Faber
	Playwright/Date	Frank McGuinness	1985
	Casting	9M	GCE Or able GCSE
	Notes, guidance and considerations for teachers/students	**Description:** Historical tragedy. **Summary:** Follows the experiences of eight men who volunteer in the 36th Ulster regiment at the start of the WW1 right up to the start of the Battle of the Somme. **Where:** Various locations. An army barracks, a field, a bridge, a churchyard and inside a church. A trench in the Somme. **When:** 1914–18, WW1. **Themes:** History; psyche; sexuality; religion; community; comradeship. **Notes:** I have concentrated on Part 3 as it contains some excellent opportunities for paired work. Parts 2 and 4 are very powerful too for the whole cast. Part 1 is a long, complex monologue/soliloquy in which Pyper sees and talks with ghosts. There are two Pypers (older and younger). **Design/tech notes:** A clever lighting design is needed for the very different locations. Simple set and projections. WW1 Army fatigues and a Lambeg drum. SFX. **Warnings:** The Northern Ireland accent is not to be confused with a Southern one! Adult themes and violence. **Workshop/rehearsal/ideas/notes:** Lends itself very well to Frantic/DV8 techniques. The Part 3 pairings are stunning with close-up Frantic Assembly duet work. Rehearsing with round-by-through. **Research:** Battle of the Boyne and Battle of the Somme. The Ulster 36th Division's sacrifice on the first day of the Battle of the Somme. Orangemen. Shipyard workers, Belfast.	
	Section or scene(s)	Part 3. Pairing. In the four locations. Monologues: Part 1 The two PYPERS. PYPER *'I am. Flesh. Stone. David. . .'*. ROULSTON *'There once was a boy'* CRAWFORD. PYPER *'What's more to be said?'* CRAIG *'You said you wanted to die'*. Part 4 MCILWAINE *'Let me finish'*.	

Play 37

	Title & publisher	*Lord of the Flies*	Faber & Faber acting edition.
	Playwright/Date	William Golding Adapted by Nigel Williams	1995
	Casting	8–12M	GCSE A range of abilities
	Notes, guidance and considerations for teachers/students	**Description:** Social tragedy. **Summary:** Stage adaptation of the famous novel of the same name. *Lord of the Flies* tracks the spiral into savagery when a group of boys, without adult influence, are marooned on an uncharted island during war time. **Where:** Various locations on an unknown tropical island in the Pacific. **When:** During a fictional world war around 1950. **Themes:** Civilization; human nature; law and order/authority; spirituality; the weak and the strong. **Notes:** Very popular text for GCSE literature. Many students will know it well. Excellent opportunities for physical work. Have seen it done with female casting. **Design/tech notes:** Great opportunities for simple yet effective set design. Use levels and part wreck of the plane. Use of lighting and sound to create the jungle/sea/sun/heat etc. Pig's head is a great design project. Marc Rees, for sense of place and the plane wreck. **Warnings:** Fight scenes and death. Fights need to be carefully and always professionally choreographed. **Workshop/rehearsal/ideas/notes:** A colleague of mine took his small cast to the seaside where they played trust and power games in the dunes and got a chance to wreck their costumes. Lots of physical opportunities. DV8. **Resources:** Excellent resource from Pilot Theatre Company.	
	Section or scene(s)	Opening scene to introduce the boys and their situation. Tensions between JACK & RALPH. Hunting, building the fire. SIMON'S visions, The death of PIGGY. Allow cast to discuss and decide. Monologues: Act 1 RALPH *'Yes' (Crosses to* PIGGY*)*. Act 2 JACK *'There. I got it. See?'* SIMON *'My mind isn't right'*. Act 3, PIGGY *'Gimme the conch!'*	

Play 38

	Title & publisher	*Journey's End*	Samuel French
	Playwright/Date	R.C. Sherriff	1929
	Casting	12M Can be reduced	GCSE A range of abilities
	Notes, guidance and considerations for teachers/ students	**Description:** Historical/biographical. **Summary:** A bleak and brutally honest insight into life in the trenches during WW1 from the point of view of a young infantry commander, and how war has changed him. **Where:** An Officers' dug-out in the trenches, Quentin, France. **When:** WW1. Takes place over four days in March 1918. **Themes:** WW1; the true nature of war; courage and cowardice; loss of innocence of youth; the wisdom of age. **Notes:** Featuring 'horror, humanity and humour,' popular with all-boys' schools/classes. Opportunities for lead or supporting roles. Builds up good suspense and fear. **Design/tech notes:** Minimal set. Table, two wooden boxes and a wooden bench. Much achieved with lighting (candlelight) and SFX sounds of war dulled by earth walls. **Warnings:** Language appropriate for WW1 soldiers. Often a set text. Check exam Board. **Workshop/rehearsal/ideas/notes:** Look at the war poetry of WW1 in particular 'A Working Party' by Siegfried Sassoon. Paul Nash's painting, *The Menin Road*, 1919. Research and look at photographs of the trenches. Differences in class between enlisted and officers. The effects of trauma, fear and severe anxiety on the mind and body. The physicalisation of fear. Responding to fear, becoming on edge. Simple exercises with blowing balloons up and overinflating. Games/exercises to explore tension. Foreshadowing and silence. **Resources:** The Heineman edition contains student notes. *Discovery Film Festival* have produced a great teacher resource pack (to accompany the film) but great for drama students too.	
	Section or scene(s)	Act 1 Opening scene HARDY & OSBORNE. Entry of MASON. The meal. Act 2 Scene 1. Act 3 Scene 1. Act 3 The final scene. Monologue: Act 2 Scene 1 STANHOPE 'I had that feeling this morning'.	

Play 39

	Title & publisher	*Black Watch*	Faber & Faber
	Playwright/Date	Gregory Burke	2006/2010
	Casting	12M	GCE Highly choreographed physical work
	Notes, guidance and considerations for teachers/ students	**Description:** Docudrama **Summary:** Based on interviews and through the eyes of those on the ground. What it means to be part of a legendary Scottish regiment, part of the war on terror and to make the journey home. **Where:** Various locations. Scotland and war zones. **When:** Various times and flashbacks. **Themes:** Nationalism; patriotism; imperialism; war. **Notes:** The Scots accent/dialect is vital. With multi-role the cast can be reduced to 10. **Design/tech notes:** Set design offers exceptional opportunities. A very busy complex set with multiple locations. Projections and SFX. **Warnings:** Strong language, adult themes. Requires sensitive selection and choices from a rich selection of material. **Workshop/rehearsal/ideas/notes:** Docudrama using choreographed movement, music, song and projection. Katie Mitchell. DV8. Godber. **Research:** BBC documentary 'Black Watch: A Soldier's Story'.	
	Section or scene(s)	Open with Tattoo. Pub 1 Camp incoming. The scene *'Fashion'*. CAMMY's monologue. Embeds. Allies. Officer email 2. TWA Recruiting Sergeants. On Patrol. Officer email 3. Pub 4. Suicide (last piece). Casualties. The future.	

Play 40

	Title & publisher	*Barber Shop Chronicles*	Oberon Books
	Playwright/Date	Inua Ellams	2017
	Casting	12–28M Multi-role	GCSE A range of abilities
	Notes, guidance and considerations for teachers/students	Description: Comedy. Black culture. Summary: For generations, African men have gathered in barber shops to discuss the world! A play of anecdote and argument. Where: Barber shops in Peckham, Harare, Johannesburg, Kampala, Lagos and Accra. When: Contemporary. Themes: 'Six cities, a thousand stories'. Newsroom, political platform, local hotspot, preacher and football stadium. Banter and the truth. Notes: Accent and dialect/language should be as genuine as possible. Design/tech notes: Minimal set. The barber shop should change slightly only to reflect location. Lighting and music will help but it's the people that give the place its identity. Warnings: Mild language. Ethnicity should be respected. Workshop/rehearsal/ideas/notes: Strong characters. Rehearse with music. Some great physical opportunities. Research: The various cultures, music and political histories. Talawa and Eclipse.	
	Section or scene(s)	Scenes 2, 3, 4, 6, 8, 11, SIMPHIWE & ANDILE. Scenes 12, 14 to end. Monologues: Scene 2 KWAME. Scene 6 MUHAMMED's story. Scene 13 OLAWALE.	

Plays with Mixed Cast

Play 41

	Title & publisher	*Two*	Methuen Drama
	Playwright/Date	Jim Cartwright	1989
	Casting	1M: 1F 2 Actors 14 roles	GCSE or GCE Challenging!
	Notes, guidance and considerations for teachers/students	Description: Comedy Summary: One night, one pub, many experiences. Where: Set entirely in a Northern working-class pub. When: 1980s. Themes: Couples and their secrets. Dealing with love and loss. Notes: There is a temptation to cast more than two performers for the many varied roles, but this is to lose the excellent opportunities for multi-role and the intent of the playwright. Short, sharp dialogue with several poignant monologues. Minimalist works best! Audience address. Design/tech notes: The set is a bar with all the glasses, pumps and optics being mimed. Warnings: Some strong pub language and themes. Workshop/rehearsal/ideas/notes: Lends itself well to physical theatre with plenty of body props. The multiple characters need careful study. Good duet work opportunities. Who am I? What do I want in the scene? Quick transitions.	
	Section or scene(s)	Opening scene with the LANDLORD and LANDLADY then scenes with MOTH and MAUDIE. Mr and Mrs IGER. FRED and ALICE. End scene with LANDLORD and LANDLADY. Monologues: MOTH, OLD MAN, LANDLORD. WOMAN, OLD WOMAN, LANDLADY.	

Play 42

Title & publisher	*Paper Flowers*	Methuen Drama
Playwright/Date	Egon Wolff	1970
Casting	1M: 1F	GCE Able (Physical)
Notes, guidance and considerations for teachers/students	\multicolumn{2}{l}{**Description:** Latin American Theatre/socio neo-realism.}

Notes, guidance and considerations for teachers/students	**Description:** Latin American Theatre/socio neo-realism. **Summary:** Eva, a kind, lonely middle-class woman, gives a tramp a place to sleep for the night. He quickly occupies her life and her home, reducing her to his state. **Where:** An apartment in a city in Chile. **When:** 1970s. **Themes:** Power and power struggles; class conflict; relationships; loneliness. **Notes:** If the two can dance Tango, even better! **Design/tech notes:** Fairly demanding set and detailed props. **Warnings:** The performers must have a good relationship and work very well together. **Workshop/rehearsal/ideas/notes:** Physicalise the duologues, how people move and look at each other. Consider dance. DV8. Boal. Imaginary Body. **Research:** The dictatorship in '70s Chile, looking at the affluent middle class and the poor *los rotos* (the broken ones). Magic Realism.	
Section or scene(s)	A six-scene two-hander. Challenging monologues, mainly BARRACUDA.	

Play 43

Title & publisher	*Blood*	Methuen Drama
Playwright/Date	Emteaz Hussain	2015
Casting	1M: 1F	GCE or Able GCSE Knowledge of Mirpuri-Punjabi

Notes, guidance and considerations for teachers/students	**Description:** Dark comedy **Summary:** 'A 21st century urban love story'. Boy meets girl and their families disapprove. 'A brutal yet funny take on Romeo and Juliet'. **Where:** Various locations. Midlands Pakistani community. **When:** Contemporary. **Themes:** Love; innocence; cultural and parental pressure; hope. **Notes:** Requires great pace. Performers should have a good understanding of Mirpuri-Punjabi. Beatbox! **Design/tech notes:** Works well in a studio space. Levels, props and lights to signify place. **Warnings:** Reference to and depiction of violence. Some adult language. **Workshop/rehearsal/ideas/notes:** Direct address and duologues. Pacey rhythm and meter. Work on the physicality of relationships. Nuance and gesture. **Research:** Tamasha Theatre Company. For tech students carefully research the locations for visual and SFX signifiers of location.
Section or scene(s)	Start of Scene 1 Nando's Scenes 2, 4, 6 and 7 (with AMMA) as monologues. Scenes 9, 10 13, 14, 15, 16, 17, 19, 27, 30, 31, 32, 34, though all scenes have merit. Respect order and timing/rhythms of the piece.

Play 44

📋	Title & publisher	*Death and Dancing*	Methuen Drama
✏️	Playwright/Date	Claire Dowie	1992
👥	Casting	1M: 1F	GCE
📋	Notes, guidance and considerations for teachers/students	**Description:** Gay theatre. **Summary:** Two people going dancing and the social categories of sexuality that try to pin them down. **Where:** London, England. **When:** 1990s. **Themes:** Gender; sexuality; identity; growing up; the labels that constrict us. **Notes:** Works well in an intimate 'black box' studio. **Design/tech notes:** Minimal set and props. Two chairs. Lots of lighting and sound opportunities. Gareth Fry. Costume should follow script. Projections. Music should be as suggested by the script. **Warnings:** Strong language of a sexual nature. **Workshop/rehearsal/ideas/notes:** Proxemics of the relationship. Swap roles/ identities. Dance. DV8. Punchdrunk. Eddie Ladd.	
🎬	Section or scene(s)	Allow students to select from Parts 1 and 2. Beware of the very long monologues.	

Play 45

📋	Title/ & publisher	*Disco Pigs*	Methuen Drama (Far from the Land Contemporary Irish Plays)
✏️	Playwright/Date	Enda Walsh	1996
👥	Casting	1M: 1F	GCE High energy
📋	Notes, guidance and considerations for teachers/students	**Description:** Irish theatre. **Summary:** Two teenage Irish misfits, Pig and Runt, who share everything, including a birthday, inhabit an intense, imaginative world of their own. But then adulthood comes along. **Where:** Cork, Ireland. **When:** Contemporary. **Themes:** Relationships and miscommunication; violence; fantasy. **Notes:** This piece almost explodes onto the stage with a mad energy which never ceases. **Design/tech notes:** Colourful, crazy, chaotic lights and sound and music. Minimal set. Works well in a studio. Forkbeard Fantasy. **Warnings:** Some strong language and sexual references. The pair have developed a distinctive language (a mix of Cork patois and gibberish) of their own which must be used as read. **Workshop/rehearsal/ideas/notes:** Lots of physical theatre. Acting and reacting to each other. Punchdrunk. **Research:** There is a 2001 movie of the play.	
🎬	Section or scene(s)	Requires a pair who are known to work very well together. Some strong, lengthy monologues. As a pair, plot the moments that share the relationship and its breakdown in the time allowed. The text is rich with opportunities. Respect the order of events.	

Play 46

	Title & publisher	*Teechers*	Methuen Drama (Godber Plays 2)
	Playwright/Date	John Godber	1985
	Casting	2M: 1F 21 characters 3 actors!	GCSE Able
	Notes, guidance and considerations for teachers/students	**Description:** Comedy. **Summary:** Using the format of an end-of-term play (within the play), Nixon, the new drama teacher, is shown battling through his first two terms of recalcitrant classes, cynical colleagues and obstructive caretakers. The 21 characters are played by three actors. **Where:** Whitewall High school. Any comprehensive in the UK. **When:** Contemporary. References may change. **Themes:** Equality and education; inspiring teachers; the play within the play. **Notes:** Godber reduced this to a bare set with minimal cast to represent the basic bare essentials available to many drama teachers. It works very well indeed. Most examiners and moderators know it intimately. Done well, it's always a winner. There are several very helpful education packs available as free downloads. **Design/tech notes:** All of the minimal set and props/costume should be readily available in any school. The Samuel French edition has useful lighting plots. **Warnings:** Don't be tempted to add more actors. It's the multi-roles that make the play work. Language is honest, as you would expect from three Year 11 students. **Workshop/rehearsal/ideas/notes:** Fast paced, plenty of audience address. Great opportunities for physical theatre. Look at stereotypes and exaggerated movement, proxemics and levels. Fast transitions. (Frantic).	
	Section or scene(s)	Total run time 110 minutes. Episodic structure. Sections from both Acts 1 and 2. As with all material, keep scenes in order. Choose sections carefully according to the abilities of the group. The fast-moving multi-role opportunities are where the marks are to be found but demand 100% focus.	

Play 47

	Title & publisher	*Death and the Maiden*	Samuel French
	Playwright/Date	Ariel Dorfman	1990
	Casting	2M: 1F	GCE Able group
	Notes, guidance and considerations for teachers/students	**Description:** Realistic political theatre. **Summary:** When dictatorships fall, the victims emerge from the shadows and some seek revenge! **Where:** A Beach house. South American dictatorship (fictional/Chile). **When:** 1981–90. **Themes:** Revenge; justice; power; politics; the transition from dictatorship to democracy; human rights abuse. **Notes:** My students once used a talented ballet dancer from the group, who wanted to dance to Schubert's string quartet 'Death and the Maiden' during some of the more disturbing descriptions of torture. It was stunning and very moving. **Design/tech notes:** Minimal but with a strong sense of confinement. Suits a black box studio. SFX/LX need planning. **Warnings:** Strong language and reference to rape as torture. **Workshop/rehearsal/ideas/notes:** Strong character work. Proxemics. Theatre of the oppressed.	
	Section or scene(s)	Act 1 Scene 1 (1M 1F). Act 1 Scene 2 (2M) Act 1 Scene 4 PAULINA'S monologue. Then (1M 1F). Act 2 Scene 1 (2M 1F) ROBERTO'S voice and monologue. Final scene.	

Play 48

	Title & publisher	*Confusions* 'Mother figure' Methuen Drama
	Playwright/Date	Alan Ayckbourn 1977
	Casting	1M: 2F GCSE A range of abilities
	Notes, guidance and considerations for teachers/students	Description: Comedy. Summary: Lucy puts her neighbours' ailing relationship to rights by telling them to behave themselves and rewarding them with a biscuit. It appears she hasn't seen her husband for weeks! Where: A suburban living room in the UK. When: The 1970s, but could be now. Themes: Relationships; power struggles/obedience; maternity. Notes: A great piece, accessible to mixed abilities. The part of Terry can be as demanding or simple as required. *Confusions* consists of five short interconnected one-act plays of which 'Mother Figure' is one. Design/tech notes: A good studio piece. A simple living room set. Needs a front door with bell and a phone with SFX. Set can be strewn with many props for Lucy (in particular) to interact with throughout the play. Warnings: Beware of trip hazards on what should be an untidy set. (Try to rehearse with all of the props in place whenever possible.) Workshop/rehearsal/ideas/notes: Character work. Study relationships between the characters. Acting and reacting exercises.
	Section or scene(s)	Opening scene with LUCY, talking to her children (off). The disarray of her life. Through to doorbell (ignored). Then, ROSEMARY & LUCY. Later TERRY enters. Read together and select with students.

Play 49

	Title & publisher	*Christmas Is Miles Away* NHB
	Playwright/Date	Chloe Moss 2005
	Casting	2M: 1F GCSE An able group
	Notes, guidance and considerations for teachers/students	Description: Comedy. Summary: Three teenagers coming of age. Luke and Christie are typical sixteen-year-olds. They like camping out, drinking and talking about girls. But when they leave school and their lives go in different directions, will they still have things in common? And then there's Julie! Where: Manchester. A tent outdoors and a small bedroom. When: Action takes place between February 1989 and October 1991. Themes: Love; sex; school; parents; the future; relationships. Notes: The two boys in particular should be of similar ability. Really a set of duologues. Design/tech notes: Set divides well between outside/trees and a bedroom. A challenging set for design students. Levels and lighting. Warnings: Select short sequences. Strong language. Death of father. Workshop/rehearsal/ideas/notes: Character work. Look at how volatile a relationship can become. Body language of relationships. Be very aware of the pace and keep it moving.
	Section or scene(s)	Great comic duologues LUKE & CHRISTIE, LUKE & JULIE, JULIE & CHRISTIE. There is one small scene with all three characters. All scenes are relevant and provoking. Choose short sharp sections. Not entire scenes.

Play 50

	Title & publisher	*4.48 Psychosis*	Methuen Drama
	Playwright/Date	Sarah Kane	1999
	Casting	1M: 2F Flexible ensemble	GCE Very challenging monologues
	Notes, guidance and considerations for teachers/students	**Description:** 'In yer face' theatre! **Summary:** Sarah Kane's account of 'a psychotic breakdown, when the barriers between reality and imagination vanish'. **Where:** Anywhere. A hospital. There are subtle hints in the script. **When:** Anytime. **Themes:** Disability/illness; loss; love; melancholia; mourning; depression; suicide. **Notes:** Unconventional script layout. Divided into 24 segments. A lack of stage directions apart from references to silence can be confusing. Students need to research and experiment with the text. **Design/tech notes:** Whatever the performers need (not want). A table, two chairs. Visual aids/projects are a good option. **Warnings:** Very strong language and disturbing subject matters, mental health, suicide, drugs. Check your school's policy. I have seen it done at GCSE. I advise against this. **Workshop/rehearsal/ideas/notes:** Artaud. Making an audience react. **Research:** Look at Belarus Free Theatre production. Glenn D'Cruz book on *4:48* published by Routledge/The Fourth Wall.
	Section or scene(s)	Encourage able students to experiment with segments and involve an ensemble. It can be a poetic monologue or a shared physical ensemble piece. Set challenges/consider original ideas through the study of short segments.

Play 51

	Title & publisher	*Colder Than Here*	Oberon Plays
	Playwright/Date	Laura Wade	2005
	Casting	1M: 3F	GCE
	Notes, guidance and considerations for teachers/students	**Description:** Comedy. **Summary:** The life of a terminally ill woman who plans her own funeral, and how her family comes to terms with her imminent death. **Where:** A living room and various woodland/greenfield burial sites around the West Midlands, UK. **When:** Mid-September 2005 to the end of March 2006. **Themes:** Loneliness; changes; sharing. **Notes:** There is not a lot of plot in this piece and Myra must lead the audience through her story. Beware of bathos! **Design/tech notes:** The living room is an important piece of the set, and perhaps on a lower level at the front could be the various burial sites. Seasons shown through lighting/projections. **Warnings:** Adult language. Death/cancer. Some Boards use this as a prescribed text. Check your specification! **Workshop/rehearsal/ideas/notes:** The coldness of emotional distance. Look at the characters and how they are alone and distanced from the other family members. Emotion memory. Realism. Stanislavski character work on these four excellent full characters.
	Section or scene(s)	Nine scenes from mid-September to late March of the following year. Great duologues, Mother, daughter, father, sister. Great material. Scene 8 ALEC'S phone conversation about the boiler. MYRA & ALEC duologue. Scene 9. Monologues: Scene 3, HARRIET *'You're always having a . . .'* Scene 8 ALEC The letter.

Play 52

	Title & publisher	*Circles*	Methuen Drama
	Playwright/Date	**Rachel De-lahay**	2014
	Casting	1M: 3F	GCSE Able group
	Notes, guidance and considerations for teachers/students	**Description:** Urban Drama. **Summary:** Three generations of women all living with domestic abuse. Circling the outskirts of Birmingham on the No. 11 bus, two teenagers develop an unlikely friendship, and a mother watches her daughter attempt to leave a violent relationship. **Where:** Birmingham. Top deck of a double deck bus and a small living room. **When:** Contemporary. **Themes:** Cycles of violence and how to break them; love; trust; family; friendship. **Notes:** The bus could circle London, Bristol, Cardiff, Glasgow...or your hometown! **Design/tech notes:** A beautifully simple set, alternating between the graffiti-scratched top deck of the No. 11 bus and a sofa in a living room. Two moveable benches representing the bus seats and the sofa is all you need. **Warnings:** Strong language, references to violence. **Workshop/rehearsal/ideas/notes:** The meter of the dialogue is what leads the piece. Lots of opportunities for paired work. Physicality of relationship. Acting/reacting.	
	Section or scene(s)	Opening scene on the bus is fast paced and funny. The Duologues on the bus between Demi and Malachi or between Angela and Phyllis in the house can be played as two separate pieces for exam purposes. However, as a complete piece its true power is realised.	

Play 53

	Title & publisher	*Entertaining Mr Sloane*	Methuen Drama
	Playwright/Date	Joe Orton	1964
	Casting	3M: 1F	GCE An able group
	Notes, guidance and considerations for teachers/students	**Description:** Black comedy. **Summary:** Kath, a lonely 'widow', invites a handsome, mysterious stranger, Mr. Sloane, to become a lodger. Both she and her brother become very attracted to the young man, but their father claims the man is a dangerous killer. **Where:** Inside a house. London, UK. **When:** 1960s. **Themes:** Sexual manipulation; blackmail; bribery; violence. **Notes:** A shocking and unexpected climax. Stage directions cannot be ignored. The pauses are vital! **Design/tech notes:** Good opportunities for set design. Doors off and a curtained window. Naturalistic set. Front room, sofa if possible. Good suits from the era and house dress. **Warnings:** Shocking and explicit in places. No bad language but strong sexual innuendo and references. The scene where Kemp is kicked (to death) by Sloane can be hidden behind the settee or be as graphic/stylised/choreographed as performers wish. **Workshop/rehearsal/ideas/notes:** Stanislavski, in depth character study. Explore the character's motivations/wants. Three strong male characters with a lot of tension on-stage. Kath should be a very able performer too. (Not for the faint hearted!)	
	Section or scene(s)	Opening scene Act 1 with KATH and SLOANE. KEMP and SLOANE, ED and SLOANE. SLOANE'S monologue to KEMP in Act 2. KATH, ED and SLOANE in Act 3.	

Play 54

	Title & publisher	*Advice for The Young at Heart*	Methuen Drama
	Playwright/Date	Roy Williams	2013
	Casting	3M: 1F	GCSE An able group
	Notes, guidance and considerations for teachers/students	**Description:** Youth Theatre. **Summary:** Candice is ordered by her boyfriend (a gang leader), to lure Clint into a trap. Haunted by her Grandfather's mistakes she has to make a decision. Will she let history repeat itself? **Where:** Outside a lockup, London, UK. **When:** 2011 and 1958. **Themes:** Race; racism; family; misguided loyalty; sexual abuse; the play examines 2011's unrest against the background of the 1958 race riots. **Notes:** Needs to be very physical in places and stylised. Strong female lead. **Design/tech notes:** Excellent opportunities for set design and lighting/projections. Costume is very important as it sets the main stories/time frames apart. **Warnings:** Racist violence. Reference to gang rape. **Workshop/rehearsal/ideas/notes:** Katie Mitchell. Try to get students to mirror the madness of the riots through physical work. Four very strong characters. Godber works. Music is important. **Research:** 1958 Race riots and 2011 London riots.	
	Section or scene(s)	The conversations between CANDICE and her GRANDFATHER are very powerful and develop as an almost independent story. Mix this with the stories of CLINT and KENNY. Respect the order. Allow cast to select.	

Play 55

	Title & publisher	*Monsters*	Oberon
	Playwright/Date	Niklas Rådström	2009
	Casting	2M: 2F	GCE A mature group
	Notes, guidance and considerations for teachers/students	**Description:** Verbatim **Summary:** Based on material from the police investigation (interview tapes and Court notes) into the murder of James Bulger. **Where:** Police interrogation rooms, a shopping mall and various outdoor locations in the UK. **When:** Any time after the event. **Themes:** The nature of evil; crime; guilt; suffering; family. **Notes:** Be very aware of everyone involved and their suitability to be taking part in this project (including techies!). **Design/tech notes:** Minimalist. Projections/light, stark lighting. **Warnings:** Very disturbing subject matter. At no time should the actors/adults play the parts of children. They should be represented. See notes in Scene 3. 'Do you know what the truth is?' **Workshop/rehearsal/ideas/notes:** Brecht /Artaud to involve audience. Greek theatre. Rehearse in a secure, safe place.	
	Section or scene(s)	30 scenes. Teacher should carefully guide students in their choices. Monologues: Scene 6 ROBERT'S MOTHER. Scene 16 JON'S MOTHER.	

Play 56

Title & publisher	*School Play*	Oberon Plays
Playwright/Date	Suzy Almond	2001
Casting	2M: 2F	GCSE Mixed ability
Notes, guidance and considerations for teachers/students	\multicolumn{2}{l}{**Description:** Comedy. **Summary:** Charlie is 15. She wants to front a gang, to ride a motorbike and mess with her teachers' heads. Until she meets her new music teacher. **Where:** Stage and playground of a South London Comprehensive in the UK. **When:** The 2000s. **Themes:** Teaching/inspiring students; music; redemption; motorbikes; showing off and being 15 with something to prove; aspiration/latent talent. **Notes:** Miss Fry and Charlie should be able to play the piano (or backs to audience). **Design/tech notes:** Set can be the backstage of the school hall. Black box studio. **Warnings:** Some sexual references and adult language. **Workshop/rehearsal/ideas/notes:** Strong characters. Look at status and proxemics. Building relationships onstage.}	
Section or scene(s)	\multicolumn{2}{l}{Scene 1, from LEE's entrance. Scene 2, from Miss FRY's entrance. Scene 3 FRY & CHARLIE at the piano. Scene 5 FRY & CHARLIE at the piano 12 bar blues. Scene 8 CHARLIE & FRY. Monologues: Scene 3 FRY 'I see it out of...' LEE Scene 4. Scene 5 FRY Scene 7 CHARLIE. Scene 8 FRY.}	

Play 57

Title & publisher	*Lovesong*	Oberon Modern Plays
Playwright/Date	Abi Morgan	2011
Casting	2M: 2F	GCE Able group. Physically challenging
Notes, guidance and considerations for teachers/students	\multicolumn{2}{l}{**Description:** Physical theatre. A love story. **Summary:** The story of one couple, told from two different points in their lives. **Where:** A house and a garden in the suburb of any city. **When:** Now and over 40 years. **Themes:** Love; youth; faith; growing old. **Notes:** Although this is a beautifully written duologue, its strength in performance is its physicality. Do not underplay this. I started with a group of students in 6th form who had started with chair duets way back in year 10. **Design/tech notes:** Semi-naturalistic set. Bed/kitchen. Costume to denote era. SFX/lighting important. **Warnings:** For students with a particular flair for physical/Frantic theatre. Highly choreographed/directed but the physical interpretation should come from the students themselves. **Workshop/rehearsal/ideas/notes:** Physical. Frantic Assembly. **Research:** *The Frantic Assembly Book of Devising Theatre*, Routledge. **Resources:** Frantic Assembly have many excellent resources including masterclasses on YouTube and will come to your school for practitioner workshops.}	
Section or scene(s)	\multicolumn{2}{l}{Having first studied the work of Frantic Assembly, students should be encouraged to experiment with scenes they find appealing. Needs strong choreographic guidance.}	

Play 58

	Title & publisher	*The Static*	Methuen Drama
	Playwright/Date	Davey Anderson	2012
	Casting	2M: 2F	GCE Physically challenging
	Notes, guidance and considerations for teachers/students	\multicolumn{2}{l}{**Description:** Alternative theatre **Summary:** Two troubled teenagers meet in school detention with explosive results. **Where:** A high school in a small town on the West Coast of Scotland, UK. **When:** Present time. **Themes:** Love; family; fantasy; supernatural; growing up; surviving; ADHD; Ritalin; violence; school. **Notes:** The performers double up as the four storytellers/voices. **Design/tech notes:** Minimal. A table, a chair. A large pair of headphones. Lighting/projections/SFX offer great opportunities. Works well as an intimate studio piece. **Warnings:** Strong language. Physically challenging. **Workshop/rehearsal/ideas/notes:** Highly choreographed physical theatre. DV8. Frantic. **Research:** ThickSkin Theatre.}	
	Section or scene(s)	\multicolumn{2}{l}{Scenes 1, 2, 3, 4, 5, 8, 9, 10 parts of 11, 12, 14, parts of 15, parts of 17, 18, 19, 20, 23. Monologues: Inside SPARKY's head. Scene 3 N *'Look at you all sitting'*. Scene 8 P from *'They're just normal kids'* to *'Some of them'*. Scene 17 B *'I'm standing here'* to end.}	

Play 59

	Title & publisher	*The Glass Menagerie*	Penguin Classics
	Playwright/Date	Tennessee Williams	1944
	Casting	2M: 2F	GCSE Able/mixed ability group
	Notes, guidance and considerations for teachers/students	\multicolumn{2}{l}{**Description:** Memory Play **Summary:** The story of a family surviving the depression and their sometimes ugly lives, by inventing a beautiful fantasy world. Told through the narration of the brother who cares for them. **Where:** An apartment and facing alley. St Louis USA. **When:** 1937 and before. **Themes:** Duty and family; weakness; the impossibility of real escape; accepting reality; the power of memory. **Notes:** A dreamlike/surreal quality. **Design/tech notes:** Nothing about the set should be too realistic. A dim stage with shafts of light to highlight certain areas/action. Set can be as odd as you like! The suggested music and projections help the real/surreal moments. **Warnings:** Laura has a disability (one leg shorter than the other). This should not be exaggerated but should be noticed and present. Some Boards use this as a prescribed text. Check your specification! **Workshop/rehearsal/ideas/notes:** This play requires a combination of realism and non-realism on stage. With this in mind, we need to show the thoughts and emotions of each character. 'Stan' meets Brecht! Look at extremes of emotion. The characters are created through real study, in particular, of the many stage directions. Not copied. The play then casts them into a non-naturalistic environment. Beginning with Tom breaking the fourth wall (Narration). Characters at times act and react with props, at others they can body prop (Physical theatre devices).}	
	Section or scene(s)	\multicolumn{2}{l}{A careful selection of TOM's narration and selected monologues and dialogues from all seven scenes. Monologues: TOM's opening audience address. AMANDA – LAURA – AMANDA in Scene 2 TOM Scene 3 'Opium dens' TOM Scene 6 opening lines. Scene 6 AMANDA × 2 Scene 7 JIM and then TOM's closing speech.}	

Play 60

	Title & publisher	*Who's Afraid of Virginia Woolf?*	Penguin Plays
	Playwright/Date	Edward Albee	1962
	Casting	2M: 2F	GCSE/GCE Challenging
	Notes, guidance and considerations for teachers/students	**Description:** Naturalism, containing elements of both comedy and tragedy. **Summary:** The secrets of two couples are savagely laid bare during a night after a faculty party. Full of dark secrets and heartbreak, humiliation, betrayals and vicious wordplay. **Where:** The living room of Martha and George's home on the campus of a New England University, USA. **When:** 1960s (takes place in one day). **Themes:** Marriage and its imperfections; appearance, secrecy and the truth; ambition/success and failure in academia; children. **Notes:** Despite being dated the script contains superb dialogue offering great performance opportunities. **Design/tech notes:** A naturalistic set of a living room. Sofa, table, chairs, drinks cabinet. **Warnings:** Adult themes. **Workshop/rehearsal/ideas/notes:** Character work. Stanislavski. What motivates them? Explore tension and sexual tension. Rapid dialogue work. **Research:** Film of the same name with Taylor and Burton captures the mood/tension well.	
	Section or scene(s)	Choose dialogues from the three Acts to suit your cast. Look at the ends of the acts where the tension is most tangible. Notable MARTHA, NICK and HONEY toward the end of Act 1. Monologues: GEORGE in Act 2 'When I was 16'. MARTHA'S opening of Act 3 and later in the act.	

Play 61

	Title & publisher	*Virgins*	Oberon Modern Plays
	Playwright/Date	John Retallack	2006
	Casting	2M: 2F	GCE All dancers
	Notes, guidance and considerations for teachers/students	**Description:** Physical and dance theatre. **Summary:** Explores issues of sexuality in young people through the lives of a family of four. **Where:** A three-bedroomed house and nearby wood in the South of England, UK. **When:** Action takes place over six Sundays in the present time. **Themes:** Sexuality; family values; growing up. **Notes:** All four performers are always visible on stage/at the side sitting when not performing. **Design/tech notes:** Excellent opportunities for design student. A model house large enough for one adult to stand in (and fully mobile). Set must also include a dance space for a dance with a reflective floor! **Warnings:** Adult themes and language. **Workshop/rehearsal/ideas/notes:** Dance is a vital component of the piece and focuses on the relationships within the family. Each dance interaction will have a different shape. The script gives the theme only. DV8. **Research:** *Company of Angels*, Boundless Theatre Company.	
	Section or scene(s)	Scene 1 Bedroom exchange 1. 2nd Sunday. 3rd Sunday 4th Sunday 4th Bedroom exchange. 5th Sunday. Scene 4 in the woods. Scenes 5, 6, 8, 9, 11, 6th Sunday. Scene 14. Monologues: 2nd Sunday ZOE then JACK Scene 9 SUZY. 6th Sunday ZOE Scene 13 JACK.	

Play 62

	Title & publisher	*Groping for Words*	Methuen Drama
	Playwright/Date	Sue Townsend	1983
	Casting	2M: 2F	GCSE A range of abilities
	Notes, guidance and considerations for teachers/students	**Description:** Comedy. **Summary:** A play about an adult literacy evening class, run by a well-meaning middle-class woman, and her students. Each have a story and a dream. **Where:** A classroom/crèche and corridor/office in a Victorian school. **When:** Evenings and one morning, over a period of several months. 1980s. **Themes:** Adult literacy; class; unemployment; hope; aspiration; love. **Notes:** Needs lots of pace and energy. **Design/tech notes:** Small primary school chairs, children's paintings on the wall, a working door can split the stage for the two spaces. Costume (quite specific). **Warnings:** Mild adult themes. **Workshop/rehearsal/ideas/notes:** Character based. Who am I and what do I want? What is my history?	
	Section or scene(s)	Act 1 Scenes 1, 2, 5, 6, 7 from GEORGE enters, and 9. Act 2 Scenes 1, 2, 3 from KEVIN's entrance, and 6 (important scene but can be cut down). Monologues: THELMA, Scene 2 *'Them!'* JOYCE, Scene 6 *'I'm going to tell you something'*. Act 2 Scene 1 GEORGE *'I would have done. . .'*, Scene 6 KEVIN *'Look I spent . . .'*	

Play 63

	Title & publisher	*That Face*	Faber & Faber
	Playwright/Date	Polly Stenham	2007
	Casting	2M: 2F	GCE An able group
	Notes, guidance and considerations for teachers/students	**Description:** Comedy/realism. **Summary:** Mia is at boarding school. She has access to drugs. They are Martha's. Henry is preparing for art college. He has access to alcohol. From Martha. Martha controls their lives. Martha is their mother. **Where:** Various. England, UK. **When:** Contemporary. **Themes:** Family; parenthood; divorce; children who care for their parents; mental illness. **Notes:** There is dark humour, but take care – this piece is not about belly laughs! **Design/tech notes:** Works well in the round. Requires a highly adaptable set. **Warnings:** Disturbing subject matter. Alcohol abuse, suggestion of mother–son incest. Adult language. Some Boards use this as a prescribed text. Check your specification! **Workshop/rehearsal/ideas/notes:** Vocal work and proxemics. How a young man is forced to be an adult and a woman becomes like a child. Pain and longing as a super objective. Explore realism whilst using naturalism to enable the audience to access the tragic humour of a family breakdown.	
	Section or scene(s)	Scene 2 from MIA's entrance. Scene 3, Scene 4 HENRY & MARTHA. Scene 8 from HUGH & MIA's entrance. Monologues: Scene 6 MARTHA. Scene 8 HENRY *'Stupid me. . .'*	

Play 64

	Title & publisher	*The 39 Steps*	Samuel French
	Playwright/Date	Patrick Bucham (adapted by P. Barlow)	2005
	Casting	3M: 1F Four performers, 139 roles!	GCSE Very able
	Notes, guidance and considerations for teachers/students	\multicolumn{2}{l	}{**Description:** Melodrama/political thriller. **Summary:** A man with a boring life meets a woman with a thick accent who says she's a spy. When he takes her home, she is murdered. Soon, a mysterious organization called 'The 39 Steps' is hot on the man's trail in a nationwide manhunt that climaxes in a death-defying finale! **Where:** The length and breadth of the British Isles, interior small hotel rooms to exterior heathlands and suspension bridges. **When:** 1914, 2 or 3 weeks before WW1. **Themes:** War; class; government; Edwardian Britain; public school; privilege. **Notes:** Pace is vital. **Design/tech notes:** A massive props list (see script). The multi-role requires set/prop and costume changes/adaptions. A very fast paced piece for a talented group. Endless opportunities for design students! Follow spots and crossfades work so well in the train scene. **Warnings:** Some Boards use this as a prescribed text. Check your specification! **Workshop/rehearsal/ideas/notes:** Brecht for characters. Physical theatre. Status games.}
	Section or scene(s)	\multicolumn{2}{l	}{Opening narration by HANNAY. Act 1 Scene 1, 2 to set the scene. Any of the fast-paced scenes. Respect the order! Great opportunities for simple physical theatre. The scene on the Flying Scotsman. The cottage on the moors. No small parts!!! HANNAY has many narrative monologues throughout.}

Play 65

	Title & publisher	*Like a Virgin*	Oberon Books
	Playwright/Date	Gordon Steele	1995
	Casting	2M: 3F	GCSE or GCE 3 Strong female parts
	Notes, guidance and considerations for teachers/students	\multicolumn{2}{l	}{**Description:** Tragi-comedy. **Summary:** Angela and Maxine are besotted with Madonna and dream of becoming famous. 'A romp through the bubble-gum years of teenage life'. **Where:** Multiple simple settings. Middlesbrough, UK. **When:** Early '90s, Thatcher's Britain. **Themes:** Growing up; divorce; depression; leukaemia; death; honesty. **Notes:** This is really about the three women. The two male parts are small and not too demanding. **Design/tech notes:** Great opportunities for design students. Costume and set in particular. **Warnings:** Adult language of a sexual nature. Teenage cancer. **Workshop/rehearsal/ideas/notes:** Stanislavski for character work. Role on wall. Emotion memory. Complete range of emotions (also, comedic timing, tickle and slap). Brecht.}
	Section or scene(s)	\multicolumn{2}{l	}{Prologue scene. Act 1 Scene 1. Good monologues. (ANGELA) Great duologue at end of Act 1, Act 2 Scene 4, including ANGELA's monologue, and Scenes 5 and 6.}

Play 66

	Title & publisher	*Joyriders*	Methuen Drama
	Playwright/Date	Christina Reid	1986
	Casting	2M: 3F	GCSE
	Notes, guidance and considerations for teachers/students	**Description:** Tragi-comedy. **Summary:** Four teenagers on a youth training programme in Belfast. The troubles and unemployment are the backdrop, but they dare to dream of better lives. **Where:** Mainly in a community centre plus brief scenes in a house, a gallery and a theatre. All in Belfast. **When:** Between February and May 1986. **Themes:** The violence of the troubles and youth unemployment; working class life in West Belfast. **Notes:** See also the sequel *Clowns* by the same author, which re-visits the characters. **Design/tech notes:** Minimalist with good opportunities for design/set graffiti and images of the troubles. **Warnings:** Violent death. Some adult language. Glue sniffing and joyriding. **Workshop/rehearsal/ideas/notes:** Katie Mitchell. Physical theatre. Improv games. **Research:** *Christina Reid's Theatre of Memory and Identity: Within and Beyond the Troubles* by Rachel Tracie. The troubles in 1970–80s Belfast. Belfast's Divis Tower flats. The play *The Shadow of a Gunman* by Seán O'Casey.	
	Section or scene(s)	TOMMY & KATE. MAUREEN & SANDRA Scene 2. ARTHUR'S monologue and conversation with KATE. SANDRA & TOMMY. Scene 3. Act 2 Scene 1 at KATE'S. SANDRA & MAUREEN, including monologues Scene 2, All of Scene 3, Scene 4 SANDRA'S monologue to end.	

Play 67

	Title & publisher	*The Persians*	Methuen Drama Aeschylus Plays 1
	Playwright/Date	Aeschylus	472 BCE
	Casting	4M: 1F Plus Chorus	GCE Or a very able GCSE group
	Notes, guidance and considerations for teachers/students	**Description:** Tragedy. Ancient Greek. **Summary:** The Persian army has been destroyed by the smaller Greek army and all the survivors but one will never see their homes again. Only the lamenting Queen's son Xerxes returns. His fate is to witness the downfall and devastation of the kingdom (Persia) he failed to defend. **Where:** The Royal Palace Susa (an ancient capital of Persia). **When:** 480 BCE. **Themes:** The horrors of war (one specific war); pride and grief; family and nation; supernatural/fantasy. **Notes:** The Western world's oldest surviving play. Excellent physical and highly choreographed dance opportunities. **Design/tech notes:** Simple set, opulent costume. Good lighting and SFX. The appearance of the king's ghost should be utterly believable. Keep it simple! This is the theatre. **Warnings:** Violence and grief. **Workshop/rehearsal/ideas/notes:** Grief and its translation to the physical. Sharing with the audience through the Chorus. Deep emotions. Explore the tension between order and unrestrained feeling. Emotion memory, Stanislavski. Dance/Chorus, Berkoff, Lecoq. **Research:** A. H. Sommerstein, *Aeschylean Tragedy* (Bloomsbury Academic).	
	Section or scene(s)	Includes many long and challenging monologues. CHORUS (PARADOS) [1-67 and 107-139] ATOSSA, [176-214] followed by CHORUS/ATOSSA/MESSENGER to [529] ATOSSA exits. The GHOST of DARIUS rises to end of play.	

Play 68

	Title & publisher	*The Usual Auntijies*	Methuen Drama & Belgrade theatre Coventry
	Playwright/Date	Paven Virk	2011
	Casting	1M: 4F (Can be without the Male scenes.)	GCSE
	Notes, guidance and considerations for teachers/students	\multicolumn{2}{l	}{**Description:** Comedy (Asian drama/feminist theatre). **Summary:** A bittersweet comedy looking at the lives of four women on an emotional and inspiring journey to overcome the past and rediscover a sense of life, love and happiness. **Where:** Coventry. A Women's refuge, a bedroom and a park bench. **When:** Contemporary. **Themes:** Women; relationships; marriage; love; cultural differences and abuse; vulnerable adults. **Notes:** Cast will need access to Punjabi. Male part can be omitted if all female cast required. **Design/tech notes:** The busy set offers great design set/prop opportunities. Costume and make up could be a good challenge too. Two distinct locations and the park where they meet. The life-size cardboard cut-out of Joan Collins as Alexis from Dynasty can be constructed from downloaded images and needn't be exact. **Warnings:** Disturbing and violent at times. **Workshop/rehearsal/ideas/notes:** Strong characters. Understanding of their history and culture. Three older women, Stanislavski. How each character moves and carries their pain is important. What do they want? **Research:** Read *Geji* by David Semple. The 'Dynasty' TV series.}
	Section or scene(s)	\multicolumn{2}{l	}{Opening scene. Act 1 Scenes 1, 3, 4, 6, 8, 9. Act 2 Scenes 1, 3, 4, 6, 7, 8. Monologues: Act 1 Scene 1 AUNTY5. *'Abusive husband' – 'Don't suppose you know any literature'* AUNTY2/JASVIR. Scene 4 AUNTY5. Scene 5 GURPREET. Scene 6 AUNTY4 Act 2 Scene 5 GURPREET.}

Play 69

	Title & publisher	*Burning Bridges*	NHB
	Playwright/Date	Amy Schindler	2016
	Casting	1M: 4F	GCSE or GCE Depending on scenes
	Notes, guidance and considerations for teachers/students	\multicolumn{2}{l	}{**Description:** Comedy. **Summary:** A young woman (Sarah), living with autism (Asperger's Syndrome) and how her behaviour affects those closest to her. **Where:** North-West London, UK. **When:** Contemporary. **Themes:** Love; family; trust; disability. **Notes:** The best dialogues take place towards the second half of the play. **Design/tech notes:** Changing venues include a flat, a cafe, a police station and a picnic. Suggest minimalist with good lighting/projections. **Warnings:** Some sexual references and adult language. **Workshop/rehearsal/ideas/notes:** Looking for the truth of the moment. I saw it done with a very Frantic Assembly direction. It really worked and got my attention due to the physical contact issues with Asperger's.}
	Section or scene(s)	\multicolumn{2}{l	}{Scenes 1, KATE & DAN Scene 4, Scene 6 KATE & SARAH. Scene 7 Police station. Scenes 8, 9, 10. Monologues: KATE at end of Scene 4. SARAH Scene 6 *'Grieving?'*}

Play 70

	Title & publisher	*Leaves*	Faber & Faber
	Playwright/Date	Lucy Caldwell	2007
	Casting	1M: 4F	GCSE An able group
	Notes, guidance and considerations for teachers/students	**Description:** Family drama (Irish theatre). **Summary:** Three teenage sisters struggle to define who they really are and why, and where they might be going. **Where:** Belfast. **When:** Present day. **Themes:** Suicide, family life, stress and loneliness. **Notes:** Good female monologues. Act 3 is set three months before Acts 1 and 2. **Design/tech notes:** Simple set can be divided between a bedroom and family living room. Front stage can be the garden. **Warnings:** Attempted suicide of a family member. **Workshop/rehearsal/ideas/notes:** Character creation work. Emotional work on the nature of suffering. Look at the relationships between the three sisters. **Research:** Belfast and 'The Troubles'.	
	Section or scene(s)	Start with the tension building in Act 1 Scenes 1, 3, 4, 5, POPPY & PHYLLIS Scenes 6, 7. Act 2 Scene 1 LORI & PHYLLIS, Scene 3, Scene 4 LORI & POPPY, Scene 5. Monologues: PHYLLIS in Scene 4, Act 2 Scene 1, LORI.	

Play 71

	Title & publisher	*Black Comedy*	Samuel French
	Playwright/Date	Peter Shaffer	1965
	Casting	1M: 1F Lead 3M: 3F support	GCSE An able group
	Notes, guidance and considerations for teachers/students	**Description:** Farce/satire. **Summary:** A Sculptor has embellished his apartment with furniture and objects d'arte 'borrowed' from the neighbour, hoping to impress his fiancée's pompous father and a wealthy art dealer. The fuse blows and the comedy begins. **Where:** An apartment in South Kensington, London, UK. **When:** Mid-1960s. **Themes:** Love; class; deception. **Notes:** Great opportunity for slapstick/physical work. Timing vital. The two lead roles have witty wordplay. There are opportunities for supporting physical work. **Design/tech notes:** Reversed lighting scheme (see script!). A good opportunity for a sound/lighting design candidate. Set should be diverse and busy. **Warnings:** No intermission. Timing is crucial. Reverse lighting means even when a match/torch is lit the set becomes dimmer and when extinguished becoming brighter. **Workshop/rehearsal/ideas/notes:** Physical theatre, slapstick. Commedia dell'arte. Watch Marx Brothers, Mr Bean, Laurel and Hardy for routines.	
	Section or scene(s)	Any of the duologues between CAROL & BRINDSLEY or THE COLONEL. The scenes revolve around darkness and light. But the witty one liners and slapstick should be considered when selecting scenes for students. 75 minutes in total.	

Play 72

	Title & publisher	*Abigail's Party*	Samuel French
	Playwright/Date	Mike Leigh	1977
	Casting	2M: 3F	GCSE A range of abilities
	Notes, guidance and considerations for teachers/students	**Description:** Comedy (Naturalistic). **Summary:** Beverly has invited her new neighbours Angela and Tony as well as long-term neighbour, Sue, around for drinks. But as the evening goes on the tensions between characters are exposed through jealousy, prejudice and insecurities. **Where:** A house in middle-class suburbia, UK. **When:** Early evening in Spring and later that same evening. 1970s. **Themes:** Love; marriage and its breakdown; class. **Notes:** Music is important. Also be aware of the way alcohol sets the tone as the party progresses. **Design/tech notes:** Written as a stage and TV play, the temptation is to replicate the complex garish 1970's set. It works very well but should not distract from performances. **Warnings:** Shows a man having a heart attack. **Workshop/rehearsal/ideas/notes:** Character based devising to build roles. For example, shyness and self-consciousness being responsible for Tony's aggression. Role on wall. Naturalism. **Research:** The TV version with Alison Steadman. Musically, listen to Donna Summers and Demis Roussos. Consumerism and 'keeping up with the Joneses'.	
	Section or scene(s)	The best performances I have seen have always included the moments of rising tension – sexual tension, disagreements over music and art and long-held marital grudges. Monologues: LAURENCE on the phone start of Act 1. LAURENCE *'You know I think musicians and artists . . .'* Act 2 BEVERLY, *'It's my fault is it?'*	

Play 73

	Title & publisher	*Antigone*	Methuen Drama
	Playwright/Date	Jean Anouilh	1944
	Casting	2M: 3F Plus, chorus. Flexible multi-role.	GCE/GCSE
	Notes, guidance and considerations for teachers/students	**Description:** Greek tragedy. **Summary:** Inspired by the Greek mythology by Sophocles of the same name. **Where:** Thebes (but could be anywhere). **When:** 5th century BCE (but could be any time). **Themes:** The nature of tragedy; rivalry (sibling); society's view of femininity. **Notes:** The original version Sophocles 440 BCE is a viable alternative. I chose the Anouilh version as the characters are more easily accessible for young actors. Suggest Sophocles at GCE. **Design/tech notes:** Set should be devoid of geographical or historical reference. Minimalist. The same applies to costume. **Warnings:** Similar in most respects to the original (Sophocles) but the characters differ in their depth, in particular Antigone herself in her dialogues with Creon. There is also less power in the Chorus in the Anouilh version. Some Boards use this as a prescribed text. Check your specification! **Workshop/rehearsal/ideas/notes:** Physical and Chorus led. Works well with Berkoff. Physical work. Lecoq. **Research:** Original by Sophocles.	
	Section or scene(s)	PROLOGUE: NURSE & ANTIGONE then ISMENE. HAEMON & ANTIGONE. CREON & JONAS- CHORUS. ANTIGONE & CREON. Monologues: CREON, ANTIGONE, CHORUS. ANTIGONE & JONAS - MESSENGER to end.	

Play 74

	Title & publisher	*The Long Road*	Methuen Drama
	Playwright/Date	Shelagh Stephenson	2008
	Casting	2M 3F	Able GCE
	Notes, guidance and considerations for teachers/students	**Description:** Research based project. Family/social theatre. **Summary:** When teenage Danny is fatally stabbed in a random attack his family struggle to find meaning and forgiveness. His mother's determination to understand brings her face to face with his killer and forces the family to confront the bitter senselessness of their loss. **Where:** London, UK. **When:** Contemporary. **Themes:** Crime; knife crime; violence; death; loss; family; moral dilemmas; forgiveness; redemption. **Notes:** Produced by Synergy Theatre Project in association with the Forgiveness Project. Designed to be performed in theatres but also in prisons. Direct audience address. **Design/tech notes:** Highly stylised requires minimum set and props. **Warnings:** The issues and subject matter require you to really know your students. Very strong language and themes. **Workshop/rehearsal/ideas/notes:** Character role on wall. Emotion memory. **Research:** Synergy Theatre Project and the Forgiveness Project.	
	Section or scene(s)	The opening monologues: MARY, ELIZABETH and DAN'S Ashes. EMMA & ELIZABETH. Scene in which MARY & JOHN slap each other and JOE'S response. ELIZABETH & EMMA 2nd meeting. EMMA & MARY'S 1st meeting. JOE, JOHN & MARY after the meeting. EMMA reads MARY'S letter.	

Play 75

	Title & publisher	*100*	NHB
	Playwright/Date	Diene Petterle, Neil Monaghan and Christopher Heimann	2003
	Casting	3M: 2F	GCSE A range of abilities.
	Notes, guidance and considerations for teachers/students	**Description:** Physical theatre/storytelling. **Summary:** You have one hour to choose one single memory from your life. Choosing this memory is the only way to pass through to eternity. An eternity made up of only that one memory. All else is permanently erased! **Where:** A void and various locations of memory. **When:** Present with flashbacks. **Themes:** Afterlife; death and dying and those we leave behind. **Notes:** For exam performance look at the individual stories and the changes between them. Respect the order. **Design/tech notes:** Create a blank void. No definition of space, make it dark but with a strong sense of light and dark available (scripted lighting). Minimal props. Four small blocks/bamboo or broomsticks. Works well if performers are all in simple grey or off-white costume. Grotowski. **Warnings:** Used by some Boards in various units. Check your specification! **Workshop/rehearsal/ideas/notes:** Work on proxemics, character development, vocal tone, pace, eye contact. Physical theatre and improvisation work. **Research:** Imaginary Body Theatre Company. Magical realism and *100 Years of Solitude* (Marquez).	
	Section or scene(s)	The introduction so that the development and purpose of the piece is evident, then concentrate on one story per person. Mixture of successful and unsuccessful memories to blackout with the GUIDE'S revelation to ALEX.	

Play 76

	Title & publisher	*Metamorphosis*	Faber & Faber
	Playwright/Date	Berkoff, adaptation of Kafka	1969
	Casting	3M: 2F	GCE Or an able GCSE group
	Notes, guidance and considerations for teachers/students	\multicolumn{2}{l	}{**Description:** Physical theatre/adaptation of a novella. **Summary:** A travelling salesman awakes from a night of uneasy dreams to find himself transformed in his bed into a giant insect **Where:** A small apartment in Austria-Hungary (today's Czech Republic). **When:** 1910s. **Themes:** Family; duty; responsibility; alienation. **Notes:** 'The animal is the mis en scène, the production' (Berkoff). **Design/tech notes:** Minimal, stark stage using scaffolding to suggest a house/cage and the skeletal body of the insect. No props, everything is mimed! (Exception: 3 stools.) For lighting candidates, look at shadow and silhouette. Sound also offers exciting challenges. **Warnings:** Stage directions are precise and deliberate. Some Boards use this as a prescribed text. Check your specification! **Workshop/rehearsal/ideas/notes:** Expressionism/physical theatre. Lecoq and Artaud and of course Berkoff himself. Ensemble, strongly choreographed, using freeze frame to capture mood and moment.}
	Section or scene(s)	\multicolumn{2}{l	}{Opening sequence of introductions. The change. CHIEF CLERK'S visit. The lodgers. GREGOR's dream. Final sequence. Consider the flow and physicality of chosen scenes and respect the order. Monologues: CLERK, '*Mr Samsa – what is the matter . . .*' GREGOR '*Could that have been you father?*'}

Play 77

	Title & publisher	*Look Back in Anger*	Faber & Faber
	Playwright/Date	John Osborne	1957
	Casting	3M: 2F	GCE Or an able GCSE group
	Notes, guidance and considerations for teachers/students	\multicolumn{2}{l	}{**Description:** Realism. Kitchen sink. **Summary:** Jimmy Porter is an 'angry young man'. The play focuses on his life and marital struggles. Intelligent, educated and disaffected, the young working-class Jimmy's life with Alison, his upper middle-class wife, is one of anger, hatred and regret. **Where:** A one-room flat in a large midlands town, UK. **When:** Mid-1950s. **Themes:** Anger; lost childhood; class; education; disillusionment; nostalgia; gender and love. **Notes:** Depending on your students and numbers, there are excellent monologues/duologues and dialogues. Having studied the play, encourage students to select sections (in order), which interest them. **Design/tech notes:** I've seen minimal and very stark which worked well. I have also seen students gain excellent grades for set design with minute detail to the time and mood of the piece. Osborne gave specific directions and details of the five characters and the set. **Warnings:** It is very important to find the right pace. Students tend to play it fast, but rushed lines lose their impact. **Workshop/rehearsal/ideas/notes:** Stanislavski, who am I, what do I want? Building of tension, explore how tension is released physically. Joan Littlewood. **Resources:** British Library.}
	Section or scene(s)	\multicolumn{2}{l	}{Act 1 JIMMY, CLIFF & ALISON. (ALISON gets burned by the iron) Act 2 Scene 1 ALISON & HELENA to CLIFF's entrance. Act 2 Scene 2, Act 3 to end. Monologues: JIMMY Act 1 '*Nobody thinks . . .*' and '*Don't try and patronise me*'. Act 2 HELENA '*Marry him?*' Act 2 Scene 2 JIMMY has two long monologues at the end of the act.}

Play 78

	Title & publisher	*Kvetch*	Methuen Drama
	Playwright/Date	Steven Berkoff	1986
	Casting	3M: 2F	GCE An able group
	Notes, guidance and considerations for teachers/students	**Description:** Comedy. **Summary:** Frank and Donna are a mundane Jewish husband and wife. They are having dinner with friends George and Hal and The Mother in Law. What happens when their fears, anxieties, desires and secrets are uncovered? **Where:** An apartment in Los Angeles. Various locations and an office. USA. **When:** Contemporary. **Themes:** Anxiety and fear. Neurosis and cultural identity in America. **Notes:** Much of the speech is 'aside' (written in italics). Spoken thought in freeze frame. (Easily adapts to British English). **Design/tech notes:** Simple set using levels. Dining table angled to represent a bed. No props. Filmic projections. **Warnings:** Strong language. Simulated sex. **Workshop/rehearsal/ideas/notes:** Sharp and dynamic movements. Expressionism/physical theatre. Lecoq and Artaud. Berkoff.	
	Section or scene(s)	Act 1 Scene 1 (Scene 2 at your discretion) Act 2 Scene 1 FRANK & GEORGE's thoughts. Scene 2 GEORGE & DONNA & HAL as the WAITER. *Remains one of the best pieces of exam performance I have seen.* Many excellent Monologues/soliloquy.	

Play 79

	Title & publisher	*Britannia Waves the Rules*	NHB
	Playwright/Date	Gareth Farr	2011
	Casting	3M: 2F Really a set of monologues with an ensemble	GCSE/GCE Challenging
	Notes, guidance and considerations for teachers/students	**Description:** Realism. **Summary:** From the sands of Blackpool to the sands of Afghanistan. A brutal story of how war changes one man. **Where:** Blackpool, Kenya, Afghanistan. **When:** Contemporary. **Themes:** Conflict and its effect on soldiers returning home. **Notes:** Much of the play is a monologue (95% is Carl). For a very talented performer. Other parts are support/ensemble. Instead of listing scenes I have listed the names of those involved in suitable dialogues. **Design/tech notes:** Multiple venues, require simple set with light/projections creating Carl's different worlds. **Warnings:** Adult themes and language. Intense and violent. **Workshop/rehearsal/ideas/notes:** The idea of running and getting nowhere, of being trapped, was cleverly captured by literally tying Carl to the set with a bungee cord. It works in rehearsals! Character/types. Suppressed energy, physical theatre. Use the idea of moving in and out of verse/hip-hop rhyming to give a dreamlike quality which is then pulled sharply back to reality (Carl's different realities).	
	Section or scene(s)	Although much of the script is a monologue, there are sections with sustained dialogues. Jobcentre with ANDY & ANTHONY. GOLDIE & KARL. DAD/RECRUITING OFFICER & CARL. SERGEANT STOKES. CARL & BILKO. CARL & MUM. CARL & LIEUTENANT. CARL & ANDY.	

Play 80

	Title & publisher	*A Taste of Honey*	Methuen Drama
	Playwright/Date	Shelagh Delaney	1958
	Casting	3M: 2F	GCSE A fairly able group
	Notes, guidance and considerations for teachers/students	**Description:** Kitchen sink realism/feminist drama. **Summary:** Jo, a teenager, lives with her single mother Helen, a woman hardened by life, an alcoholic and 'a good time girl'. The play begins with them moving into a shabby flat. Jo wants to be an artist, but they've moved so often, it's made education impossible. Now she just wants to leave school and find a job and independence. **Where:** Salford, Manchester. **When:** 1950s. **Themes:** Identity; gender; race; class; care; responsibility; friendship; love; sex; popular culture. **Notes:** The relationship between Jo and Helen onstage is electric, with stinging ferocious interchanges which exploit every syllable of the dialect. The use of music/jazz music onstage or during set/scene changes can be very pleasing. **Design/tech notes:** The original set was fairly busy (kitchen sink) but a contemporary more bleak open set works well today. **Warnings:** Sexual references. Pregnancy and abortion. Some Boards use this as a prescribed text. Check your specification! **Workshop/rehearsal/ideas/notes:** Stanislavski for narrative, themes, characters and relationships. Joan Littlewood.	
	Section or scene(s)	F/F from the beginning or M/F/F from where JO finds out that HELEN is getting married. Monologues: HELEN has a number of brief monologues in Act 1 and one longer one at the end of the play 'You know when I was young'.	

Play 81

	Title & publisher	*Beside Herself*	Methuen Drama
	Playwright/Date	Sarah Daniels	1996
	Casting	3M: 2F	GCSE An able group
	Notes, guidance and considerations for teachers/students	**Description:** Social tragedy. **Summary:** Evelyn, an MP's wife, is struggling to make people like her, helping her father round the house, work and absorbing the stress she feels. Her innermost thoughts are voiced to the audience by the otherwise unseen Eve. Evelyn is not well, the spectre of mental illness haunts her as she puts on a timid, polite manner and faces the world. St. Dymphna's Community Group Home becomes not just a place of work for her, but a place where she can tackle the problems afflicting her and confront her father. **Where:** Various indoor scenes. A halfway house and a home. **When:** The 1990s. **Themes:** Mental illness and child abuse in families; child abuse; guilt and secrets in families. **Notes:** A very moving and intense piece which lends itself well to non-naturalism coupled with stark realism. The scene where Evelyn confronts her father is often represented with the little Girl Eve being seen by the audience as a visual torment in Evelyn's mind. Can be two female, one male. I did this with Eve dancing, which worked very well and gained high marks. **Design/tech notes:** Simple set with easy changes of location. **Warnings:** Some strong language, sexual references/child abuse. **Workshop/rehearsal/ideas/notes:** I have used physical theatre DV8 for the movement and emotion memory work for the guilt and pain. Rehearse in a small safe place.	
	Section or scene(s)	Scene 1 In her father's house. Scene 2 from GREG *'However, the real story has since emerged . . .'* Favoured scenes for exam performances are when EVELYN and the unseen EVE confront the father, Scene 9 to End of play. Monologues: Evelyn Scene 9.	

Play 82

	Title & publisher	*Sink the Belgrano*	Methuen Drama
	Playwright/Date	Steven Berkoff	1986
	Casting	4M: 1F and multi-role ensemble	GCE Or a very able GCSE group
	Notes, guidance and considerations for teachers/students	**Description:** Satire (verse). **Summary:** The decision to sink the Belgrano. The events and the personalities. **Where:** UK, Argentina, Falkland Islands, various locations, including onboard a submarine. **When:** 1982 during the Falklands war. **Themes:** 'The underlying values and attitudes revealed during the war at all levels of society'. **Notes:** Written in verse. **Design/tech notes:** Divide set into three areas: upstage rostrum Political; downstage main area and submarine; then SL The British Pub. Above the rostrum a large screen for projections. Props should be kept to a minimum, with minimal costume solely to denote character changes. **Warnings:** Strong language, some racist remarks. **Workshop/rehearsal/ideas/notes:** Expressionism/physical theatre. Lecoq and Artaud and of course Berkoff. Exaggerated facial expression and vocal work, stylised mime. Perhaps masks.	
	Section or scene(s)	It is possible with just a few cuts to perform the whole piece (respect the order). Monologues: CHORUS and many characters have significant monologues.	

Play 83

	Title & publisher	*Risk*	Oberon Modern Plays
	Playwright/Date	John Retallack	2006
	Casting	3M: 2F	GCE A very able physical/dance group
	Notes, guidance and considerations for teachers/students	**Description:** Dance based theatre. **Summary:** A series of soliloquy and monologues from young people at risk. Told through five voices. **Where:** Various locations (Glasgow) but anyplace. **When:** Anytime. **Themes:** Risk (physical/mental and identity) and how young people are drawn to danger/thrill seeking. **Notes:** The five innocents are played by the same actors. **Design/tech notes:** Minimalist set, open stage (audience on three sides), a bed, a table/levels. Scaffolding perhaps. Lighting/projects and sound very important. **Warnings:** Very physical. Violence. Adult content. **Workshop/rehearsal/ideas/notes:** Each of the five named characters have an objective (see script) these should be pursued through rehearsal. Highly choreographed. DV8. Ensemble. Punchdrunk. Off Balance. **Research:** David Le Breton, 'The Anthropology of Adolescent Risk-Taking Behaviours', *Body and Society Journal*, 2014.	
	Section or scene(s)	Study the text, find what you like and let your body talk. Respect each character's objective. Keep to the order of the piece but use what you want from each soliloquy for your performance.	

Play 84

	Title & publisher	*Holloway Jones* NHB
	Playwright/Date	Evan Placey 2011
	Casting	3M: 3F GCE Or able GCSE group
	Notes, guidance and considerations for teachers/students	**Description:** Storytelling. **Summary:** Holloway Jones dreams of competing in the Olympics as a top-class BMX racer. But she is held back by the tough realities of her life, like having a mother in prison, being in foster care and living in a tough unforgiving world. **Where:** Various locations. Mainly London, UK. **When:** 2008–12. **Themes:** Teenagers, gangs, BMX, Foster care and parents in prison. Choices. The role of the Bystander. Relationships. **Notes:** Chorus should be played by members of the cast (except Holloway). There are no individually assigned lines for the chorus who should attempt to speak them rather like a Greek chorus, together or as directed. The chorus should always be present, either on stage or watching the action. **Design/tech notes:** Minimal set incorporated into which should be a large screen. Projections and SFX vital. **Warnings:** Needs a strong choreographer and a real sense of both the rhythm and the poetry to do it justice. **Workshop/rehearsal/ideas/notes:** Focus on the story, recall all the main events in rehearsal. High energy, fluid scene to scene. Keep up the pace, always in the race. Try reflecting subtext through movement. Non-naturalism. Hot seating. **Resources:** Teacher resource pack available online from Synergy Theatre Project.
	Section or scene(s)	Prison visit duologues and CHORUS. Club/training scene with AVERY/COACH/HOLLOWAY Skipping rope. HOLLOWAY & AVERY, HOLLOWAY & GEM. Use CHORUS and show multi-role. Monologues: TEACHER (Members of the CHORUS in various roles). HOLLOWAY with the police. GEM *'When I grow up'*.

Play 85

	Title & publisher	*Kindertransport* NHB
	Playwright/Date	Diane Samuels 1995
	Casting	1M: 5F GCSE A range of abilities
	Notes, guidance and considerations for teachers/students	**Description:** Modern history play. **Summary:** The story of 9-year-old Jewish girl, Eva, who was sent from Germany in 1939 to Manchester to be raised by the Miller family – an act of kindness that saved her life – while others remained to perish in the Holocaust. Later, her own daughter discovers that her mother (Eva) concealed her history from her in a locked storeroom/attic. The shadow of the rat catcher is ever present. **Where:** Spare storage room of a house in a London suburb. Also time shifts to Hamburg and London. **When:** Mid-1980s, but jumps between three time periods. **Themes:** Fear; identity; mother–daughter relationships; memory; survival. **Notes:** The sole male performer plays five parts. **Design/tech notes:** Set and costume should not overcomplicate. Good opportunities for lighting/projections and sound. Some very important props. **Warnings:** Deals with the Holocaust. Some Boards use this as a prescribed text. Check your specification! **Workshop/rehearsal/ideas/notes:** Each character has to establish their 'want' within the play and pursue this throughout. Each rehearsal should begin with a statement of what you want. The style of the play is really quite naturalistic. However, the scenes where the characters from other times occupy the same stage need planning (for example, the idea that the play is timeless and the events are taking place all at once). The character of the rat catcher can be in a more stylised way. Repressing emotions and the physical outcomes. Shared Experience. **Research:** Read *We Came as Children* edited by Karen Gershon. Timelines of WWII Anti-Semitic propaganda. **Resources:** UK history, '6 stories of the Kindertransport' (IWM.org.uk). OCR Resources. Shared Experience have produced an excellent resources pack.
	Section or scene(s)	Act 1 the story of the journey to England. The interchanges between the women at different ages. YOUNG EVA & LIL. The confrontation between EVELYN & FAITH. EVA & EVELYN at end of Act 1. Act 2 EVA & HELGA. EVA & THE POSTMAN. LIL & EVELYN. EVA & STATION GUARD. LIL & EVA post-liberation. EVELYN & FAITH. HELGA & EVA at 17. Final scene. Monologues: Act 1 Scene 1 EVA on the train. *'The border!'*. Act 1 Scene 2 EVELYN *'My father was called Werner Schlesinger'*. To *'Yes. In Auschwitz'*.

Play 86

	Title & publisher	*Chatroom* Samuel French
	Playwright/Date	Enda Walsh 2005
	Casting	3M: 3F GCSE Mixed ability
	Notes, guidance and considerations for teachers/ students	**Description:** Dramatic comedy. **Summary:** Six teenagers communicate solely through the internet and deal with everything from pop culture to suicide. **Where:** The virtual space of an internet chatroom. **When:** 2004. **Themes:** Teenage life; parents; pop culture; suicide; anonymity; isolation; responsibility; technology. **Notes:** Lighting plots and effects plot are all in the Samuel French edition. However, more recent interpretations have done their own thing. **Design/tech notes:** Six identical chairs. A screen for projections at the back (though I've seen it done as a far more physical GCE piece on a bare stage). Lighting/SFX important/projections/technical option opportunities are excellent. **Warnings:** Discussions about suicide. Some strong language and sexual references. **Workshop/rehearsal/ideas/notes:** Look at the idea of faceless freedom/'Disguise I see thou art a wickedness'. A more physical interpretation enables the text to stay more 'of the moment'.
	Section or scene(s)	Good starting duologues. McDonald's sequence through to black-out. Monologues: JIM'S (DAD and the Zoo). Followed by EVA & WILLIAM'S *'notes'* with JIM, & later JACK.

Play 87

	Title & publisher	*Things I Know to be True* NHB
	Playwright/Date	Andrew Bovell and Frantic Assembly 2017
	Casting	3M: 3F GCE Able group. Physically demanding.
	Notes, guidance and considerations for teachers/ students	**Description:** Suburban drama. Dark comedy. **Summary:** Fran and Bob Price are two doting parents whose lives centre around their four children. When their children start facing complex life decisions, can they cope and are they ready for their children to make their own decisions? Over one year, each season tells one of their children's story. Each season/story brings its own crisis, a turning point. **Where:** Suburban Adelaide, Australia. **When:** Present time, over one year with flashbacks. **Themes:** Expectations; family love; parenting; the cycles of life. **Notes:** This is a well written piece and can be used as a straight text (Australian realism) but the physical work that comes from it can be breath-taking and very enabling. Students should be encouraged to experiment rather than copy. **Design/tech notes:** Dining table and six chairs. Set required to represent indoor and outdoor. Suburban living room and garden. Other locations through sound and light and levels. **Warnings:** Adult themes and language (death in a car accident). Some Boards use this as a prescribed text. Check your specification! **Workshop/rehearsal/ideas/notes:** Stanislavski for characters and naturalism. Frantic for physical work. **Research:** The Australian dream. Transitioning. The music is important: listen to 'Famous Blue Raincoat' by Leonard Cohen. **Resources:** There is an excellent downloadable resource from Frantic Assembly and Arts Council England.
	Section or scene(s)	Divided into seasons of a year. Watch the Frantic Assembly material. Lots of fast and funny exchanges. Six unique struggles. Monologues: ROSIE Berlin. PIP, Autumn. As Autumn turns PIP *'Dear mum'*. Winter MARK *'On the weekends'*. As Winter turns MARK *'Then stay there'*. Spring BEN *'In the chaos of our home'*. Summer, BOB *'It wasn't meant to be like this'*. ROSIE *'And it ends like this'*.

Play 88

	Title & publisher	*Those Legs*	Methuen Drama NT connections
	Playwright/Date	Noel Clarke	2017
	Casting	3M: 3F	GCE
	Notes, guidance and considerations for teachers/students	**Description:** Youth Theatre. **Summary:** It's two years after Georgia's accident, in which she lost the use of her legs, and her fiancé and flatmates are trying hard to support her. Georgia cannot see beyond her own struggle and how it affects the lives of those around her. **Where:** A house, several rooms, UK. **When:** Contemporary. **Themes:** Friendship; loyalty; love; the cracks that appear in relationships. **Notes:** The final scene is a flip back to the past before the accident. This should be made obvious even before we see Georgia walking. **Design/tech notes:** Good challenge for set designers. Stage is upstairs section of a house. We see living room, dining area, a bathroom, Georgia's room and Lana's room. A wheelchair. **Warnings:** Adult themes and language. **Workshop/rehearsal/ideas/notes:** Hard hitting and honest, each character should spark debate within the audience. As a group, explore previous circumstances/last two years since the accident. Excellent workshop/rehearsal ideas follow the text in the Connections 2011 copy. Performers should read their character descriptions and discuss them together.	
	Section or scene(s)	Scenes 1, 2, 6, 7, 8, 9, 10, 11, 12, 13. Monologues: Scene 10, GEORGIA. Scene 13, GEORGIA.	

Play 89

	Title & publisher	*Pink Mist*	Faber & Faber
	Playwright/Date	Owen Sheers	2013
	Casting	3M: 3F	GCE An able group
	Notes, guidance and considerations for teachers/students	**Description:** Physical theatre. **Summary:** The story of three young Bristol men deployed to Afghanistan returning to the women in their lives who must now share the physical and psychological aftershocks of their service. ARTHUR, HADS and TAFF find their journey home is their greatest battle. **Where:** Bristol/Afghanistan various. **When:** New millennium/21st century with flashbacks. **Themes:** War; love; grief; revenge. **Notes:** Written in verse (Bristol accent). Movement, mime and gesture. **Design/tech notes:** Contemporary costumes/street clothes/blacks/uniforms. Minimal set/levels. SFX Lighting opportunities. Wheelchair. **Warnings:** Violent images of war in Afghanistan. Intense adult themes and strong language. **Workshop/rehearsal/ideas/notes:** Six performers/ensemble physical, strongly Choreographed. DV8/Frantic. **Research:** Afghan war (UK involvement). Blue on Blue. PTSD. British Army.	
	Section or scene(s)	The sequences in verse consist of fairly long monologues which will need to be shortened and carefully selected for exams. Encourage students to read and select from the whole. Very powerful and highly dependent on good choreography.	

Play 90

🎭	Title & publisher	*Shades*	Methuen Drama
✏️	Playwright/Date	Alia Bano	2009
👥	Casting	4M: 2F	GCE
📋	Notes, guidance and considerations for teachers/students	**Description:** Romantic comedy. **Summary:** Explores the tolerance within and without the Muslim community. **Where:** London, UK. **When:** Contemporary. **Themes:** Being a young, single Muslim woman living in modern London; racism; faith; tolerance. **Notes:** Nazir can also play the waitress. **Design/tech notes:** Set is challenging with multiple locations. Keep it simple. Lighting will be important. Costume as suggested by script. **Warnings:** Respect the ethnicity of the piece when casting. **Workshop/rehearsal/ideas/notes:** Naturalism. Stanislavski. Declan Donnellan. Complex characters. Status and taboo.	
🎬	Section or scene(s)	Scenes 1, 3, 6, 9, 10, 11, 12, 13–end. Monologues: Scene 6 REZA.	

Play 91

🎭	Title & publisher	*The Memory of Water*	Methuen Drama
✏️	Playwright/Date	Shelagh Stephenson	1997
👥	Casting	2M: 4F *Many all-female scenes*	GCSE An able group
📋	Notes, guidance and considerations for teachers/students	**Description:** Tragi-comedy. **Summary:** Three sisters meet on the eve of their mother's funeral. **Where:** A cliff-top bungalow on the north eastern coast of England. **When:** 1990s. **Themes:** Coping with death; conflict and strains in family relationships; memory. **Notes:** A great pace is needed throughout with witty interchanges and good comic lines. Emotional arguments with good opportunities for outstanding performances. Excellent scenes for strong female roles, in particular Mary, Catherine and Teresa. Many all-female opportunities. The two male roles come later in the play and can be omitted. **Design/tech notes:** A simple set with several props/costume. A full mirror. Window to outside. Table, chairs, a bed. Door to kitchen/outside. Simple lighting FX. Phone. **Warnings:** Some adult themes and language. Reference to smoking a joint. Death of mother. **Workshop/rehearsal/ideas/notes:** Character based. Acting and reacting. Objectives and super objectives in each scene. Stanislavski.	
🎬	Section or scene(s)	Act 1 to CATHERINE'S entrance, then to MIKE at the window Act 2 Scene 3 to *'Mum don't go just yet'*. 12 mins CATHERINE & VI have good monologues in Act 2.	

Play 92

	Title & publisher	*Bruised*	Methuen Drama Contemporary Welsh Plays
	Playwright/Date	Matthew Trevannion	2012
	Casting	4M: 2F	GCE
	Notes, guidance and considerations for teachers/students	\multicolumn{2}{l}{**Description:** Welsh theatre. Social drama. **Summary:** Noah returns to the family home after 10 years away to find his place taken by Shane, a crazed drug dealer and violent abuser. A mixture of powerful monologues and complicated dramatic scenes lead to a slow yet unexpected reveal. **Where:** A room in a flat. Pontypool, South Wales. **When:** Contemporary. **Themes:** Guilt and blame; secrets in families; domestic violence; dominance. **Notes:** Coming from Pontypool myself I am partial to the accent and believe it should be respected! It's a very real part of the story (Valleys Welsh). **Design/tech notes:** The whole play takes place in one room of a council flat. Simply furnished. Drab non-matching furniture. Another space/level is needed for the monologues/memories of Noah and Adam. **Warnings:** Strong language, violence. Stabbing scene. **Workshop/rehearsal/ideas/notes:** Strong character study. Stanislavski. Eddie Ladd for physical work/tension/resistance and status games. Safe fight choreography.}
	Section or scene(s)	\multicolumn{2}{l}{ADAM'S monologue introduction. Followed by scene with SHANE & WENDY. NOAH'S arrival. ADAM and NOAH'S monologues. SHANE & NOAH meeting. Last scenes as tension builds to reveal and stabbing.}

Play 93

	Title & publisher	*Language Roulette*	Methuen Drama (Far from the Land Contemporary Irish Plays)
	Playwright/Date	Daragh Carville	1996
	Casting	4M: 2F	GCE An able group
	Notes, guidance and considerations for teachers/students	\multicolumn{2}{l}{**Description:** Irish theatre. **Summary:** A reunion of old school friends on the night of the ceasefire to welcome home the one who went away. They drink too much, pop pills and then the game starts. **Where:** Inside a pub and a house Belfast, UK. **When:** 1994 (first eve of the ceasefire). Northern Ireland. The troubles from a different viewpoint. **Themes:** Friendship and change. **Notes:** Carefully select scenes. It's the pithy dialogues that make this piece work. Lots of pace and energy needed throughout with slick scene changes. **Design/tech notes:** The set is a good opportunity for a design student with a pub doubling as a front room. **Warnings:** Scene in which a joint is smoked. Very strong language and drugs culture. **Workshop/rehearsal/ideas/notes:** Character work. Objectives/super objectives and how they influence mood/tone and movement.}
	Section or scene(s)	\multicolumn{2}{l}{Scenes 1, 3, 4 (with cuts) Scene 5 (the game) 6. Careful choices should be made. Experiment with moments and tension. Respect the order and the reprises.}

Play 94

	Title & publisher	*Four Nights in Knaresborough*	NHB
	Playwright/Date	Paul Webb	1999
	Casting	5M: 1F	GCE and GCSE
	Notes, guidance and considerations for teachers/students	**Description:** Black comedy/historical. **Summary:** Historical drama for the Tarantino generation. The four knights who killed Thomas Becket hide out in Knaresborough castle for 12 months hoping that the heat will die down. **Where:** Knaresborough Castle, Yorkshire, and Canterbury Cathedral in a dream. **When:** 1170. **Themes:** Loyalty; religion; God's existence; love; lust; and dentistry! **Notes:** Opening dream sequence can be with projections. **Design/tech notes:** Set should not be complicated. A large hall, as dingy and dull as possible. Lighting important. A fire (light) and a large table, some chairs. Props and costume as described. A stained-glass church window gobo will be useful. **Warnings:** Strong and bawdy language. **Workshop/rehearsal/ideas/notes:** Comic timing, finding each character's desire (want). Fast and physical. Naturalistic with dreamlike sequences. Tickle and slap.	
	Section or scene(s)	Many very funny yet demanding scenes. Needs the opening dream sequence then Scene 2 MORVILLE's monologue, Scene 3. The tooth extraction scene is great. Act 2 Scenes 1, 3, 4, 5 to end.	

Play 95

	Title & publisher	*Accidental Death of an Anarchist*	Methuen Drama
	Playwright/Date	Dario Fo (Translated by Simon Nye) or Adaption by Gavin Richards translated by Gillian Hanna	1970
	Casting	5M: 1F	GCE Or an able GCSE group
	Notes, guidance and considerations for teachers/students	**Description:** Political farce/satire. **Summary:** An incident in 1969 – in which an anarchist railway worker, arrested in connection with a terrorist bombing in Milan, fell to his death from a fourth-storey window of police headquarters during the course of an interrogation – is investigated by a series of satirical fictional characters played by 'The Maniac'. **Where:** A room on the third floor of a central Police headquarters (England but see Fo's own notes). **When:** Contemporary. **Themes:** Crime; death; politics; corruption. **Notes:** Very fast pace, physical and high energy clowning. Set and performance must allude to being high up in a building. **Design/tech notes:** A filing cabinet with papers. A desk. A window to the outside! A large bag full of disguises as dictated by script. **Warnings:** Some four-letter words sprinkled throughout. Threat of a bomb. Some Boards use this as a prescribed text. Check your specification! **Workshop/rehearsal/ideas/notes:** Brecht/'Breaks the fourth wall'. Often slapstick in appearance. Try to avoid any subtlety! Look at pantomime and the clown figure. Commedia dell'arte.	
	Section or scene(s)	The nervous tick of the INSPECTOR and the duality of THE MANIAC lend themselves to memorable performances. THE MANIAC's monologue. Act 1 Scene 1 sets the scene but it's all gold.	

Play 96

	Title & publisher	*The Gut Girls*	Methuen Drama
	Playwright/Date	Sarah Daniels	1988
	Casting	2M: 6F	GCSE A range of abilities
	Notes, guidance and considerations for teachers/students	**Description:** Comedy/feminist. **Summary:** The lives of the girls who work in the gutting sheds of a Cattle Market and how their lives are changed when the sheds are closed down. They become unwilling members of a club founded by Lady Helena to find alternative employment, which has tragic consequences. **Where:** Deptford Cattle Market and a drawing room of an upper-class home. London, UK. **When:** 1900. **Themes:** Strong contrasts between the lower and upper classes of the time. The exploitation and marginalisation of women. Solidarity. **Notes:** Some good multi-role opportunities. Focus on the blood and mess of independence and solidarity and contrast with the seemingly perfect lives of the upper classes. **Design/tech notes:** Usually done with full set, costume and props. White aprons and blood. Hanging carcasses, excellent opportunities for design students. **Warnings:** Strong language, some violence. **Workshop/rehearsal/ideas/notes:** Close attention must be paid to the character differentiation (Stanislavski). Role on the wall. Hot seating. Status games/workshops.	
	Section or scene(s)	Act 1 Scene 1 in the gutting shed, Scene 2 LADY H's drawing room. EMILY & LADY H. Scene 4 POLLY & EDNA. Scene 6 JIM & KATE. Act 2 Scene 1, Scene 3 LADY H & PRISCILLA, Scene 10 ARTHUR & PRISCILLA. Scene 12 LEN & JIM. all of Scene 13. Monologues: LADY H's prayer at the end of Scene 3. Scene 5 ANNIE's 'I was in service'. Scene 10 MADJACKO 'You're a friendly couple'. Act 2 Scene 1 LADY H 'That's quite enough'. Scene 5 LADY H 'Rarely will you be required...' Scene 7 ELLEN 'I pawned all my books today...'	

Play 97

	Title & publisher	*Scratching the Surface*	Pping
	Playwright/Date	Mark Wheeller	2016
	Casting	4M: 2F and Flexible ensemble	GCSE or GCE
	Notes, guidance and considerations for teachers/students	**Description:** Verbatim. **Summary:** Dramatisation of interviews with self-harmer and his family and a youth drama group who share their experiences. **Where:** A theatre studio. **When:** Now. **Themes:** Self-harm. **Notes:** Much of this can be seen as devising. Interpretation is so much a part of the art of making theatre. Careful selection and experimentation with scenes by the cast is essential to the process. **Design/tech notes:** A studio. A bare set. **Warnings:** Deals with self-harm and mental health issues. **Workshop/rehearsal/ideas/notes:** Improvisation. Physical theatre. Emotion memory.	
	Section or scene(s)	Section 1 is important (with music as suggested in the text). After this, choices of scenes to include should stem from experimenting with ideas/feelings shared by the cast as a whole. Use dialogue between family and friends.	

Play 98

	Title & publisher	*La Chunga*	Methuen Drama
	Playwright/Date	Mario Vargas Llosa	1986
	Casting	4M: 2F	GCE Able/mature group
	Notes, guidance and considerations for teachers/students	**Description:** Feminist/Latin American theatre. **Summary:** La Chunga's bar and its regulars present a distilled picture of the low life in a low-down gambling den in a demoralised community. **Where:** A bar/restaurant Piura, Peru. **When:** 1945. **Themes:** Morality; gender identity; fantasy and illusion vs. reality; love and sexuality; devils and miracles; magic realism. **Notes:** The four male characters are very strongly defined and all characters lend themselves to both characterisation and physical work. **Design/tech notes:** Minimalist. Tables and chairs. Stark lighting. Good opportunities for set/props/costume. SFX. **Warnings:** Some sexual reference and fantasy. Teachers should read this first and make a judgement as to its suitability for their students/school/college. Some scenes may need to be avoided. Act 2 Scene 2 should be sensitively approached or sections omitted. Use illusion. **Workshop/rehearsal/ideas/notes:** Stanislavski for characterisation but lends itself to Frantic style physical work with the changes between fantasy and reality. Boal.	
	Section or scene(s)	Run time 105 minutes in total Act 1, 1, 4 MECHE & LA CHUNGA, 5 and 6. Act 2 1, LA CHUNGA and JOSÉ. Whichever speculations and variations the cast selects and you sanction! Monologues: Act 2 Scene 9 JOSEFINO various. LA CHUNGA.	

Play 99

	Title & publisher	*The Homecoming*	Faber & Faber
	Playwright/Date	Harold Pinter	1964
	Casting	5M: 1F	GCE Or a very able GCSE group
	Notes, guidance and considerations for teachers/students	**Description:** Kitchen sink. **Summary:** Teddy returns from the USA to his London home with his wife Ruth, to meet his father, Max, and his two brothers and uncle. Ruth's presence uncovers a tangle of confused sexuality and rage in the all-male household. **Where:** An old house in North London, UK. **When:** A Summer in the 1960s. **Themes:** Power; survival; truth; memories and illusion; family; the outsider; women and sexuality. **Notes:** Pay particular attention to stage directions. **Design/tech notes:** A well-worn, comfortable living room with views off including a hallway and staircase. Costumes as scripted. But see also rehearsal ideas on minimalism. **Warnings:** Abusive language and sexual references. **Workshop/rehearsal/ideas/notes:** Role on wall Stanislavski character work. Proxemics. Students should explore the language/dialogue and what makes us laugh. The Pinter pause. 'You never heard such silence!' Try minimalism. Characters caught in space. Draw lines on stage and play territory games. **Resources.** Royal exchange theatre student notes.	
	Section or scene(s)	Opening Scene, LENNY & MAX to SAM'S entrance. JOEY'S entrance to Blackout. TEDDY & RUTH'S entrance to RUTH'S exit. TEDDY & LENNY, RUTH. MAX & SAM in the kitchen. MAX & TEDDY. MAX & JOEY fight. TEDDY & MAX, LENNY'S monologue. *'One night down by the docks'* to *'some kind of proposal'*. with RUTH & TEDDY.	

Play 100

	Title & publisher	*The Birthday Party*	Faber & Faber
	Playwright/Date	Harold Pinter	1959
	Casting	4M: 2F	GCE Range of abilities
	Notes, guidance and considerations for teachers/students	\multicolumn{2}{l	}{**Description:** Tragi-comedy. **Summary:** Stanley's life at a rundown seaside boarding house is interrupted by the unexpected arrival of two sinister strangers who terrorise him before abducting him. **Where:** The living room of a house in an English seaside town, UK. **When:** 1950s. **Themes:** Power games; identity; cruelty; the terrors of the outside world. **Notes:** The play is divided by a series of blackouts and fades. There are two different styles within the play, from the very definite naturalism of the breakfast in Act 1 to the absurd Goldberg/McCann brainwashing of Acts 2 and 3. **Design/tech notes:** The set has quite specific requirements (see script). Good design opportunities. **Warnings:** Very able group, small pieces, respect the order of the piece. **Workshop/rehearsal/ideas/notes:** Ensure each character has a strong awareness of their patterns of speech/accent/tone. Tension games. Explore the beat/pace of the word play. Look at repetition and comedy. Proxemics. **Research:** British Library articles on early performances of the play.}
	Section or scene(s)	\multicolumn{2}{l	}{For exam performances Act 1 Opening scene with PETEY & MEG. Act 2 onwards. The interrogation scene. Act 3 GOLDBERG, MCCANN sequence to the prone STANLEY.}

Play 101

	Title & publisher	*A Doll's House*	Methuen Drama
	Playwright/Date	Henrik Ibsen	1879
	Casting	3M: 4F Plus minor roles	GCSE/GCE
	Notes, guidance and considerations for teachers/students	\multicolumn{2}{l	}{**Description:** Realism. **Summary:** Torvald and Nora seem happy; she is indulged by her successful husband. But pride and her class/gender conspire to destroy their perfect life when a loan is taken out with a disreputable individual. Nora's journey of self-discovery. **Where:** The Helmer's apartment. A town in Norway (we believe). **When:** Late 1870s. **Themes:** Social and legal equality between men and women; moral laws; pride; love; duty; determinism and free will; betrayal. **Notes:** Explores the tension between appearance and reality. **Design/tech notes:** The apartment should be warm and seemingly comfortable. A good study of naturalism with some symbolic references. However, all aspects of design are open to the interpretation of the cast. **Warnings:** Seen as an example of realism (Ibsen). If a different approach is decided upon it should be well argued. **Workshop/rehearsal/ideas/notes:** Stanislavski. Realism. Strong emphasis on the main protagonists and their motivations. Can be done in a very different way, for example by physicalising the emotions and hidden subtext (shared experience).}
	Section or scene(s)	\multicolumn{2}{l	}{Act 1 NORA and HELMER *(TORVALD)*. Look at main areas of conflict/rising tension. Act 1 NORA & Mrs LINDE. KROGSTAD's visit. Act 2 the letter *(Blackmail)*. End of Act 2. Act 3 Mrs LINDE, NORA & HELMER. HELMER discovers the letter. NORA's monologue *'That may be . . .'* to end.}

Play 102

	Title & publisher	*Blue Remembered Hills*	Samuel French
	Playwright/Date	Dennis Potter	1979
	Casting	5M: 2F	GCSE A range of abilities
	Notes, guidance and considerations for teachers/students	**Description:** Tragi-comedy. Television play. **Summary:** A simple tale of the activities of seven, seven-year-olds on a summer afternoon during WW2. The children play, fight, fantasize and swagger. Their world becomes a reflection of the adult lives they see. **Where:** A wood, a field and a barn in the West Country, UK. **When:** One summer afternoon in 1943. **Themes:** Childhood and its darker side; lost innocence; memory; friendship; being bullied; war and parents. **Notes:** The children are around 7 and traditionally played by adults, or in this case older students aged 15–17 so the author's intent remains. **Design/tech notes:** The Samuel French script has detailed set and props lists plus lighting /effects plots. I have seen it done very successfully for exams, with little more than a mattress and excellent lighting. The mattress was used extensively by the children to land on, play on and ultimately be lifted to form the fateful barn doors! Costume: boys in shorts, girls in summer dresses of the era. SFX A siren. **Warnings:** The death of a child. **Research:** BBC DVD of the same name. **Workshop/rehearsal/ideas/notes:** Memory workshops, when you were 7. Running and playing as a company as unrestrained children. Naturalism, but not! A naturalistic illusion!	
	Section or scene(s)	60 minutes, 30 scenes. Scenes 1–4 PETER & WILLIE joined later by RAYMOND & JOHN Scene 5 ANGELA, AUDREY & DONALD. Scene 8 '*Come back dad*' Scene 8 ANGELA & AUDREY. Scenes 10 and 11 Everyone except DONALD 12–14 PETER & DONALD in the Barn. Scene 23 to end.	

Play 103

	Title & publisher	*Family Planning*	Samuel French
	Playwright/Date	Frank Vickery	1981
	Casting	3M: 4F	GCSE A range of abilities
	Notes, guidance and considerations for teachers/students	**Description:** Comedy. **Summary:** When Tracy discovers she is pregnant, she doesn't know how to break the news to her mother or father or to her boyfriend. Gran, who is permanently in bed on stage, knows all, and tries to prepare everyone for Tracy's announcement. Misunderstandings and mishaps abound! **Where:** In a house, in three areas (hallway, living room, a bedroom). South Wales perhaps? UK. **When:** Contemporary. **Themes:** Misunderstanding and mishap; communication; pregnancy; relationships and family ties. **Notes:** Gran is always in bed. **Design/tech notes:** A composite set: A living room, bedroom and hallway. Gran's room on a higher level. Script contains quite specific instructions. Some good opportunities for design candidates. **Warnings:** Fast duologues. Comic timing/awareness and delivery is vital. **Workshop/rehearsal/ideas/notes:** Acting and reacting, fast comic exchanges. Stanislavski for character work.	
	Section or scene(s)	Opening scene GRAN, TRACY and ELSIE Act 2 GRAN upstairs with IDRIS then downstairs with TRACY & BOBBY then back and forth action upstairs and down. Act 3 TRACY, MASIE & GRAN. Monologues: MASIE Act 2 '*Well anyway . . . I'd gone to bed*' GRAN's long monologue at the start of Act 3.	

Play 104

	Title & publisher	*Tonypandemonium*	Methuen Drama (Contemporary Welsh plays)
	Playwright/Date	Rachel Trezise	2013
	Casting	3M: 4F	GCE
	Notes, guidance and considerations for teachers/students	**Description:** Welsh theatre. **Summary:** A raucous, funny yet heart-breaking account of a daughter's decade with her beautiful alcoholic mother. **Where:** South Wales Tonypandy, Pontypridd, UK. **When:** Jumps back and forth in time between 1987, 1992, 1994 and 1996. **Themes:** Mother–daughter relationships; alcohol dependency; poverty; mental illness. **Notes:** Three different performers play the character of Danielle at 9, 15, and 18 years of age. There is some multi-role with the male characters. **Design/tech notes:** Works well in the round. Locations shared and simple. **Warnings:** Strong language and sexual references. Alcoholism, death of a mother. (Valleys Welsh) **Workshop/rehearsal/ideas/notes:** Works well with some Frantic ideas or Eddie Ladd. Rehearse the three Danielles together and let them try each other's roles out.	
	Section or scene(s)	Start with opening sequence in tattoo parlour. Allow students to choose scenes but respect the scripted order. Excellent monologues and shared role opportunities. TOMMY's early monologue *'Well this happened back when I . . .'* DEBORAH *'Well you shouldn't have bothered'*. TOMMY's Phil Collins monologue followed by DEBORAH's in Scene 15. The Danielle's #1 and #2 duologue. Scene 16.	

Play 105

	Title & publisher	*An Inspector Calls*	Samuel French or Heinemann School edition.
	Playwright/Date	J.B. Priestley	1937
	Casting	4M: 3F	GCSE A range of abilities
	Notes, guidance and considerations for teachers/students	**Description:** Crime thriller. **Summary:** A wealthy family's dinner party is interrupted by a police inspector who is investigating the grisly death of a young working-class woman. It soon appears every member of the family knew her or someone like her. Or did they? **Where:** Various locations. Predominantly in a well-to-do home. Burnley, England, UK. **When:** 1912. **Themes:** Youth and age (time); responsibility; class; social duty; the supernatural; cause and effect. **Notes:** Popular with English GCSE literature. **Design/tech notes:** The script carries a very detailed description of the set. It is not necessary to follow it to the letter but it does offer some excellent opportunities for set/costume designers. **Warnings:** Some Boards use this as a prescribed text. Check your specification! **Workshop/rehearsal/ideas/notes:** Stanislavski. Character study. Role on wall. Characters must be strongly aware of and influenced by their history and class. Establish and play to objectives. Actors should keep a record of what they discover about their character as rehearsals continue. What others say about them and how they react. **Research:** Britain/Europe just before WW1. There are a few versions of the film 2017 Movie/2015 TV and the original 1954 film each have something to offer. Look at class divisions at that time. *Titanic* is a good example and referenced in the play. **Resources:** Many education resources packs available including TES, Theatre Royal teacher resources, Trailers for Wyndham Theatre among others and many of the exam Boards. Chat to the English department of your school!	
	Section or scene(s)	The moments leading up to the INSPECTOR's 1st entrance. Flashbacks. BIRLING's monologues. SHEILA's monologue, enacted (the same with other characters if you wish). The INSPECTOR's various accusations. End of Act 2 MRS B, SHEILA and the INSPECTOR. Final scenes from Act 3.	

Play 106

	Title & publisher	*Fences*	Samuel French
	Playwright/Date	August Wilson	1985
	Casting	5M: 2F	GCSE An able group
	Notes, guidance and considerations for teachers/ students	\multicolumn{2}{l	}{**Description:** American period drama. **Summary:** Troy Maxson was once an outstanding baseball player at a time when the major leagues were closed to black players; he bitterly resents his lost opportunities. An ex-convict as well, Troy is now a garbage collector/driver who has struggled to become the city's first black to hold the job. He is married to Rose and father to a teenage son, Cory. Though he loves his son, they feud continually. Troy refuses to permit Cory to accept a football college scholarship. An emotional, hard-drinking man, Troy ranges from tyrannical fury to delicacy as his preconceived ideas are challenged. **Where:** The backyard of a house in Pittsburgh, USA. **When:** Mid- to late 1950s up to 1965. **Themes:** The African American experience; race relations; men and masculinity; dreams and hopes; betrayal; father–son conflict; self-delusion. **Notes:** The sixth of Wilson's 10 Pittsburgh cycle. The title works on several levels, which should feature symbolically at least as a part of the set. **Design/tech notes:** Dirt backyard, porch and steps/levels from house to backyard as the main performance area. A fence. A baseball bat and ball. **Warnings:** Racist themes and language. Choreograph fight scenes with care. Some Boards use this as a prescribed text. Check your specification! **Workshop/rehearsal/ideas/notes:** Each scene ends on a point of either physical or verbal tension. Look at the physicalisation and proxemics of this. Character work. Rehearsal warm-ups with Blues music. **Research:** 1950s' USA and black men in sports (the Negro Leagues). Denzel Washington's 2016 movie of the same name.}
	Section or scene(s)	\multicolumn{2}{l	}{Act 1 Scene 1 TROY & BONO, later ROSE. Scene 2 GABE, ROSE & TROY. Scene 3 TROY & CORY. Then ROSE & TROY. Act 2 Scene 1 TROY & BONO. TROY tells ROSE. Scene 2 TROY & ROSE. Scene 4 TROY & CORY fight. Scene 5 GABRIEL's final words. Monologues: Act 1 Scene 3 TROY *'Like you? . . .'* Scene 4 TROY, two strong monologues. Act 2 Scene 1 BONO. ROSE. Scene 2 TROY's Soliloquy. Scene 5 CORY then ROSE's}

Play 107

	Title & publisher	*Children of Killers*	Methuen Drama NT Connections 2012
	Playwright/Date	Katori Hall	2012
	Casting	4M: 3F and the silenced 3–10 M/F	GCSE A range of abilities
	Notes, guidance and considerations for teachers/students	\multicolumn{2}{l	}{**Description:** Youth theatre. **Summary:** Three friends in the aftermath of the Tutsi genocide prepare to meet their fathers upon their release from prison for crimes they committed during this time. **Where:** A village in Rwanda. **When:** Contemporary. **Themes:** Genocide and the survivors, on both sides; fear; forgiveness; love; family. **Notes:** Historically the play takes place ten years after the genocide of 1994. **Design/tech notes:** A minimalist set with projections and sound. Katie Mitchell. Costume is also another good opportunity. **Warnings:** A disturbing and powerful play. Students must be aware of the history of Rwanda (1994 genocide). **Workshop/rehearsal/ideas/notes:** Ensure that the story, the characters and their intentions are super objectives and clearly visible at all times. Explore the tension of silence. Allow students to warm down after stressful encounters with the script. Singing together! **Research:** Students should be prepared by watching films like *Hotel Rwanda* or *Shooting Dogs*. (There is a lot of information about the genocide. Please be careful to manage young people's exposure to some of the information/pictures which are very harrowing.) **Reading:** *Machete Season* by Jean Hatzfield and the documentary 'My neighbour, my killer'. **Extra notes on casting:** The writer is happy for actors of any ethnicity and accent to play the characters. (See notes on inclusion of music/songs in the connections script.)}
	Section or scene(s)	\multicolumn{2}{l	}{Scene 1 (enough to introduce the boys and themes) Scene 2 with the GAHAHAMKUTA. End of Scenes 3, 4, 5 ESPERANCE's monologue. Scenes 6, 7, 8 to end (encourage students to identify the main moments/events in the play). Look to the silences.}

LISTING OF 200 PLAYS 117

Play 108

Title & publisher	*Five Kinds of Silence*	Methuen Drama
Playwright/Date	Shelagh Stephenson	1996
Casting notes	2M: 5F	GCE Or an able GCSE group
Notes, guidance and considerations for teachers/students		

Notes, guidance and considerations for teachers/students	**Description:** 'In yer face theatre' psycho drama. **Summary:** Three women living under the vicious control of Billy (father/husband) escape the only way they can, by killing him. **Where:** Various locations, single rooms and outdoor. England. **When:** Present time with short, interconnecting scenes, jumping back and forth in time, as the characters deliver contrasting soliloquies. **Themes:** Physical, emotional and sexual abuse; power struggles within families; survival. **Notes:** A short but very disturbing play! Good opportunities for monologue/soliloquy. Excellent physical theatre opportunities. The struggle for power within the family is a stunning creation of tension. Some multi-roles. **Design/tech notes:** Simple set, able to change locations quickly. Outside scene can be upstage or auditorium. Lighting important for location changes. SFX gunshot. **Warnings:** Sexual references and violence with strong language in places. Gun shots! Murder of a father. Incest and rape. **Workshop/rehearsal/ideas/notes:** Strong character work. Works well with Frantic style physicality.	
Section or scene(s)	Opening scene to end of BILLY's 2nd monologue. MARY's monologue 'I'm 6 years old . . .' and following scene 12 mins. JANET's letter, and SUSAN with THE PSYCHIATRISTS.	

Play 109

Title & publisher	*Oxford Street*	Methuen Drama
Playwright/Date	Levi David Addai	2008
Casting	5M: 2F Plus, various shoppers and two boys	GCSE Various abilities
Notes, guidance and considerations for teachers/students	**Description:** Comedy **Summary:** At Total Sports, security guard Kofi and his workmates are making sure everything runs smoothly, easing the daily grind with plenty of jokes and chat about the future. Young or old, they all want more from life. The only difference is how they go about getting it. **Where:** A security office, sports shop, Oxford Street, London W1, UK. **When:** Early December, present time. **Themes:** Looks beyond the glossy facade of the high street at the stories and ambitions of the workers within. **Notes:** Much use of urban (London) slang. **Design/tech notes:** Table, chairs, computer, tannoy, radios. London street sounds. Shopping trolley, footballs/stock. Staff in same colour tops. Lighting harsh/constant. Sports store muzak! Security window to staff entrance/projected or framed. **Warnings:** Careful consideration of ethnicity when casting/considering this material. **Workshop/rehearsal/ideas/notes:** Research busy retail. Lots of pace/improv/character work. Status games. The pecking order.	
Section or scene(s)	Scene 1 EMMANUEL & KOFI. To HUSNAD's entrance. Scenes 2, 3, 4, 7, 8, 10. Monologue: Scene 6 LORAINA 'On my second day . . .'	

Play 110

	Title & publisher	*Animal Farm*	NHB
	Playwright/Date	George Orwell adapted by Ian Wooldridge	1982
	Casting	5M: 2F Very flexible casting	GCSE A range of abilities
	Notes, guidance and considerations for teachers/students	**Description:** Satire, adaptation of a novel. **Summary:** Allegoric tale of a power-hungry pig who takes over a farm and convinces the other animals to rebel against the humans. **Where:** A fictitious farm. **When:** Any time. **Themes:** Revolution; injustice; brutality; heroism; loyalty; privilege and power; media, truth and democracy. **Notes:** Dressing up as animals is not the way; the performers take on the animal characteristics but also the personality chosen for that animal. Very physical. **Design/tech notes:** Costumes may suggest the animal nothing more. Set and lighting important, with good design opportunities for mood and various locations/times. Sound and music play an important role. **Warnings:** There are many adaptations out there. Some not suitable for exam purposes. Very popular with GCSE English too. **Workshop/rehearsal/ideas/notes:** Take on physical qualities of the animals both movement and vocally. Berkoff. Well-considered costume or props can also extend the illusion. Narration. Ensemble. Physical, stylised, highly choreographed scenes work well. Look at soundscapes, repetition. **Resources:** The NHB edition contains production notes for schools.	
	Section or scene(s)	OLD MAJOR'S address Act 1 Scene 1. Scene 3 the rebellion. Scene 4 the seven commandments. Scene 6 Sunday meeting. Scene 7 COWSHED. Scene 8 SNOWBALL. Act 2 Scene 1 The windmill. Scene 2 Pigs break rules. Scene 3 Hens revolt. Encourage students to choose scenes to end the piece for exam.	

Play 111

	Title & publisher	*Billy Liar*	Samuel French
	Playwright/Date	Waterhouse and Hall	1960
	Casting	3M: 5F	GCSE A range of abilities
	Notes, guidance and considerations for teachers/students	**Description:** Tragi-comedy. **Summary:** Teenager Billy Fisher weaves a world of his own out of his daydreams. He is an incurable liar, idle and dishonest. **Where:** Stradhoughton, a fictional industrial town in Yorkshire, UK. **When:** Act 1 Saturday, Act 2 Saturday evening, Act 3 Saturday night. 1960. **Themes:** Escaping the mundane; family dynamics; women of the era. **Notes:** Popular with Exam Boards. Take care to select scenes where students can work to their strengths. Pairs/larger groups/fantasy scenes etc. **Design/tech notes:** Single set depicting the Fisher household's living room, hallway and porch/garden. Can all take place in one space. Good opportunities for levels or lighting to set up the fantasy scenes (subtly). Costume of the era. No changes. The Samuel French edition carries a full furniture and props list. **Warnings:** In particular, the fantasy scenes should be directed for reality rather than comedy. It is not a farce. Mild bad language. Dated racist remarks. **Workshop/rehearsal/ideas/notes:** Naturalism. There are many funny lines but they must be played subtly and carefully, naturalistic. The five characters should all be very detailed. Pay attention to their physicality, tone, accent and proxemics on stage. Explore the tension within them (in particular dad). Pursue the truth of the piece. Joan Littlewood. **Research:** Extracts of the original novel should be read. See the original 1963 movie, as well as the film *Rebel Without a Cause* for teenage angst. **Resources:** Royal exchange theatre.	
	Section or scene(s)	Opening scene of Act 1 Breakfast. BILLY & FLORENCE in their dream worlds. BILLY & ARTHUR. BILLY & BARBARA. Phone call from DUXBURY. Act 2 BARBARA with the family. RITA'S entrance. BARBARA & ALICE. End of Act 2 RITA, BILLY, ALICE & BARBARA. Act 3 GEOFFREY & ALICE. BILLY ARTHUR & LIZ. Dialogue led. Monologues: Act 1 FLORENCE 'I don't know' Opening scene. BILLY on phone to DUXBURY. ALICE Act 2 'I don't know where he'll end up'. ACT 3 GEOFFREY 'Well she did at first'. BILLY 'I want a room, in the house'.	

LISTING OF 200 PLAYS 119

Play 112

	Title & publisher	*Equus*	HarperCollins
	Playwright/Date	Peter Shaffer	1973
	Casting	5M: 3F	GCE Range of abilities
	Notes, guidance and considerations for teachers/students	**Description:** 'Suspense thriller meets Greek tragedy'. **Summary:** The story of a psychiatrist who attempts to treat a young man who has a pathological religious fascination with horses. **Where:** Psychiatric ward and multiple settings. **When:** Contemporary. **Themes:** Sexuality; religion; definition of normality; duty vs. morality; pain; freedom; passion vs. materialism. **Notes:** It is crucial that Shaffer's notes on set and lighting are made available to design students in particular. **Design/tech notes:** Works well in the round. Bare set with minimal props. Clever use of projections/lighting and shadows. **Warnings:** Highly sexual interpretations needing sensitive teacher supervision. Some Boards use this as a prescribed text. Check your specification! **Workshop/rehearsal/ideas/notes:** Greek theatre. Ensemble physical work. Berkoff. Lecoq.	
	Section or scene(s)	ALAN & DYSART/ DYSART & HESTER. Patient/Dr interviews, Comic yet disturbing throughout the play. Dr and his friend, discussing ALAN and DYSART'S failings, Monologues: ALAN, DYSART, DORA.	

Play 113

	Title & publisher	*Dancing at Lughnasa*	Faber & Faber
	Playwright/Date	Brian Friel	1990
	Casting	3M: 5F	GCSE/GCE Mixed groups
	Notes, guidance and considerations for teachers/students	**Description:** Memory play/realism. **Summary:** Told from the perspective of an adult Michael, who recalls one summer he spent at his aunts' home when he was seven years old. The five Mundy sisters, all unmarried, live in a big cottage just outside of a small village. **Where:** County Donegal, Ireland. **When:** Harvest Time, 1936. **Themes:** Memory; pagan/Celtic ritual; Christianity; secret longings and shattered dreams. **Notes:** Michael the young man is also the narrator, i.e. himself, as a 7-year-old boy. **Design/tech notes:** Works well in the round. Great opportunities for design students with set and costume notes in Faber & Faber edition. **Warnings:** The accents are important – Southern Irish and Welsh. The part of Michael has many long narrative monologues. **Workshop/rehearsal/ideas/notes:** Very specific stage directions call for study of text and character work. If you choose to set this in the round it should be rehearsed that way from the start. The character of Michael is vital at rehearsal as a constant voice. The Mundy sisters need to be distinct characters. Workshops to bond the sisters with shared experiences. Polly Teal.	
	Section or scene(s)	MICHAEL'S opening narration following into Act 1 with the five sisters. Opportunities for all female cast if desired. Duologue between GERRY and CHRIS. Monologues: any of MICHAEL'S narrations, Act 1 MAGGIE *'When I was 16'*. Act 2 JACK *'Well, they begin very formally'*.	

Play 114

	Title & publisher	*Biloxi Blues*	Samuel French
	Playwright/Date	Neil Simon	1984
	Casting	6M: 2F	GCE Or an able GCSE group
	Notes, guidance and considerations for teachers/students	**Description:** Comedy/historical/biographical. **Summary:** A young army recruit is determined to use his army experiences to help his writing career. **Where:** A boot camp, Biloxi, Mississippi, USA. **When:** 1943, during WW2. **Themes:** Authority; sex and homosexuality; assimilation; Judaism; love and bigotry; mental health. **Notes:** US accent not absolutely essential but adds authenticity. However, if it is attempted it should be by the whole cast and sustained throughout. **Design/tech notes:** Quite specific set and props lists contained in the script. Great opportunities for design students. **Warnings:** Language and themes in line with a play about serving wartime soldiers. **Workshop/rehearsal/ideas/notes:** Improv, explore tension, status.	
	Section or scene(s)	Excellent opening scenes in Act 1 with Sgt TOOMEY and the recruits. Act 2 scene with drunken TOOMEY & ARNOLD & the .45 pistol. Many quick-fire scenes with excellent duologues. Monologues: Act 1 EUGENE *'Arnold Epstein was the worst soldier in WW Two . . .'* TOOMEY *'You get a good night's sleep'*. ARNOLD *'I'm getting out . . .'* Act 2 ARNOLD *'Sure Kowski . . .'* TOOMEY *'Everybody up!'* EUGENE's final memoir to end . . .	

Play 115

	Title & publisher	*Hard to Swallow*	Dbda
	Playwright/Date	Mark Wheeller	1989
	Casting	3M: 6F plus 16 either M or F	GCSE Mixed ability group
	Notes, guidance and considerations for teachers/students	**Description:** Verbatim/physical theatre. **Summary:** Adaptation of the book/film 'Catherine', the life story of an anorexic. **Where:** Various locations. **When:** 1973–84. **Themes:** Anorexia; social pressure on teenagers. **Notes:** With careful multi-role the play can be performed by five performers (see script). **Design/tech notes:** Minimal for most scenes. Body props. Section 9 'Bingeing' is a scene which benefits from a naturalistic approach to staging (see notes in script). **Warnings:** Catherine eventually dies. Her death is narrated by her sister and mother. This is a very emotional scene! **Workshop/rehearsal/ideas/notes:** Stylise robotic movement to emphasise ritual and repetition, or experiment with other ways of representing this. Freeze frame and story within a moment. Experiment with physical body props and challenge students to create their own. **Resources:** The script is a fantastic resource full of much research and helpful information. Wheeller plays.	
	Section or scene(s)	Section 1 Billy goats. Scene 2 Christmas 1973 Scenes 2, 6, 8 Brussels sprouts, Scenes 11, 12, 13. Students should select what moves them for exam performance but the whole play/project has to inform their choices. The script has many powerful monologues/diary extracts.	

Play 116

	Title & publisher	*The Pillowman*	Faber & Faber
	Playwright/Date	Martin McDonagh	2003
	Casting	6M: 2F	GCE Or an able GCSE group
	Notes, guidance and considerations for teachers/students	\multicolumn{2}{l	}{**Description:** Black comedy/horror. **Summary:** Katurian, a writer, is being interrogated by two detectives. In the next cell his mentally disabled brother waits. The detectives want to know why Katurian's stories feature gruesome plots about child murder and torture, and why they mirror a string of recent child murders in the area. **Where:** An interrogation room in an unnamed totalitarian dictatorship. **When:** Anytime. **Themes:** The line between truth and fairy tale: is a life of horror worth living at all? **Notes:** The brother, Michael, is a particularly demanding role, as he has childlike qualities but hidden power. The policemen carry the threat of executioner and real power. **Design/tech notes:** A bare room. Chair and table at most. Stark lighting. **Warnings:** Horror, murder and strong language. **Workshop/rehearsal/ideas/notes:** Look at Grimm's Fairy Tales, Kafka, and Artaud.}
	Section or scene(s)	\multicolumn{2}{l	}{3 Acts: Act 1 Scene 1, Act 2 Scene 1, Act 3. A number of excellent monologues: Act 1 Scene 1 KATURIAN *'I mean I agree...'* and TUPOLSKI *'A man wakes up in the iron gibbet...'* And many longer pieces. Scenes/Monologues should be selected with abilities in mind. Respect the order.}

Play 117

	Title & publisher	*Blood Brothers*	Methuen Drama (non-musical version Oxford Playscripts)
	Playwright/Date	Willy Russell	1983
	Casting	5M: 3F Multi-role	GCSE A range of abilities
	Notes, guidance and considerations for teachers/students	\multicolumn{2}{l	}{**Description:** Tragedy/comedy (Musical Theatre and Play version). **Summary:** Twins separated at birth, later to become blood brothers only to discover the truth with tragic consequences. **Where:** Various locations in and around Liverpool, UK. **When:** 1960s. **Themes:** Social class; education; nature vs. nurture; growing up; fate and destiny; money; superstition. **Notes:** Non-musical version differs slightly in script in addition to having an alternative ending. Richard Pilbrow. **Design/tech notes:** Designed for a Proscenium arch stage. Minimalism lends itself well to a minimalist uncluttered stage; however, there are many excellent opportunities for props/set, lighting and sound. Costume to reflect times/characters changing. **Warnings:** Some Boards use this as a prescribed text. Check your specification! Some adult themes. Gunshots. **Workshop/rehearsal/ideas/notes:** Stanislavski for character work. Multi-role. Non-naturalistic devices. Breaking the 4th Wall. Experiment with narrative and status. **Resources:** OCR's Teacher guide is excellent.}
	Section or scene(s)	\multicolumn{2}{l	}{Opening scene with NARRATOR and other multi-role cast members. Giving away the babies. Mrs LYONS & Mrs JOHNSTONE. EDDIE & MICKEY meet and become blood brothers. Great duologues and monologues. The boys in their respective schools. The final scene.}

Play 118

	Title & publisher	*Beautiful Burnout*	Faber & Faber
	Playwright/Date	Bryony Lavery	2010
	Casting	6M: 2F	GCE/GCSE Physically demanding
	Notes, guidance and considerations for teachers/students	\multicolumn{2}{l|}{**Description:** Physical theatre. **Summary:** Cameron is a boxer and he's going places. He's going to make the world take notice. He fights for his club, his mum and his place in the world. **Where:** Various locations, boxing gym, Scotland, UK. **When:** Contemporary. **Themes:** Conflict; boxing and the three minutes when men become gods and gods, mere men. **Notes:** The accent is scripted and should be honoured. **Design/tech notes:** Simple set. Ropes. Washing machine (overlarge model). Good use of lighting/projections. **Warnings:** Adult themes. Take care – as with any fight sequences, a strong safety conscious, professional choreography is required. **Workshop/rehearsal/ideas/notes:** Frantic Assembly, highly choreographed. **Resources** Frantic Assembly and National Theatre of Scotland.}	
	Section or scene(s)	\multicolumn{2}{l|}{Scenes 4, 5, 7, 10, 12, 13, 15, 18, 20, 22, 24, 25, 28. Monologues: CARLOTTA *'Food'*. BOBBY *'A split second'* Scene 7 DINA *'Right away'*. Scene 9 DINA. Scene 11 CARLOTTA. Scene 21 AJAY. Scene 26 CAMERON. Scene 29 CARLOTTA to end.}	

Play 119

	Title & publisher	*Bedroom Farce*	Samuel French
	Playwright/Date	Alan Ayckbourn	1975
	Casting	4M: 4F	GCSE Various abilities
	Notes, guidance and considerations for teachers/students	\multicolumn{2}{l|}{**Description:** Comedy/farce. **Summary:** Trevor and Susannah, whose marriage is on the rocks, inflict their miseries on three couples whose own relationships are tenuous at best. **Where:** Three bedrooms in suburbia, UK. **When:** One night and the following morning. Any time. **Themes:** The secrets of how middle-class married couples communicate; self-centred men and sensitive women – the usual Ayckbourn stuff! **Notes:** Look at the sound of the words. Simple sounds like 'oh' can, if repeated enough, take on new meaning. Lots of door slamming. **Design/tech notes:** Challenging set/props. Three differing bedrooms. Lots of cross fading. Sturdy doors! **Warnings:** Needs a lot of pace and a real understanding of the door-slamming farce. **Workshop/rehearsal/ideas/notes:** Character work. Naturalism. Try some physical work to inject a more contemporary feel to the piece. Allow the characters to become larger than life. I've seen it given a Berkoff flavour and it worked!}	
	Section or scene(s)	\multicolumn{2}{l|}{Intro to the three bedrooms. ERNEST & DELIA / NICK & JAN / MALCOM & KATE. KATE in bed as guests arrive. TREV & SUSANNAH's fight. The kiss. JAN helps NICK off the floor . . . Act 2 KATE, MALCOM and the dressing table. SUSANNAH & DELIA. Then the cross fades to the action in the other bedrooms – end.}	

Play 120

	Title & publisher	*Rosencrantz and Guildenstern are Dead*	Faber & Faber
	Playwright/Date	Tom Stoppard	1966
	Casting	6M: 2F Plus tragedians, courtiers and attendants	GCE Or an able GCSE group
	Notes, guidance and considerations for teachers/students	**Description:** Absurdist tragi-comedy. **Summary:** Rosencrantz and Guildenstern, two minor figures from Shakespeare's Hamlet, share the story retold through their eyes and from the juxtaposition of a fantasy world. **When:** A featureless wilderness. **Where:** Elizabethan era but could be any time. **Themes:** Death; friendship; memory; life and the stage; the human struggle to understand the world. **Notes:** Although the focus is on the meaning of death, the comedy lightens things just enough. Guide performers when looking for the comic elements. **Design/tech notes:** Absolutely bare. Light and dark. A structure that can be a ship or a castle with clever lighting. Richard Pilbrow. **Warnings:** A very witty and fast-paced, demanding performance. **Workshop/rehearsal/ideas/notes:** I used a lot of Frantic Assembly ideas for the pair. Start with dialogue and chair duets and build it from there. Some of the monologues work better by starkly contrasting the physical with character work. Stanislavski. Rosencrantz's 'Dead in a box', for example, using the 'Magic if'.	
	Section or scene(s)	Opening of Act 1 (Flipping coins) The arrival of the TRAGEDIANS. First change of lights. ROS & GUIL after POLONIUS. Act 2 ROS & GUIL with HAMLET. ROS & PLAYER. Act 3 morning to end. Monologues: Act 1 GUIL *'I have no desires . . .'* Act 2 ROS 'Dead in a box . . .' A3 ROS *'The position as I see it'*.	

Play 121

	Title & publisher	*Butcher, Butcher Burning Bright*	Oxford Playscripts
	Playwright/Date	Mark Wheeller	2014
	Casting	5M: 3F and flexible ensemble	GCSE or GCE
	Notes, guidance and considerations for teachers/students	**Description:** Ensemble based physical theatre. **Summary:** Molly and Ian are hot for each other. The cost of messing with fire becomes all too clear. **Where:** UK (anywhere). **When:** Now. **Themes:** Arson; love; death; school. **Notes:** Has much of the stylistic qualities of other Wheeller plays but this one is a fiction. **Design/tech notes:** Set should be minimal, all props mimed (body props). Good opportunities for design of sound/light and projections/PowerPoint. Hoodies, but costume not important. **Warnings:** Death of a young girl in a fire. **Workshop/rehearsal/ideas/notes:** A strength of this material in rehearsal/study is to facilitate experimentation! Encourage students to try sound/visuals and physical theatre/music to set a scene/event or mood. Set tasks to challenge them to 'show' the audience a moment. Physical theatre. Experiment with soundscape/ montage/chorus. The use of juxtaposition to intensify feelings and moods. Research arson/school arson, pantomime, naturalism, pastiche. Ensemble. **Resources:** The Oxford playscript is a fantastic resource for students and teachers alike.	
	Section or scene(s)	Part of Scene 1 which is repeated later. 3 Mealtime, 5 Sparks, 7 Fairground. 9 is a repeat of 1, 11 MOLLY's death, 12 MOLLY's monologue and her parents getting the news of her death. Sections 13 and 14 to end. Allow students to experiment and decide. Respect order.	

Play 122

	Title & publisher	*The Guffin*	Methuen Drama NT Connections
	Playwright/Date	Howard Brenton	2013
	Casting	4M: 4F 1N	GCSE A range of abilities
	Notes, guidance and considerations for teachers/students	\multicolumn{2}{l	}{**Description:** Youth theatre/fantasy. **Summary:** A youth theatre workshop group discover a magical reality. **Where:** Anywhere. **When:** Now. **Themes:** Self-awareness; identity; magic/reality. **Notes:** The part of the Guffin can be played by a male or female. There are two male adult parts, Dexter and a security guard (unseen and unheard). **Design/tech notes:** Play with light/sound and projections. Body props/physical theatre. **Warnings:** Mild language, blood and reference to a fatal stabbing. **Workshop/rehearsal/ideas/notes:** Be brave and experiment. Ensemble playing, approach the text through games. Complicité. Define a moment when the playing stops. Main driving force is the Guffin. Give him/her energy/dimension by how the other characters react to him/her. Imaginary Body.}
	Section or scene(s)	\multicolumn{2}{l	}{40 minutes. A four-scene structure. Challenge the students to identify the routines of play and make their own mark on it. Explore the physical language of the play. Monologues: Scene 1 and Scene 4.}

Play 123

	Title & publisher	*Find Me*	Samuel French
	Playwright/Date	Olwen Wymark	1977
	Casting	3M: 5F Multi-role	GCSE Mixed/high ability group
	Notes, guidance and considerations for teachers/students	\multicolumn{2}{l	}{**Description:** Stylised social drama. **Summary:** The story of Verity Taylor (based on fact) explores personality change, its treatment and the effects on Verity's family. **Where:** Various indoor. Wards/home/prisons. UK. **When:** Contemporary. **Themes:** Mental illness; what society calls normal; child–parent relationships. **Notes:** A disturbing play based on real events and people. The play works without any chronological time of conventional space, with several actors playing the main role of Verity. Narrated in places. **Design/tech notes:** Open stage, minimal set. No special costume. The Samuel French copy contains lighting plots. **Warnings:** Some strong language and disturbing moments. Some Boards use this as a prescribed text. Check your specification! **Workshop/rehearsal/ideas/notes:** Episodic, Brecht, Epic. Also see poor theatre, Grotowski, physical expression and vocal work. Zero set and props ideas. Wymark has given the characters numbers to indicate where changes of role take place, making characters representational. If taking on more than one role, demonstrate skills such as variation of body language, facial and vocal expression.}
	Section or scene(s)	\multicolumn{2}{l	}{Episodic, respect the order. Ideal for studio space performance. EDWARD & the INTERVIEWER. Playground Scene, French Restaurant Scene. Encourage students to read and make sensitive choices. Monologues: Opening narration and introduction of the five VERITYS. MARK *'I wish I didn't have to live at home'*. JEAN *'What are we going to do?'* Swimming Gala. VERITY 1 *'Dear reader'*.}

Play 124

	Title & publisher	*The Beauty Manifesto*	Methuen Drama NT Connections 2011
	Playwright/Date	Nell Leyshon	2011
	Casting	3M: 6F Gender swapping possible.	GCSE Mixed ability group
	Notes, guidance and considerations for teachers/students	\multicolumn{2}{l	}{**Description:** Youth theatre. **Summary:** The world of extreme physical conformity where teenagers celebrate their 16th birthday with cosmetic surgery. **Where:** Various locations in a cosmetic surgery facility. **When:** The near future/now. **Themes:** Physical conformity; beauty; cosmetic surgery; questions contemporary ideas of beauty, self-image, loneliness and sadness. **Notes:** Try to create a safe, trusting group and environment for all rehearsals. **Design/tech notes:** Set should be simple and uncluttered. Projections/multimedia. Katie Mitchell. Music should not interfere with the text. **Warnings:** Casting, gender, ethnicity and sexual orientation choices are completely open but be aware that your choices will make a statement. **Workshop/rehearsal/ideas/notes:** Great ensemble piece, choreographed physical theatre/unison and coordinated movement. Ensemble group-building games, moving as one, finding moments of stillness. Character exercises. Movement and stylisation for The Ambassadors. **Research:** Look at the differences between cosmetic and plastic surgery.}
	Section or scene(s)	It's possible to perform the whole piece.	

Play 125

	Title & publisher	*Jumpy*	Faber & Faber
	Playwright/Date	April de Angelis	2011
	Casting	4M: 5F	GCE
	Notes, guidance and considerations for teachers/students	\multicolumn{2}{l	}{**Description:** Comedy/family drama. **Summary:** Hilary once protested at Greenham. Now her protests tend to focus on persuading her teenage daughter to go out fully clothed. **Where:** Various locations, mainly in a suburban house, some outdoor. London, UK. **When:** 2010 onwards but not vital. **Themes:** Adolescence; modern middle-aged women; parental anxieties; life after fifty. **Notes:** Great as fast-paced duologues and several larger scenes. **Design/tech notes:** Can be minimal with good lighting/projections and SFX to create location. Music is fairly important. Costume can be as relevant as you want. **Warnings:** The end of Scene 16 will need to be avoided/covered or alluded to. Some adult language sprinkled throughout. **Workshop/rehearsal/ideas/notes:** Characterisation work. Each character must have a good history. Pace and comic timing. Keep rehearsals fluid. **Research:** Greenham Common women's peace camp. **Resources:** There is a good resource pack available from The Royal Court.}
	Section or scene(s)	18 scenes which can be performed as duologues allowing for great comic timing and characterisation work. Monologues: HILARY Scene 1, ROLAND, Scene 13 LYNDSEY, Scene 16 CAM.	

Play 126

	Title & publisher	*Tomorrow I'll be Happy*	Methuen Drama NT Connections 2013
	Playwright/Date	Johnathan Harvey	2013
	Casting	5M: 4F	GCSE A range of abilities
	Notes, guidance and considerations for teachers/students	**Description:** Youth theatre. **Summary:** When a stranger comes to a crumbling seaside town looking for his friend, he discovers that he was killed in a homophobic hate crime. As the secrets of the past are revealed it becomes apparent that all is not as it first appears. **Where:** A run down seaside town anywhere in the UK. **When:** Contemporary. **Themes:** Homophobic hate crime; difference and the bravery/fear associated with being different. **Notes:** The play is set in <u>reverse order</u> with a very significant timeline. **Design/tech notes:** Challenging locations, sets/lighting. **Warnings:** Murder, homophobia, strong language. **Workshop/rehearsal/ideas/notes:** Suggest rehearsing in the correct chronological order then put it back into the sequence in which it is written to make events/structure clear to the cast. Study the characters, none of them are stereotypes! Hot seating and improv. There are excellent production notes in the Connections script. Keep it truthful and real, avoid the abstract. The stage directions are vital and should not be ignored, rather studied for meaning.	
	Section or scene(s)	The opening scene is important and should be included. DIOR & CYPRUS Prison Nail room scene 2F The prison visit 2M SIDDIE & CYPRUS. DIOR & SCOTT. The murder in the old school. Final scene. Good duologues. Monologues: DARREN Hilltop 6 months earlier. *'If you wanna know the truth.'*	

Play 127

	Title & publisher	*The Importance of Being Earnest*	Penguin Classics
	Playwright/Date	Oscar Wilde	1895
	Casting	5M: 4F	GCSE A range of abilities
	Notes, guidance and considerations for teachers/students	**Description:** A comedy of manners. **Summary:** John (Jack) Worthing leads a double life. In the country he is a fine upstanding man, but he needs to visit London often to help his troubled younger brother, Ernest. Once in London however, Jack becomes Ernest and through a confusion of identity, romance, melodrama and farce, the conduct of the Victorian upper classes is wittily and ironically uncovered. **Where:** London and an estate in Hertfordshire, UK. **When:** Victorian. **Themes:** Love; family; identity; society; class; marriage; deceit. **Notes:** Witty wordplay and great characters offer great opportunities. **Design/tech notes:** Lavish costumes and set offer great opportunities for design students. Set requires a versatility for the main locations. Indoors and out, in the city and the country. **Warnings:** A much quoted play, with the potential for some of the more famous lines to fall flat if not delivered just right! **Workshop/rehearsal/ideas/notes:** Character work. Status games. Stanislavski, Boal.	
	Section or scene(s)	Act 1 ALGERNON'S flat. Act 2 In the garden. CECILY, JACK & ALGERNON. MISS PRISM. All of Act 3 Monologues: ALGERNON Act 1 *'I haven't the smallest intention...'* and *'Why does your aunt call you her uncle?'* LADY B *'Well I must say...'*	

LISTING OF 200 PLAYS

Play 128

	Title & publisher	*The Servant of Two Masters*	Methuen Drama
	Playwright/Date	Carlo Goldini Adapted by Lee Hall	1746
	Casting	6M: 3F	GCE Or very able GCSE
	Notes, guidance and considerations for teachers/students	**Description:** Commedia dell'arte. **Summary:** Underpaid and overstretched, a wily servant gets the chance to live off two masters with disastrous results for everyone concerned. **Where:** Various locations, Venice, Italy. **When:** 1700s. **Themes:** Self-interest; Venetian society; the disparity between what people say and really feel; status; thwarted love. **Notes:** Central character TRUFFALDINO needs excellent comic timing and awareness. **Design/tech notes:** Set needs to show changing locations, not really a minimalist piece! Costume and lighting important. **Warnings:** A very demanding script requiring great energy, pace and timing. There are some minor, less demanding roles. Some Boards use this as a prescribed text. Check your specification! **Workshop/rehearsal/ideas/notes:** Stock commedia characters. Multi-role. Characters say one thing and think another (shown by many comic asides to the audience). **Research:** Richard Bean's play 'One Man, Two Guvnors'. The Lazzi.	
	Section or scene(s)	Act 1 Scenes 1, 2, 3, 7, 8, 11. Act 2 Scenes 4, 9-17 through. Act 3 Scenes 1, 6–end. Monologues: TRUFFALDINO Act 1 Scene 4. Dr LOMBARDI Act 2 Scene 1. TRUFFALDINO Act 3 Scene 1 TRUFFALDINO Act 3 Scene 15–end.	

Play 129

	Title & publisher	*Punk Rock*	Methuen Drama
	Playwright/Date	Simon Stephens	2009
	Casting	5M: 4F	GCE
	Notes, guidance and considerations for teachers/students	**Description:** Teenage drama 'In yer face' theatre. **Summary:** Sixth former William is clever and Oxbridge bound. He falls for the mysterious new girl, but she wants someone else. A power struggle begins amid the pressure of exams. Aggression and desire uncover some ugly traits. **Where:** Sixth form library of a fee-paying grammar school in Stockport. Final scene is set in a UK hospital. **When:** Contemporary. **Themes:** Identity and sexuality; violence; youth and growing up; expectation and stress/pressure. **Notes:** The suggested songs at the start of each scene and punk dancing during changes are important. **Design/tech notes:** The simple creation of a sixth-form library. The windows are important and some careful lighting in some scenes adds to this. Books/shelves (could be projected), open set with tables, chairs and lockers. Change to last scene in hospital. Music/costume as per script. **Warnings:** Extreme violence (school shooting by a pupil). **Workshop/rehearsal/ideas/notes:** Very character driven. Each one very different and driven. Rehearse to the suggested music for each scene. Physical and fast.	
	Section or scene(s)	Scenes 1, 2, 4, 5, 6, 7. Monologues: Scene 2 WILLIAM. LILLY. Scene 3 CHADWICK. Scene 4 CHADWICK. Scene 5 LILLY. Scene 7 WILLIAM.	

Play 130

	Title & publisher	*Sparkleshark*	Faber & Faber
	Playwright/Date	Philip Ridley	1997
	Casting	6M: 3F	GCSE Mixed abilities
	Notes, guidance and considerations for teachers/students	\multicolumn{2}{l}{**Description:** Youth Theatre. **Summary:** A boy who tells stories to stop being bullied. **Where:** On the roof of a council tower block, UK. **When:** Contemporary. **Themes:** Bullying; fantasy and the redemptive quality of storytelling; fitting in; youth culture. **Notes:** The juxtaposition of violence and vulnerability in young people. **Design/tech notes:** An old sofa or armchair onstage. A metal step ladder. A good set design opportunity which can really exploit levels. A bare brick wall, graffiti etc. Lighting can be very influential. **Warnings:** Some Boards use this as a prescribed text. Check your specification! **Workshop/rehearsal/ideas/notes:** Role on the wall/sub-text, character interaction, creation of mood, pace and rhythm. Physical theatre.}	
	Section or scene(s)	\multicolumn{2}{l}{60 minutes. Good opportunities when everyone is on stage. Pick as you need. It's all good stuff!}	

Play 131

	Title & publisher	*Gone too Far*	Methuen Drama
	Playwright/Date	Bola Agbaje	2007
	Casting	6M: 4F	GCSE Physically able group
	Notes, guidance and considerations for teachers/students	\multicolumn{2}{l}{**Description:** Comedy. **Summary:** When two brothers from different continents go down the street to buy milk, they expose a disunited nation where everyone wants to be an individual but no one is willing to stand out from the crowd. **Where:** Various outdoor locations (and one bedroom) on a large estate, inner-city London, UK. **When:** Contemporary. **Themes:** Youth; identity; racism; history and culture. **Notes:** Ethnicity should be respected for this piece to work. Allow students to choose and explore the rich language and comedy moments. **Design/tech notes:** Minimal set with clever use of lighting and levels. **Warnings:** Racist attitudes. Strong language. Knife crime. **Workshop/rehearsal/ideas/notes:** Physical theatre, DV8. Creation of strong characters. Research the language of inner-city London's diverse communities and making meaning of it physically.}	
	Section or scene(s)	\multicolumn{2}{l}{1 Act, 11 Scenes. Scene 1 bedroom, Scene 2 with the SHOPKEEPER, Scene 4 OLD LADY, Scene 5, Scene 7 The POLICE, Scene 10 to end. No long monologues.}	

Play 132

	Title & publisher	*Our Country's Good*	Methuen Drama
	Playwright/Date	Timberlake Wertenbaker	1988
	Casting	5M: 5F Doubling as 22 roles	GCE Or an able GCSE group
	Notes, guidance and considerations for teachers/students	**Description:** Historical comedy. **Summary:** A play about a play within a play. Adapted from the Thomas Keneally novel *The Playmaker*. A group of Royal Marines and convicts in a penal colony in New South Wales, in the 1780s, put on a production of 'The Recruiting Officer'. **Where:** Australia's first penal colony. **When:** 1789. **Themes:** Redemption; dignity; power; guilt; the theatre and its civilising effect. **Notes:** One of my favourites! Often seen at A level (GCE), this play offers outstanding opportunities for very able GCSE students. 'Theatrical, often funny and at times dark and disturbing'. Designed to be multi-role, with the officers also performing as the convicts. Great opportunities to show differing characters. Accents are important. Some really gritty monologues! **Design/tech notes:** Minimalist set but offers opportunities for some imaginative set and lighting designs. The 5–5 male-female split works well, with some male roles taken by women who play a female convict and a male officer. Costume signifies changes in roles i.e. a marine's jacket or an officer's wig. **Warnings:** Some very strong language of a sexual nature. Some Boards use this as a prescribed text. Check your specification! **Workshop/rehearsal/ideas/notes:** Max Stafford-Clark/Out of Joint. Ensemble. Multi-role work needs great character study. **Research:** 'Letters to George', by Max Stafford Clark.	
	Section or scene(s)	Act 1 Scene 6 The authorities discuss the merits of the theatre. Scene 7 HARRY & DUCKLING go rowing. Act 1 Scene 9 RALPH & KETCH. Act 1 Scene 10 MARY & WISEHAMMER. Act 1 Scene 11. Act 2 Scene 2 RALPH & PHILLIP. Act 2 Scene 3 HARRY sees the dead. Act 2 Scene 6 KETCH, HARRY & LIZ. Monologues: Act 1 Scene 5 SIDEWAY *'Top of my profession'*. Act 1 Scene 6 PHILLIP *'The theatre is an expression of civilisation'*. Act 1 Scene 9 KETCH Monologue interrupted by RALPH. Act 2 Scene 1 LIZZIE MORDEN *'Luck'*.	

Play 133

	Title & publisher	*Tartuffe*	Methuen Drama
	Playwright/Date	Moliere	1664
	Casting	6M: 4F	GCE Or an able GCSE group
	Notes, guidance and considerations for teachers/students	**Description:** Comedy/satire. **Summary:** Orgon has everything a man could wish for. But he begins to wonder at the point of it all. Then he meets Tartuffe, a charismatic conman, trickster and villain, or is he? **Where:** Orgon's house in Paris, France. **When:** Mid-17th century. **Themes:** Hypocrisy and how to recognise it in yourself and others; sin, morality and ethics; religion; truth and lies; women and femininity. **Notes:** The rhyming couplets used in Moliere's original help the piece move at a crazy mad-cap-paced meter and make the lines memorable. I used Roger McGough's adaptation. **Design/tech notes:** Lavish works well. Great opportunities for costume and set designers. **Warnings:** Mild adult themes. Nudity (obviously to be avoided!). **Workshop/rehearsal/ideas/notes:** Comic timing workshops – so why is this funny? Study of caricature. Building the complex characters – what do they want? Status. Stanislavski.	
	Section or scene(s)	Act 1 Scenes 1, 3, 4. Act 2 Scenes 1, 2, 3. Act 3 Scenes 1, 2, 3. Act 4 Scenes 1, 2, 3, 7, 8. Act 5 to end. Monologues: ORGON *'Ah! If you had seen him ...'* MADAME PARNELLE *'The kind of rigmarole ...'* CLEANTE *'No, brother, I am not a sage'*. TARTUFFE *'Piety'*.	

Play 134

	Title & publisher	*Female Transport*	Samuel French
	Playwright/Date	Steve Gooch	1973
	Casting	4M: 6F	GCE Or an able GCSE group
	Notes, guidance and considerations for teachers/students	**Description:** Naturalistic/immersive theatre. **Summary:** Transportation of six female convicts to the penal colony of Australia. During the 6-month voyage they learn truths about themselves and their class. **Where:** A cell, then below and above decks on a convict ship. **When:** 1870. **Themes:** Oppression; the class system; female incarceration. **Notes:** Important that the London working-class dialect is studied and used. **Design/tech notes:** Stage split between two levels, above and below decks. White, dirty women's costumes, guards and sailors. Shackles can be used to great theatrical effect. I have seen it done in orange boiler suits to modernise it. Either works. Minimal set. **Warnings:** Adult language and themes. **Workshop/rehearsal/ideas/notes:** Ensemble. Explore the creation of tension. Study the accent, rehearse from an early stage with the shackles. Experiment with the levels.	
	Section or scene(s)	Scene 1 in the cell. Scene 3 all of the women in the cell. Scene 4 SARGE and TOMMY. Scene 10 PITTY's hanging to song. But really any scenes in sequence. Select as your cast explores the text. Brief monologues: NANCE, SARGE CAPTAIN.	

Play 135

	Title & publisher	*Too Much Punch for Judy*	dbda
	Playwright/Date	Mark Wheeller	1988
	Casting	5M: 5F Multi-role possibilities	GCSE A range of abilities
	Notes, guidance and considerations for teachers/students	**Description:** Verbatim. Physical theatre. **Summary:** Based closely on real events. A car crashes, the drunken driver is unhurt, but her sister dies at the scene. Through physical theatre and grim comedy, the play explores the impact drinking and driving has on people's lives. **Where:** Various locations including a night-club, a car, a hospital, a home and a police station. **When:** 1983 or now. **Themes:** Drink driving; alcohol; guilt; responsibility; shock and how we deal with it. **Notes:** The opening scene should be exaggerated, fast and funny. The following scenes will shock and shock again. **Design/tech notes:** A very simple set. The scaffold poles from the crash scene can be used imaginatively throughout the play. You will need a wheelchair. Two sets of car keys. Two beer glasses. Try to make other props/costumes symbolic. The use of visual slides and music offers good opportunities for design students. Lots of sound effects! Gareth Fry. **Warnings:** Drink-drive death. The play is very hard hitting and needs to be sensitively handled in schools. **Workshop/rehearsal/ideas/notes:** Physical theatre, DV8, Gecko work with mime and exaggerated movement. Good examples of tickle and slap. See Brecht's 'V effect' (*Verfremdungsefferek*). Multi-role. Encourage students to experiment with the material, physically and with soundscapes, projections/PowerPoints.	
	Section or scene(s)	Must include opening scene then move on to the documentary-style notes in section 2. JUDY & JO section 2 Section 3 Police account of accident. The accident and breaking the news. Section 5. Good monologue is DUNCAN, an eyewitness describing finding the car with JO dead inside and trying to help JUDY. A good mix of emotions. Although I have made suggestions do try to challenge students to pick the pieces that move them most, how the pieces are presented should come from the students too. Respect the order of the play.	

Play 136

	Title & publisher	*People, Places and Things*	Oberon Modern plays
	Playwright/Date	Duncan Macmillan National Theatre	2015
	Casting	5M: 5F	GCE An able group
	Notes, guidance and considerations for teachers/students	**Description:** Dark humour. **Summary:** Beginning on stage in a performance of 'The Seagull', we follow Emma, an actress suffering from drug and alcohol abuse, who falls apart and eventually sheds the masks she wears, in order to confront her addictions. **Where:** Begins on a naturalistic set on stage, moves to a rehab clinic/various locations. **When:** Contemporary. **Themes:** Addiction; identity and performance; anger; confession; therapy and recovery. **Notes:** Demands a vast amount of energy. **Design/tech notes:** The piece can demand a great deal from a theatre design team both in terms of staging and light/sound and projection. Katie Mitchell. However, the main strength for exam performers is the dialogue and opportunities for carefully choreographed movement. **Warnings:** Deals with adult themes. Dangers of substance abuse. **Workshop/rehearsal/ideas/notes:** A great deal of mature and guided research into the physical and mental effects of the highs and lows of addiction is required.	
	Section or scene(s)	Opening sequence of Act 1 up to EMMA noticing the audience/theatre change. One-way conversation with mum. EMMA & FOSTER. DOCTOR & EMMA. Then any of the excellent dialogues/monologues of the group/therapy sessions.	

Play 137

	Title & publisher	*DNA*	Oberon Plays
	Playwright/Date	Dennis Kelly	2007
	Casting	7M: 3F Some multi-role	GCSE A range of abilities
	Notes, guidance and considerations for teachers/students	**Description:** Youth theatre. **Summary:** A group of teenagers do something bad, really bad! Then they make it worse. **Where:** Three locations, outside. A street, a field, a wood. **When:** Contemporary. **Themes:** Gangs; cruelty; power, bullying and responsibility; violence; friendship. **Notes:** Divided into 14 short scenes moving between the mundane and shockingly horrific cruelty. Some significant speeches. A selection of characters. Some have a lot to say, others very very little. **Design/tech notes:** Minimalist set works well, but opportunities for creative set design and lighting. Costume and make-up for Adam. **Warnings:** Some Boards use this as a prescribed text. Check your specification! Mild language in some scenes. One particularly violent scene. **Workshop/rehearsal/ideas/notes:** Status games/improv. Greek chorus. Look at how circumstances in the play changes mannerisms, interaction/proxemics and choice of words. Guilt/fear/insecurity etc. Each character can create a montage of their character's thoughts/feelings/history and place them in the rehearsal space. Building on them as they progress. **Resources:** The Oberon School edition has good sections at the back of the script on structure, setting, style and language. Educas/WJEC produced a fine resource. The BBC have also produced a useful resource for GCSE Lit and Drama.	
	Section or scene(s)	Total run time is 60 minutes, divided into 14 short scenes. Scenes 3, 7 and 11 are scenes with a large cast in which status is a significant theme. Monologues: Scene 1 LEAH *'What are you thinking?'* MARK *'Only because you had to'*. PHIL's Plan. LEAH *'Apparently bonobos are our nearest relative'*. Scene 2 LEAH *'Are you happy?'* Scene 3 LEAH *'I'm going. I'm out of here'*. Scene 4 RICHARD *'Phil watch this Phil'*. To end.	

Play 138

	Title & publisher	*Of Mice and Men*	Josef Weinberger plays
	Playwright/Date	John Steinbeck	1937
	Casting	9M: 1F	GCSE Range of abilities
	Notes, guidance and considerations for teachers/students	**Description:** Tragedy. Adaptation of American literature **Summary:** The tragic story of two migrant drifters, George and mentally challenged Lenny, and their dreams of owning a farm. **Where:** Soledad, Californian Agriculture Belt, USA. **When:** 1930s, The Great Depression. **Themes:** Friendship; loneliness; powerlessness; hope; belonging. **Notes:** An American classic. No attempts at realism should be made in the outdoor scenes. See set notes. **Design/tech notes:** Outdoor scenes should be minimal, relying almost entirely on lighting. Inside the bunkhouse one entrance which all characters use and a window close by and upstage. Chairs and boxes. A hanging lamp referred to in the text. Dog on stage can be simply referred to and seen by performers. There is a list of props. Costume should be simple and of the time/setting. **Warnings:** Mild adult themes. A gunshot. Death. Some dated racist remarks. **Workshop/rehearsal/ideas/notes:** Stanislavski. Characterisation work. Emotion memory. Status. **Research:** The Great Depression. Read the novel of the same name.	
	Section or scene(s)	Opening scene with GEORGE & LENNY by the river. Scene 2 CANDY & GEORGE, BOSS & CURLY. SLIM, CARLSON and the old blind dog. CURLEY'S WIFE & LENNIE. LENNIE & GEORGE Final scene. Monologues: Act 2 CROOKS 'A guy can talk to you . . .' Act 3 CURLEY'S WIFE 'My old man was a sign painter'.	

Play 139

	Title & publisher	*At the Black Pig's Dyke*	Methuen Drama (Far from the Land Contemporary Irish Plays)
	Playwright/Date	Vincent Woods	1992
	Casting	6M: 4F and Cross casting	GCE Various demanding roles
	Notes, guidance and considerations for teachers/students	**Description:** Irish Theatre. Tragedy. **Summary:** At the Black Pig's Dyke is a story of murder, mystery, fairy tale and tragic love. **Where:** Border of Northern and Southern Ireland where family feuds are passed down through generations. Leitrim and Fermanagh. **When:** Past and Present. **Themes:** Family feuds; poetic/gothic political; comedy; murder; mystery; fairy tales; violence; resurrection. **Notes:** The story is told using the pagan ritual of the mummers' play. Multi-role opportunities. Some help from musicians. **Design/tech notes:** Set should be just a sense of the space, interior and exterior. Neither should be over defined. Can be performed promenade. Simple costume, straw masks. **Warnings:** Sexual acts referenced/simulated. Sectarian violence. **Workshop/rehearsal/ideas/notes:** Ensemble rehearsals, use music and rhythm. Experiment with physical theatre and choreograph throughout. Marianne Elliott. **Research:** Mummers traditional folklore plays in rhymed verse (Culture Cavan Project).	
	Section or scene(s)	Prologue: Act 1 Scenes 1, 2, 4, 5, 6 Act 2: Prologue. Scenes 1, 2, 4, 5, 6, 7, 9, Epilogue. Some large shared monologues and verses. TOM FOOL & MISS FUNNY.	

Play 140

	Title & publisher	*The Curious Incident of the Dog in the Night-Time* Methuen Drama
	Playwright/Date	Mark Haddon 2012 Adapted by Simon Stephens
	Casting	5M: 5F **GCSE/GCE** Flexible multi-role High energy/physically demanding
	Notes, guidance and considerations for teachers/students	**Description:** Mystery (stage adaptation of a novel). **Summary:** A gifted boy, Christopher Boone, investigates the killing of a dog and embarks upon a difficult journey of self-discovery. **Where:** Various locations in Swindon and London, UK. **When:** 1998. **Themes:** Autism spectrum; family; crime fiction; isolation; lies; freedom and confinement; love. **Notes:** Presented as a play within a play. Christopher's condition is not explicitly stated; however, he demonstrates many traits associated with Autistic spectrum disorder. **Design/tech notes:** For exam performance, minimalist studio space works well. Good opportunities for design students, particularly projections and lighting (Forkbeard Fantasy). **Warnings:** Do not try to replicate the National Theatre. Let students explore and experiment with this great text. References the killing of a family pet. **Workshop/rehearsal/ideas/notes:** Can be very physical. All performers on stage all the time/multi-role. Strong characterisation work. Ensemble. **Resources:** Great resources online from National Theatre and curiousonstage.com.
	Section or scene(s)	Opening sequence. CHRISTOPHER & POLICE. SIOBHAN & metaphors. CHRISTOPHER investigates. SIOBHAN & JUDY longer sequences physicalised. Journey to London. The company at the start of part 2 'Everyone plays a part in it!' CHRISTOPHER & JUDY. Final sequence ED & CHRISTOPHER. Many monologues.

Play 141

	Title & publisher	*Translations* Faber & Faber
	Playwright/Date	Brian Friel 1980
	Casting	7M: 3F **GCE** A range of abilities
	Notes, guidance and considerations for teachers/students	**Description:** Irish theatre/ensemble. **Summary:** *Translations* explores the troubled lives of a group of characters struggling to adjust to a changing world. A subtle yet radical change as the hard fist of British regulation seeks to impose itself on local tradition. In 1883 Ireland, item No. 1 was the mapping of the country and translating the Gaelic place names into 'proper' English (labelling new anglicized maps). **Where:** Ballybeg (Baile Beag), County Donegal, Ireland. **When:** August 1883. **Themes:** Language, love and alienation; Nationalism/British Imperialism and history. **Notes:** A Level Literature set text. The various accents should be respected. **Design/tech notes:** Simple versatile set. Good lighting plot. Costume important. **Warnings:** Latin and Greek as well as Gaelic needs to be well rehearsed. **Workshop/rehearsal/ideas/notes:** Complex characters. Ensemble work. Irish music/dance. Realism. **Research:** Hedge Schools of Ireland.
	Section or scene(s)	Act 1 Scene 1 MANUS & SARAH. MAIRE. Entry of DOALTY & BRIDGET. HUGH enters. OWEN enters with LANCEY & YOLLAND. Act 2 Scene 1 OWEN & LANCEY. YOLLAND, OWEN & MAIRE. Scene 2 MAIRE/YOLLAND. Act 3 to end. Monologues: Act 2 Scene 1 YOLLAND. HUGH, OWEN. Act 3 MAIRE. HUGH.

Play 142

	Title & publisher	*Womberang*	Methuen Drama Plays 1
	Playwright/Date	Sue Townsend	1979
	Casting	2M: 9F	GCSE Range of abilities
	Notes, guidance and considerations for teachers/students	**Description:** Comedy. **Summary:** It's afternoon in a gynaecology waiting room. All is grimly quiet, then Rita turns up! **Where:** A hospital outpatients' waiting room, UK. **When:** Contemporary. **Themes:** Pregnancy; work; courage; truth; love and marriage; anarchy; poverty and politics. **Notes:** Respect the pauses. **Design/tech notes:** Minimal props. Set can be simple with posters etc. to suggest a hospital waiting room. Costume opportunities. **Warnings:** Mild adult themes. **Workshop/rehearsal/ideas/notes:** Character work. Hot seat/role on wall. Super objectives. Age and class differences. Proxemics.	
	Section or scene(s)	Opening scene RITA'S entrance. AUDREY & JAMES. The women dance. RITA & MRS CORNWALLIS. JAMES returns. Through to final scene with DR RILEY and Blackout.	

Play 143

	Title & publisher	*A View from the Bridge*	Methuen Drama
	Playwright/Date	Arthur Miller	1955
	Casting	7M: 4F and minor roles	GCSE/GCE Range of abilities
	Notes, guidance and considerations for teachers/students	**Description:** American drama/tragedy. **Summary:** Eddie has an obsession, a love for his young niece. When she begins to fall in love and talk of marriage to a young Italian immigrant, Eddie takes matters into his own hands with tragic consequences. **Where:** Red Hook Docks, Brooklyn. Poor Italian/American neighbourhood near the Brooklyn Bridge, New York City, USA. **When:** 1950s. **Themes:** Emigration; law and justice; codes of honour and love. **Notes:** Popular choice for GCSE English Literature. Direct audience address. **Design/tech notes:** Offers many opportunities for design students, depending on scenes chosen. Set should be versatile. Projections on to the cyclorama. **Warnings:** Knife fight resulting in a death at the end. Some Boards use this as a prescribed text. Check your specification! **Workshop/rehearsal/ideas/notes:** Stanislavski character work. Study their objectives. Rising tension and conflict games. Breaking 4th wall with audience address. **Research:** 1950s' US immigration. Ellis Island records and photographs. **Resources.** BBC have created some good resources for literature studies. Useful for background and character study.	
	Section or scene(s)	Open with ALFIERI'S audience address. CATHERINE & EDDIE *'He blesses you Eddie'*. EDDIE'S meeting with ALFIERI. Act 2 CATHERINE & RODOLPHO. EDDIE & CATHERINE. Final scene. Monologues: EDDIE'S final address to the crowd. ALFIERI'S addresses.	

Play 144

	Title & publisher	*Pronoun*	NHB
	Playwright/Date	Evan Placey	2014
	Casting	7M: 4F Plus 1 Transgender M Flexible casting	GCE A sensitive able group
	Notes, guidance and considerations for teachers/students	**Description:** Romantic comedy/a love story. **Summary:** A love story about transition, testosterone, and James Dean. Josh and Isabella are childhood sweethearts. They were meant to spend their gap year together; they were meant to be together forever. But Isabella has now become a boy. **Where:** Various locations, UK. **When:** Over 13 months from May of one year to June of the next (present). Contemporary. **Themes:** Gender transition; transgender/love/sexuality/friendship; growing up; conformity; transgender man (female to male). **Notes:** Dean is a transgender man (female to male), played by a female or a transgender man. **Design/tech notes:** Set should include/represent a wardrobe/closet or at least contain a costume rail from which the actors retrieve items in order to change adult/teenage character. Large poster/projection of James Dean from the film *Rebel without a Cause*. Lighting is an important scene/location changer. **Warnings:** Sensitive treatment of transgender themes. **Workshop/rehearsal/ideas/notes:** Multi-role, anti-naturalism. Some physical theatre.	
	Section or scene(s)	Scene 3 MUM & DAD duologue. Scene 4 JOSH & DEAN to DEAN's Monologue /MUM & DAD Scene 5 SMT. Scene 6 JOSH & DEAN. Scene 8 physical theatre. Scene 10 DEAN & JOSH. SMT Scene 11 Scene 13 JOSH & DEAN fight. Scene 14. Monologue: DEAN's assembly. 16 DEAN & JAMES DEAN Final scene.	

Play 145

	Title & publisher	*Oedipus the King*	Methuen Drama
	Playwright/Date	Sophocles	420 BCE
	Casting	8M: 3F Plus Chorus and minor roles	GCE Or an able GCSE group
	Notes, guidance and considerations for teachers/students	**Description:** Greek tragedy. **Summary:** A plague has stricken Thebes. Oedipus consults a prophet for the reason and discovers he has cursed his city by marrying his mother, having murdered his father. **Where:** Thebes, ancient Greece. **When:** Based on myths from 5th century BCE. **Themes:** Religion; ritual; divine law; heroic humanism; free will; politics. **Notes:** There are many versions and takes, both modern and ancient, on this piece of work. The audiences of ancient Greece were very familiar with the story before watching the performance – this was part of the experience. **Design/tech notes:** A simple set using levels, perhaps even a circular space (arena). Angles and shadow/light screens. White sheets/robes are simple and versatile. Good opportunities for costume/make-up design. **Warnings:** For exam purposes, only sections can be chosen; however, these sections should be kept as intact as possible and the order not altered at all. **Workshop/rehearsal/ideas/notes:** Chorus work, ensemble. Berkoff approach to the movement and masks (not the Berkoff script). **Resources.** National Theatre has a great resource for their production.	
	Section or scene(s)	Opening scene. OEDIPUS addresses the people. The PRIEST Then CREON & OEDIPUS. 2nd CHORAL song. OEDIPUS & TEIRESIAS 4th scene with the OLD SHEPHERD. 5th Song and final scene. Monologues: See chorus OEDIPUS, TEIRESIAS, CREON & JOCASTA.	

Play 146

	Title & publisher	*The Exam* Collins
	Playwright/Date	Andy Hamilton 2008
	Casting	6M: 6F GCSE A range of abilities
	Notes, guidance and considerations for teachers/students	**Description:** Comedy. **Summary:** Three teenagers re-sit a paper, struggling with nerves and facing very different parental pressures. **Where:** A school anywhere, and front rooms of a house, UK. **When:** Contemporary. **Themes:** Exam pressure; stress; parents and parental pressure; emotions; self-doubt; revision; exams. **Notes:** The author is very specific with stage directions. Written with school productions in mind. **Design/tech notes:** A very minimal set. Three plain chairs plus a 'swivel chair' on a higher level. Lightweight small tables. Sharply focussed spotlights with hard cuts to natural and soft interiors. There are very strong pointers concerning the staging, and the Collins National Theatre edition gives excellent notes. One voice off. Use costume and props to differentiate the eight main characters perhaps with subtle links to each family. Sheets of paper, exercise books, pens etc. A violin. **Warnings:** Where music is suggested, pay attention to the needs of the piece at that moment. There are suggestions in the script. **Workshop/rehearsal/ideas/notes:** Stylised with a good rhythm. The script has a good exercise for this. Hot seating and body language exercises. Character work. **Resources:** The Collins NT edition has a great section on staging the play.
	Section or scene(s)	Divided into three fairly short scenes. The opening scene has great pace and energy. A good stylised piece. Scene 2 in the exam with quick fire changes. Scene 3 is short with quick changes between the three families, post-exam. Monologues: Scene 1 CHAS & MRS C both have good monologues.

Play 147

	Title & publisher	*What are they Like?* Methuen Drama NT Connections 2013
	Playwright/Date	Lucinda Coxon 2012
	Casting	5M: 7F GCE Or an able GCSE group
	Notes, guidance and considerations for teachers/students	**Description:** Youth theatre. **Summary:** What if you as a teenager had to walk in your parents' shoes? **Where:** Anywhere. **When:** Now. **Themes:** Time; performance; lying; children and parents; change; empathy. **Notes:** The stage directions can at times seem very specific. However, they should be viewed as suggestions only. **Design/tech notes:** The play should be explicitly theatrical in its setting. A large toy box full of toys. Adult shoes. **Warnings:** Not a linear story. **Workshop/rehearsal/ideas/notes:** Non-naturalistic. All 12 performers on stage all of the time with transitions between performer and character being seen by audience. Look for the intention behind the directions and as a group explore the physicality of the piece. Each actor needs to develop a very detailed sense of who their character is. They will also need to study the patterns of adult speech and tone, gesture and posture. Teacher should read through and model for the cast. Walking the text/pointing lines exercises. Fast familiarity with the text is important. **Research:** Ask students to bring in photos of their parents when they were teenagers.
	Section or scene(s)	Another one of those plays where students should be challenged to experiment with the material, using the props from the first rehearsal and choosing what to use.

Play 148

	Title & publisher	*Black Harvest*	Collins
	Playwright/Date	Nigel Gray	1986
	Casting	7M: 3F	GCSE
	Notes, guidance and considerations for teachers/students	**Description:** Adaptation of a novel. **Summary:** A family holiday in a beautiful location. But it soon becomes clear that all is not well. A holiday turns into a nightmare! **Where:** West coast of Ireland. **When:** Contemporary (before mobile phones!). **Themes:** The Irish potato famine; the horrors of the past; haunting; hunger; Irish history. **Notes:** Could be studied in conjunction with the History and English departments. **Design/tech notes:** A number of interiors, levels. Lighting and SFX will be important. See the many notes in the Collins edition. Great opportunities for design candidates, including costume. **Warnings:** Can be quite harrowing and frightening for sensitive students. **Workshop/rehearsal/ideas/notes:** Explore building tension, unseen threat/ghosts and horror. Read Thomas Hardy's poem 'The Glimpse'. **Research:** The great hunger 1845–51. **Resources:** The Collins educational copy contains many teaching resources.	
	Section or scene(s)	Cast should work together to identify key moments. Look at moments of tension and ones that hold the stories together. There are some short monologues that help tell the history and explain events.	

Play 149

	Title & publisher	*Blood Wedding* *Bodas de sangre*	Methuen Drama
	Playwright/Date	Federico García Lorca	1933
	Casting	4M: 6F Plus multi-role	GCE Or an able GCSE group
	Notes, guidance and considerations for teachers/students	**Description:** Tragedy. **Summary:** A young woman and two men fighting for her love. She loves Leonardo but their families hate each other so he marries another and she is made to marry a man she doesn't love. **Where:** Rural Spain. **When:** Circa 1900. **Themes:** Love; passion; control; isolation; religion; blood; revenge. **Notes:** Music can and should be used in this play. It is a translation from the original Spanish. **Design/tech notes:** Set can be almost bare, few props (uncluttered). Lighting should play an important part. **Warnings:** The passions and tension of the play can lead some inexperienced performers to simply shout at each other. Try to internalise! **Workshop/rehearsal/ideas/notes:** Explore the tension of confrontation. Perusing opposite wants/objectives. Experiment with the violence/tension in movement dance/flamenco. Works well as a stylised minimalist piece. Look at death scenes as fantastical, full of imagery and poetic (can be offstage). **Research:** Lorca. Surrealism and Spanish folk culture. Flamenco music of Andalucía, African American Gospel. (Letters to Dali.) Generación del 27. **Resources:** Sydney Theatre Company produced a great Pre-production Education Resource.	
	Section or scene(s)	Act 1 Scenes 1, 3, Act 2 Scenes 2, 3. Act 3 Scenes 1, 2. Monologues: Act 3 Scene 1 LEONARDO TO BRIDE. Act 3 Scene 2 BRIDE TO MOTHER. The MOON'S monologue. Look at the poetry of the piece.	

Play 150

	Title & publisher	*The Playboy of the Western World*	Methuen Drama
	Playwright/Date	J.M. Synge	1983
	Casting	6M: 5F	GCSE/GCE
	Notes, guidance and considerations for teachers/students	**Description:** Comedy. **Summary:** Christy Mahon stumbles into a tavern on the coast of Mayo, claiming to have killed his father. Instead of calling the police, the bored villagers hail him as a hero. The barmaid and publican's daughter falls for his glamour, and her betrothed, who tries to set the stranger up with a local widow. But is the romantic dashing hero all he seems? **Where:** A rough country tavern in County Mayo (on the West coast of Ireland). **When:** Circa 1906/7. **Themes:** Darkness; community (Republic of Ireland); crime; death; family. **Notes:** Depending on your students, the text offers physical comedy moments and very funny lines in abundance. **Design/tech notes:** Good opportunities for set design of the tavern's interior. **Warnings:** Take care with the language and pronunciation. **Workshop/rehearsal/ideas/notes:** Farce. Some good farcical comedy moments. Comic timing/delivery. Facial expression, tone and pause/changes in emotion.	
	Section or scene(s)	Act 1 (enough to set scene then from entry of CHRISTY) Then PEEGAN, CHRISTY and the WIDOW to end of the Act. Act 2 CHRISTY as MAHON turns up. Act 3 SHAWN & CHRISTY. Monologues: CHRISTY Act 1 MICHAEL Act 3.	

Play 151

	Title & publisher	*Andorra*	Methuen Drama
	Playwright/Date	Max Frisch	1961
	Casting	8M: 3F and 4 silent	GCSE A variety of opportunities
	Notes, guidance and considerations for teachers/students	**Description:** Epic theatre (symbolic drama). **Summary:** 'In Andorra there lived a young man who was believed to be a Jew'. A play about political and personal issues, race and national prejudice ... and love. **Where:** A fictional Andorra (not the real one). **When:** Any time. **Themes:** Anti-Semitism; People trapped in their public image; racism; stereotypes; collective guilt. **Notes:** Some elements of satire. Parallels with Nazi Germany. **Design/tech notes:** The script has very specific requirements for costume. The set is the town square under a gloomy sky! Alison Chitty. **Warnings:** No anti-illusionism needs to be demonstrated. The audience must always be aware they are in the theatre. **Workshop/rehearsal/ideas/notes:** Brechtian epic theatre. Also stylised movement. Minimalist. Some Berkoff influences with the ensemble/soldiers and the silent.	
	Section or scene(s)	Scenes 1, 2, 5, 6, 7, 8, 9, 11, 12. Monologues: Scene 3 ANDRI then CARPENTER Scene 4 DOCTOR × 3. Scene 6 ANDRI. Scene 7 PRIEST. Scene 9 SEÑORA, ANDRI × 2. Scene 12 TEACHER & SOLDIER.	

Play 152

	Title & publisher	*Stags and Hens*	Methuen Drama
	Playwright/Date	Willy Russell	1978
	Casting	7M: 5F	GCSE A range of abilities
	Notes, guidance and considerations for teachers/students	**Description:** Social comedy. **Summary:** Unknown to each other, Linda and Dave decide to have their hen and stag parties in the same night club – well in its toilets, where the groom is throwing up and the bride-to-be is getting cold feet! **Where:** Alternates between the Ladies and Gents toilets in a seedy Liverpool nightclub. **When:** Now (or 1970s). **Themes:** Working-class society; misogyny; class issues; friendship; love; popular culture. **Notes:** Music and topical references can be updated as necessary. **Design/tech notes:** Good opportunity for technical/design students. Two toilets in a nightclub. Distinctly Ladies and Gents. Doors to the nightclub. LX/FX: Music fades and swells as the doors open and close. Disco lights glimpsed. **Warnings:** Strong language and adult themes. **Workshop/rehearsal/ideas/notes:** Cross cutting and freeze frame/action/thought tracking.	
	Section or scene(s)	Two Acts. Opening of Act 1 with girls and on to the lads. EDDY'S monologue in Act 1. Act 2 BERNADETTE & CAROL then MAUREEN, FRANCES & CAROL. Make choices according to M/F cast requirements.	

Play 153

	Title & publisher	*Living with Lady Macbeth*	Cambridge University Press
	Playwright/Date	Rob John	1992
	Casting	3M: 9F	GCSE Range of abilities
	Notes, guidance and considerations for teachers/students	**Description:** Youth theatre/Play within a play. **Summary:** Lily is a very 'ordinary' girl. Everyone laughs when she tells them she's going to audition for Lady Macbeth in the school play. **Where:** School various locations and Lily's home, UK. **When:** Contemporary. **Themes:** Fitting in; peer pressure; ambition; women's roles in society. **Notes:** Multi-role/multi-age opportunities. Play within a play. The character of Lily is realistic but her situations are not. The play has two types of stage directions (essential and less essential). **Design/tech notes:** I have seen some excellent design work done with this text, in particular, costume. Moves back and forth in time and between reality and dreams/fantasy. **Warnings:** Take care with the knife and tape the blade (make safe). Don't use an obvious plastic fake, it has to be threatening not funny. **Workshop/rehearsal/ideas/notes:** Improv to develop characters. Physical theatre/body props. Work through scenes by closely following the stage directions and then again with improv. Freeze frame tableaux to capture moods/moments and feelings. **Research:** Macbeth and film clips of Lady Macbeth.	
	Section or scene(s)	Opening sequence where all the characters are introduced, including monologues. LILY and BARRY discuss Macbeth. Five-girl group scenes. LILY & MON'S imagined sticky ends for the five girls. The audition.	

Play 154

🎭	Title & publisher	*Too Fast*	Methuen Drama NT Connections 2011
✏️	Playwright/Date	Douglas Maxwell	2011
👥	Casting	4M: 8F	GCSE Strong vocal work/singers
📋	Notes, guidance and considerations for teachers/students	**Description:** Ensemble comedy. **Summary:** A vocal group led by DD has a plan! The group is going to win next year's Britain's Got Talent. But first they need a gig and, more importantly, a heart-breaking backstory that will win them votes. **Where:** Backstage at a funeral/church hall. **When:** Contemporary. **Themes:** Loyalty; betrayal; ambition; hopes and fears. **Notes:** The final scene contains huge theatrical reveal. Very much an audience-involved piece. The ensemble should be singers. The song, which is very important, needs to be chosen sensitively by the cast. **Design/tech notes:** There are fantastic, though complex opportunities for design option students. Performed in a school uniform. **Warnings:** Some strong language. **Workshop/rehearsal/ideas/notes:** Subtext shown through the action not articulated. Lots of pace. Strong character work. Performers should know precisely who they are. **Resources:** The NT Connections 2011 script carries useful suggestions for workshops and rehearsals.	
🎬	Section or scene(s)	Good monologues: SPOKE'S BROTHER; ALI; DD, SEAN & CALLUM. Performances must include final scene. Encourage cast to select.	

Play 155

🎭	Title & publisher	*Ghetto*	NHB
✏️	Playwright/Date	Joshua Sobol	1984
👥	Casting	9M: 3F and various others	GCE A variety of challenging opportunities
📋	Notes, guidance and considerations for teachers/students	**Description:** Historical satire. Play within a play. **Summary:** A play within a play based on diaries written during the holocaust, it tells of the unlikely flourishing of a theatre at the very time the Nazis began their policy of mass extermination. **Where:** Vilna Jewish ghetto, Lithuania. **When:** 1939–43. **Themes:** The holocaust; Nazi madness; Jewish resilience; power struggles; responsibility; resilience and the preservation of a culture. **Notes:** Some characters need to be able to sing well and/or play a musical instrument. NHB edition includes songs and music. **Design/tech notes:** Puppet/dummy, complex SFX. Some quite technical yet rewarding challenges. As many costumes/rags/uniforms as possible. **Warnings:** Deals with mass murder of the Jews during WW2. Contains some sexual references. **Workshop/rehearsal/ideas/notes:** Read together the extracts of the Ghetto diaries included in the book. Brechtian techniques work perfectly with this powerful piece. Also consider Berkoff.	
🎬	Section or scene(s)	All scenes are demanding. Look to your cast and choose wisely as a company having studied the diaries and researched in some depth. The songs are vital. Monologues: NARRATOR Scene 1 *'Our last performance?'* Scene 8 GENS *'Herman Kruk, permit me'* to *'I insist'*. Scene 9 WEISKOPF *'Times are hard?'* Scene 10 WEISKOPF *'Costumes . . .'* Scene 12 GENS *'They still don't see'*. Part 2 Scene 14 PAUL *'There's an old Hassidic legend'*.	

Play 156

	Title & publisher	*Volpone*	Methuen Drama
	Playwright/Date	Ben Jonson	1606
	Casting	12M: 2F Flexible cast	GCSE/GCE Many varied opportunities
	Notes, guidance and considerations for teachers/students	**Description:** Comedy/satire. **Summary:** Volpone, a philanderer and conman, and Mosca, his servant cause chaos with a cheeky fraud to part the city's wealthiest from their fortunes. The tale twists and turns, as all the characters attempt to deceive each other, until the whole scheme finally collapses, with disastrous consequences. **Where:** Venice, Italy. **When:** 17th century (action takes place over the course of one day). **Themes:** Greed; morality; money; class. **Notes:** *Volpone* is Jonson's most performed work. High-energy, intensely theatrical comedy. **Design/tech notes:** Encourage the animal qualities of the characters to influence not only performance but costume and make-up. Real opportunities for set and costume design students. **Warnings:** The comedy requires high energy interchanges and precise timing. **Workshop/rehearsal/ideas/notes:** Commedia dell'arte tradition of the comic relationship between master and servant. Status workshops. The physicalisation of the characters (animal qualities, fox etc.) The antihero. Super objectives and scene objectives. **Resources.** The British Library, *Discovering Literature: Shakespeare and Renaissance. An Introduction to Volpone*.	
	Section or scene(s)	Prologue. Act 1 Scenes 1, 2. Act 3 Scenes 6, 7. Act 4 Scenes 1, 4. Act 5, Scenes 4, 5, 6, 7, and 12. *(disguise-reveal)*. Monologue: Act 2 Scenes 5 CORVINO. Act 3 Scene 1 MOSCA's soliloquy. Act 3 Scene 7 VOLPONE, and then CELIA '*If you have ears*'.	

Play 157

	Title & publisher	*The History Boys*	Faber & Faber
	Playwright/Date	Alan Bennett	2004
	Casting	11M: 1F	GCSE/GCE Range of abilities
	Notes, guidance and considerations for teachers/students	**Description:** Comedy. **Summary:** Eight sixth-form boys prepare to take their entrance exams for Oxbridge. Hector, their Master, an eccentric ageing teacher, has a unique take on their General Studies. His teaching is brought into question, however, by the young, newly appointed Irwin, brought in specifically to ensure that the boys excel at interview. **Where:** Cutler's Grammar School, Sheffield, England, UK. **When:** 1980s. **Themes:** Education; sex; ambition; rebellion. **Notes:** Quite a bit of French to be learned. In addition, a good grasp of RP. **Design/tech notes:** No real stage directions or set instructions. Good opportunities for a set design that allows for quick changes between the various locations. The boys carry out the scene/set changes. Some projection work could be used. SFX and subtle lighting. A wheelchair. A piano on stage. **Warnings:** Adult language. **Workshop/rehearsal/ideas/notes:** Character work on age and status in order to clearly set teacher and student apart with a young cast. Use of prop/costume to establish status and age. Some great opportunities for physical work. Explore relationships between Headmaster and the teachers and teachers and students. **Resources.** Sell A Door Theatre Company has produced a very detailed education pack with Alan Bennett.	
	Section or scene(s)	Many great scenes for exam. Allow students to select through study. My personal favourite is the Act 1 poetry/history lesson. Notable monologues: HEAD '*What's wrong with Hector*'. IRWIN '*Has anybody been to Rome?*' HECTOR '*I've got this idea of buying a van*'. LINTOTT '*I'll tell you why there are no women historians*'.	

Play 158

	Title & publisher	*Refugee Boy*	Methuen Drama
	Playwright/Date	Benjamin Zephaniah Adapted by Lemn Sissay	2013
	Casting	9M: 3F	GCSE A range of abilities
	Notes, guidance and considerations for teachers/students	\multicolumn{2}{l}{**Description:** Tragedy. **Summary:** Alem is a 14-year-old refugee boy. Left in England in an act of love by his father, the play follows his turbulent life in the British care system while a bloody civil war rages in his home country. **Where:** UK/London and war-torn Ethiopia/Eritrea. **When:** 2001, but works in present time. **Themes:** What it means to be a refugee in the UK; arriving, belonging and finding home; Immigration and migration; control; father–son relationships; human rights; our need for peace; the darkness that surrounds us. **Notes:** Based on the teen novel by Benjamin Zephaniah. **Design/tech notes:** Great opportunities for set design and lighting/projections. Old suitcases and rucksacks. Levels. **Warnings:** Mild bad language. Knife attack. **Workshop/rehearsal/ideas/notes:** Role on wall. 'Hot seat' to develop characters/improv based on movement of people. **Research:** the meaning of refugee/emigration/immigration. Read the novel *Refugee Boy*.}	
	Section or scene(s)	\multicolumn{2}{l}{29 scenes. ALEM & MUSTAPHA's monologues and duologues. Scene 11 The FITZGERALDS, RUTH and ALEM. Dad's letter. Scene 12 Mr KETO & THE SOLDIER. Scene 14 ALEM & RUTH. ALEM, SWEENEY and 'HOODED' scenes 15–16. Scene 25. Final scenes.}	

Play 159

	Title & publisher	*Pigeon English*	Methuen Drama
	Playwright/Date	Stephen Kelman Adapted by Gbolahan Obisesan	2013
	Casting	8M: 5F	GCSE A range of abilities
	Notes, guidance and considerations for teachers/students	\multicolumn{2}{l}{**Description:** Tragi-comedy. **Summary:** Newly arrived from Ghana with his mother and older sister, Harri lives on the ninth floor of a block of flats on a London housing estate. Unaware of the danger growing around him, he decides to solve a vicious knife crime and in so doing, exposes himself and his family to very real danger. **Where:** A playground and surrounding flats. London, UK. **When:** Contemporary. **Themes:** Loss; home and immigration; language and culture; guilt/innocence; masculinity; violence; death. **Notes:** Multi-role. Music plays an important part in the fabric/choreography of the piece and in particular beat box ability a must for this one! Audience address. **Design/tech notes:** Levels and imaginatively used scaffolding. Lighting and SFX/projections. **Warnings:** Gang-related crime/violence and language. Knives – make them safe! **Workshop/rehearsal/ideas/notes:** Physical theatre. Display of character/status through movement. Improv with social groups. Match music to spoken word. Tableau. Physicality of objects. Use of sound (beat box). Use of objects in a symbolic manner, e.g. knives, choreographed, stylised. **Research:** Events of the original novel (Damilola Taylor, 2000). **Resources:** NYT has a fantastic resource online plus film footage.}	
	Section or scene(s)	\multicolumn{2}{l}{Scene 1. Scene 4 Any of HARRI & NEVER NORMAL GIRL's narrations. Scene 9. Scene 12–13 Scene 29. Scene 31, 32, 33 and 33b. However, most scenes offer great opportunities. Read as a group and decide according to preferences and skills/talents of cast. Respect the order.}	

Play 160

	Title & publisher	*Once a Catholic*	Amber Lane Press
	Playwright/Date	Mary O'Malley	1977
	Casting	4M: 10F	GCSE A range of abilities
	Notes, guidance and considerations for teachers/students	\multicolumn{2}{l	}{**Description:** Comedy/satire. **Summary:** Three teenage girls, all by the name of 'Mary', attend a girls' convent school (the 1950s). As they enter puberty, they beginning to question their faith, amongst other things. They are taught by hilariously strict nuns and a priest with a drink problem. **Where:** Catholic convent school and various locations in and around London NW10, UK. **When:** Late 1950s. **Themes:** Growing up; a satirical look at Catholicism; faith and indoctrination. **Notes:** I first saw this in a girls' convent school and loved the irreverent comedy. Can be performed by just the female cast or use the male characters too. A number of very engaging monologues of varying length. The nuns are all large parts. They are scripted as Irish but could be from anywhere. **Design/tech notes:** Try to divide areas of the stage/performance area. Classroom, desks and chairs, and outside. Distinction made by level, light etc. Nun costumes. Girls in pinafore/uniform/austere. **Warnings:** Some mild sexual references and strong language. (This play makes no reference to any of the current serious allegations levelled against the Catholic church.) **Workshop/rehearsal/ideas/notes:** Ensemble, singing/praying/learning together. St Trinian's. Comic timing.}
	Section or scene(s)	\multicolumn{2}{l	}{Act 1 Scene 1 (but cut down MOTHER PETER'S opening monologue) followed by Scenes 2, 6, 7, 8. 13. Any of FATHER MULLARKEY and the quick-fire scenes with The MARYS MAGINTY, MOONEY & GALLAGHER.}

Play 161

	Title & publisher	*Road*	Methuen Drama
	Playwright/Date	Jim Cartwright	1986
	Casting	8M: 6F	GCSE/GCE Challenging
	Notes, guidance and considerations for teachers/students	\multicolumn{2}{l	}{**Description:** Comedy. **Summary:** A working-class collection of stories of survival, told through a journey up a semi-derelict road and its inhabitants. A celebration of human endurance. **Where:** Various locations (on multiple-use set): a bar, a bedroom, a front room, a street in Lancashire, UK. **When:** Any Friday night. **Themes:** Repressed dreams; a desire to escape mundane poverty. **Notes:** Strong stage direction which should be followed. Good opportunities for powerful performances. A good physical piece. Great characters for students to get into. Written for a Northern accent. Good fast-paced dialogue and interchanges. A grim humour with tender and vicious moments. **Design/tech notes:** See the script's many notes and select. Can be as flexible as you need. Unless you have a design candidate, keep the set simple. **Warnings:** Strong language of a sexual nature. **Workshop/rehearsal/ideas/notes:** Strong character work, with a focus on the mental torment of the characters. Grotowski.}
	Section or scene(s)	\multicolumn{2}{l	}{Pre-show (important) then Act 1 to BRINK'S exit and Blackout. Act 2 from CHANTEL'S song. Any scene in Act 2 **Duologue** between CAROL & BRENDA/ LOUISE & BROTHER. Monologues: JERRY, PROFESSOR, EDDIE & BRINK MOLLY, VALERIE, CAROL & LOUISE, SCULLERY & DOR.}

Play 162

	Title & publisher	*Jerusalem*	NHB
	Playwright/Date	Jez Butterworth	2009
	Casting	9M: 5F	GCE Range of abilities
	Notes, guidance and considerations for teachers/students	**Description:** Comedy. **Summary:** The gritty side of life in contemporary rural England. **Where:** A clearing in a wood. Flintock, Wiltshire, UK. **When:** St George's day. Any time (contemporary). **Themes:** Secrets; the destruction of nature; Englishness; myth and folklore; drugs; teenagers at risk; music; love; nomads. **Notes:** There are fantastic opportunities for duologues, monologues and fast-paced comic performances. Sound plays a massive role in this piece and must be considered carefully. Gareth Fry. **Design/tech notes:** A very busy set and props list. Use of sound and light to create a real sense of place. Some great costume opportunities. **Warnings:** Adult themes and language. Some Boards use this as a prescribed text. Check your specification! **Workshop/rehearsal/ideas/notes:** Character work. Hot seat and status games. Listen to the Hymn 'Jerusalem'. Imagine a place, imagine a set. **Research:** English myth and folklore, legends. Watch *Shameless* (UK version) to study characters and poverty in affluent England.	
	Section or scene(s)	Three Acts. Good double-act comedic opportunities between JONNY & GINGER LEE, GINGER DAVEY & PEA tell JONNY'S story followed by his monologue in Act 1. JONNY and DAWN Act 2 Final scenes with PHAEDRA.	

Play 163

	Title & publisher	*Cloud 9*	Methuen Drama Caryl Churchill Plays 1
	Playwright/Date	Caryl Churchill	1978
	Casting	6M: 10F Flexible	GCE An able group
	Notes, guidance and considerations for teachers/students	**Description:** Satire. **Summary:** A view of the sexual politics and relationships of a family and their lovers, with an interval of twenty-five years of their lives, and around a hundred years of history. **Where:** Act 1, British colony in Victorian Africa. Act 2, London, UK. **When:** Act 1, Victorian times. Act 2, 1979/2004. **Themes:** The confusion of gender; present and past; identity; hypocrisy; violence; oppression; race; sex. **Notes:** Pay particular attention to vital casting notes in the script. **Design/tech notes:** Great set design opportunities. Costume varied and challenging. **Warnings:** Quite explicit in places. Adult themes. Some not appropriate for school audience. Some Boards use this as a prescribed text. Check your specification! **Workshop/rehearsal/ideas/notes:** Working with a dummy in Act 1. Act 1 lends itself well to farce. Great comic characters. Commedia and music hall. There are dark stories behind the laughs and these should not be lost.	
	Section or scene(s)	Act 1 Scene 1 CLIVE, BETTY & JOSHUA. ELLEN brings the children. CLIVE & Mrs SAUNDERS- hide and seek. Scene 4 ELLEN & BETTY – CLIVE & HARRY. Scene 5. Act 2 Scenes 1 VITORIA & LIN, Scene 2 VICTORIA, Scene 3 CATHY & LIN. Monologues: HARRY Act 1 Scene 2. CLIVE Scene 3. JOSHUA Scene 4. BETTY Act 2 Scenes 1. GERRY Scene 2. MARTIN Scene 2.	

Play 164

🎭	Title & publisher	*The Suicide*	Methuen Drama
✏️	Playwright/Date	Nikolia Erdman Adapted by Suhayla El-Bushra	2016
👥	Casting	7M: 9F	GCSE/GCE Many interesting opportunities
📋	Notes, guidance and considerations for teachers/students	**Description:** Comedy. **Summary:** Things are getting tough for Sam: no job, no benefits and stuck in a tiny flat with his girlfriend. There may only be one way out, and everyone from the corrupt politicians to the media-savvy kids in the street want a piece of the action. **Where:** Inner-city tower block, 'Clement Attlee House', UK. **When:** 2011. **Themes:** Suicide; moral dilemma; celebrity; parody. **Notes:** I believe Act 5 Scene 1 should be omitted from any exam performance. **Design/tech notes:** Fantastic opportunities for set design. A very busy, colourful production. **Warnings:** The very title/theme will not be suitable for some student groups. Strong language and adult themes. **Workshop/rehearsal/ideas/notes:** Large cast possible but keep it sane for performance exam with main characters and scenes. Define characters. Role on wall. Hot seat.	
🎬	Section or scene(s)	Act 1 Scene 1, Act 2 Scene 1, Act 3 Scene 1 SAM & ISAAM Scene 2, Scene 3 SAM & PATRICK. Act 4 Scene 1, Act 5 Scene 2 Carefully select scenes for exam which are not over-confusing out of context. Monologues: End of Act 2 ERICA. Act 3 Scene 1 SAM. End of Act 5 SAM.	

Play 165

🎭	Title & publisher	*Adrian Mole 13³/⁴*	Methuen Drama Plays 1 Sue Townsend (School edition Heineman plays)
✏️	Playwright/Date	Sue Townsend	1985
👥	Casting	12M: 6F Very flexible casting/ multi-role	GCSE A range of abilities
📋	Notes, guidance and considerations for teachers/students	**Description:** Comedy/physical theatre. **Summary:** The dramatisation of a boy (Adrian's) turbulent and excruciating teenage years. **Where:** Leicester and Ashby de la Zouch. Various locations, UK. **When:** 1980s. **Themes:** The torment of being a thirteen and three-quarter-year old intellectual. **Notes:** A very popular choice with mixed-ability groups. Some students will have already experienced the text as far back as Year 8 and may need convincing of its validity as a performance piece at GCSE. There are plenty of challenging opportunities. The multi-role and audience address and its physical style may need re-exploring after Year 8 English. Music is scored at the back. There is also a musical adaptation of the play. **Design/tech notes:** The set can be as simple as you need or a great opportunity for design students with different locations of the house separated by light/levels/positions on and off stage. Puppet dog is another great challenge. Voice-over recordings. **Warnings:** The character of Adrian is very demanding. (But voice over for diary extracts helps.) **Workshop/rehearsal/ideas/notes:** Physical theatre. Some direct audience address. Pace! The selected extracts should follow the order of the play and maintain a good pace and energy throughout. Beware that the dog puppet doesn't steal the show. Breaking the 4th wall and multi-role combined with some natural and tender moments are a great opportunity to demonstrate skills.	
🎬	Section or scene(s)	Act 1 to LUCAS family exit. ADRIAN was an ugly baby scene. Parents and flu. ADRIAN meets PANDORA. The disco. ADRIAN meets BERT. BARRY KENT. BERT'S monologue. PAULINE & MRS LUCAS. The separation! Act 2 GRAN & ADRIAN. NIGEL & ADRIAN. Visit to Sheffield. DOREEN SLATER! PANDORA & the red socks. A visit to BERT. PAULINE'S return.	

Play 166

	Title & publisher	*The Government Inspector*	Methuen Drama
	Playwright/Date	Nikolia Gogol	1836
	Casting	14M: 5F Can be reduced	GCSE A range of abilities
	Notes, guidance and considerations for teachers/students	**Description:** Satire/black comedy. **Summary:** A penniless nobody from Moscow is mistaken for a government inspector by the corrupt and self-seeking officials of a small town. **Where:** Russia (but could be anywhere). **When:** Tsarist Russia (but could be any time). **Themes:** Human greed; vanity; folly; corruption. **Notes:** Can be treated as a realistic satire, or a more physical fantasy. **Design/tech notes:** Minimal, uncluttered set. Table and chairs. Experiment with levels for different locations or simply use light. Costumes can be as flamboyant as the characters demand and should inform rehearsals and character work. Experiment with multi-role with some characters. **Warnings:** Some Boards use this as a prescribed text. Check your specification! **Workshop/rehearsal/ideas/notes:** A great opportunity to show off physical theatre. Elements of commedia and physical comedy. Performers must really study the physicality of their character – how they walk and move about the stage. Vocal tone and pace. See notes on costume in rehearsal. Games of leadership and deception. Meyerhold. **Research:** Gogol, St Petersburg in the 1800s. **Resources:** Birmingham Repertory Theatre in association with Ramps on the Moon have produced an excellent and detailed resources pack.	
	Section or scene(s)	Sections of the following: Act 1 Scene 1 The news of the visit, including the GOVERNOR'S dream and the letter. Scene 3 B&D Scenes 4, 6, Act 2 Scene 1 OSIP'S monologue (in part) then with KHLESTAKOV. Scenes 3, 6, 9, Act 3 Scenes 1, 4, 5, 7, 10, Act 4, Final scenes of Act 5 and the silent scene with the GOVERNOR.	

Play 167

	Title & publisher	*Jane Eyre*	Oxford Playscripts
	Playwright/Date	Charlotte Brontë Adapted by Barlow and Skidmore	1998
	Casting	5M: 16F Very versatile	GCSE A range of abilities
	Notes, guidance and considerations for teachers/students	**Description:** Period drama adaptation/Gothic novel. **Summary:** Jane becomes drawn toward Mr Rochester but as she does she realises he is tormented by his past – a past which is about to catch up with him. **Where:** Lowood School, Marsh End and Thornfield Hall. England, UK. **When:** 1840s. **Themes:** Love; social class; the place of women; power and love. **Notes:** Brontë's dialogue was meant to be read and in order to remain in part faithful to the Gothic novel, it is important to keep Jane's narration/audience address in the performance. **Design/tech notes:** Can be played in a black box set. Limited props/furniture, only to suggest not recreate. Lighting can be a good opportunity, with Jane stepping out of role to narrate/address audience isolated by light. Lighting very important too in the Red Room scene and the fire. **Warnings:** Stage fights should be handled professionally or in slow motion. **Workshop/rehearsal/ideas/notes:** Character work. Improv. Still imaging, thought tapping, hot seating/the Judgement chair. Shared Experience. **Research:** Images of Gothic novels/Mary Shelley. The place of women in Brontë's time.	
	Section or scene(s)	Act 1 Scene 1 to HELEN coughs again and fade. JANE hits JOHN REED & The Red Room. HELEN, JANE, MISS TEMPLE and HELEN'S death Act 2. Scenes 2, 3, The fire and GRACE POOLE Act 3 Scene 1, JANE & THE GYPSY, The Attic prison. Act 4 Scene 1, Act 5. Select scenes with the students in mind.	

Play 168

	Title & publisher	*Woyzeck*	NHB
	Playwright/Date	Georg Büchner	1913
	Casting	15M: 4F	GCE Or an able GCSE group
	Notes, guidance and considerations for teachers/students	**Description:** Expressionist German theatre (psychological realism). **Summary:** Based on a real-life murder trial which took place in Germany in the 1820s. In a series of short self-contained scenes, we follow events in the life of the lowly and abused soldier Woyzeck, who murders his common-law wife in a fit of jealous rage. **Where:** A small town and surrounding countryside Germany. **When:** 1821 (approx.). **Themes:** Madness; the human condition; politics and poverty/class/status and sexuality; religion. **Notes:** Unfinished by Büchner with many versions offered. Very open to interpretation of time and setting. A popular German theatre piece. **Design/tech notes:** Stark and minimalist. Alison Chitty. **Warnings:** Violence/sexual content and murder. Some Boards use this as a prescribed text. Check your specification! **Workshop/rehearsal/ideas/notes:** Berkoff ideas of exaggerated movement / characteristics for the stereotype/caricature. Status games. Brechtian techniques to highlight Woyzeck's suffering. **Research:** Werner Herzog's 1979 movie of the same name. **Resources:** The Old Vic have produced an excellent teaching resource offering their interpretation.	
	Section or scene(s)	Scene 1 WOYZECK & THE CAPTAIN. Scene 2 Outside the town. Scene 3 The town. Scene 9 DOCTOR & THE CAPTAIN. Scenes 10, 11, 13, 17, 18, 24. Monologues: BARKER Scene 4. THE SHOWMAN in Scene 5 DOCTOR Scene 7. GRANDMOTHER Scene 21.	

Play 169

	Title & publisher	*The Rover*	Harper Collins
	Playwright/Date	Aphra Behn	1677
	Casting	12M: 7F Plus various minor parts	GCE Or an able GCSE group
	Notes, guidance and considerations for teachers/students	**Description:** Restoration comedy. **Summary:** The comical yet dark exploits of a band of banished English cavaliers as they enjoy themselves at a carnival in Naples. Multiple plotlines revolve around their amorous adventures as they pursue a pair of noble Spanish sisters, a mistress and a prostitute. **Where:** Naples, Italy. **When:** Carnival time 1600s. **Themes:** Love; lust; marriage; courtship; prostitution; rape; all mixed with general buffoonery; the sexual politics of the 1600s. **Notes:** The Prologue and Epilogue are both in rhyming couplets and directly address the audience. **Design/tech notes:** Complex and challenging set/props. Including places for 'Discovery' scenes (screen scene) for the many eavesdroppers. Costume and mask offer great design opportunities too. **Warnings:** Bawdy and rather dark in places. Rape and prostitution. **Workshop/rehearsal/ideas/notes:** Commedia dell'arte/pantomime, exaggerated eavesdropping and audience asides. **Research:** BBC in conjunction with Open University and Routledge Video recording available. Restoration theatre. **Resources:** British Library.	
	Section or scene(s)	Act 1 Scene 1 FLORINDA, HELLENA & PEDRO, Scene 2 BELVILE, FREDRICK & BLUNT, then WILLMORE & HELLENA. Act 2 Scene 1, Act 3 Scene 3, 4, Act 4 Scene 1, 2, Act 5 Scene 1. Monologues: Prologue: Act 2 Scene 2 WILLMORE. BLUNT. Act 4 Scene 1 BELVILE. Scene 4 BLUNT. Epilogue.	

Play 170

	Title & publisher	*Walking with Shadows* Nelson Thornes
	Playwright/Date	Ben Myers 2002
	Casting	9M: 10F GCSE and Chorus A range of abilities
	Notes, guidance and considerations for teachers/students	**Description:** Psychological thriller for stage. **Summary:** 'When you are alone, in your darkest moments, what do you see?' A frightening portrayal of teenage stress and vulnerability. **Where:** A school and a house (fictional small town), UK. **When:** Contemporary. **Themes:** Friendship; families; peer pressure and bullying; school; divorce; guilt; stress and mental health. **Notes:** The build up of tension is the key to the horror element. Look at plays like the *Woman in Black* etc. **Design/tech notes:** Blacks and masks for the chorus seem obvious but it really works. Mirror frame. lighting effects. SFX and music will help to create/build the tension. **Warnings:** Be aware that there is other material out there with the same name. **Workshop/rehearsal/ideas/notes:** Experiments with building tension/suspense and breaking it. Delivery of some lines will be challenging to avoid them sounding 'cheesy'. Use screens and back light to create and experiment with shadows. **Resources:** The script has a good selection of exercises and resources at the back.
	Section or scene(s)	Act 1 Scenes 1, 2, 3, 4, 6, 8, End of 9, 10, 13, 14. Act 2 Scenes 1, 2, 3, 6, 8, 10, 11, 13 and 14. Act 2 Scene 1 LORNA. Scene 13 Mr BARNESS's story.

Play 171

	Title & publisher	*The Magdalen Whitewash* Smithscripts.co.uk
	Playwright/Date	Valerie Goodwin 2002
	Casting	4M: *up to* 16F GCE Can be played by 9F with multi-role. Or an able GCSE group
	Notes, guidance and considerations for teachers/students	**Description:** Historical play with music. **Summary:** The play focusses on eight 'Maggies' (girls signed in to the convent laundry) and their stories. **Where:** Set in a Magdalen Laundry attached to a convent near Dublin. **When:** 1929. **Themes:** Irish nuns; motherhood; female lives; adoption; religious institutions; Priests. **Notes:** A two-act play. Songs, ensemble physical theatre sequences (optional). **Design/tech notes:** Versatile. Can be very simply done with sheets, stools, benches, baskets. Aprons and head scarves, shirts and dark skirts or as detailed as wished. **Warnings:** Death of a baby during childbirth. **Workshop/rehearsal/ideas/notes:** Brechtian elements but mainly Stanislavski. Some physical theatre. The song 'This woman's work' by Kate Bush and 'The Magdalen Laundries' by Mary Coughlan are ideal 'ways in' to introduce the themes. Sheet folding 'ballet' and ensemble scenes. Mary's monologue in which it is clear she doesn't know how she got her baby. Photographs of the actual Maggies.
	Section or scene(s)	For groups: Delivery men Act 1 Scene 6/ASSUMPTA's baby adopted Act 2 Scene 2/The Dormitory/childbirth scene and SISTER GABRIEL's answers to them. Act 1 Scene 8/Mrs DOOLAN for a two-hander. Act 2 Scene 1/The last two pages, the handprints left on the sheets while she's singing Danny Boy. There are a number of good duologues. The priests' scenes are a good challenge for boys. Act 2 Scene 3, also the scene in the Nun's parlour Act 1.

Play 172

	Title & publisher	*The Crucible*	Penguin
	Playwright/Date	Arthur Miller	1950
	Casting	11M: 10F (or fewer)	GCSE Mixed/able group
	Notes, guidance and considerations for teachers/students	**Description:** Historical tragedy. **Summary:** A fictionalised account of the Salem witch trials. **Where:** Salem, Massachusetts, USA. **When:** One year around 1692. **Themes:** Guilt; hysteria; reputation; power and authority; misogyny; deception. **Notes:** Scenes which explore relationships between two or three characters work well. Look at power – who has it and who has not. **Design/tech notes:** The text has much on the set and props; however, for exam performance purposes, much of this can be dispensed with in favour of a simple bare stage perhaps with just table and chairs and levels. The costumes, however, should be accurate (unless resetting the whole play). **Warnings:** Some Boards use this as a prescribed text. Check your specification! **Workshop/rehearsal/ideas/notes:** Character work Stanislavski/Role on wall/ Mapping. **Research:** The events of the Salem witch trials, images. 1966/96 movies of the same name.	
	Section or scene(s)	Good scenes to consider are those which deal with relationships. MARY WARREN & JOHN PROCTOR. ABIGAIL & PROCTOR, ELIZABETH & PROCTOR. The three of them in Act 2. DANFORTH & PROCTOR. The courtroom Scene in Act 3. The cell in Act 4 to end. Monologues: DANFORTH, PROCTOR, HALE.	

Play 173

	Title & publisher	*Blue Stockings*	NHB
	Playwright/Date	Jessica Swale	2013
	Casting	12M: 9F Most parts can be doubled.	GCSE A range of good abilities
	Notes, guidance and considerations for teachers/students	**Description:** Historical/biographical drama. **Summary:** The story of the first female university, its struggle and its students and staff. **Where:** Multiple locations, Girton College, Cambridge, UK. **When:** 1896. **Themes:** Love over knowledge; chauvinism; Suffragettes/feminism; rejection; equality and education. **Notes:** With the exception of Elizabeth Welsh and Tess all other parts can be doubled. **Design/tech notes:** Good SFX/lighting opportunities. Use levels and lighting to signify different locations. Costume matters, excellent design opportunities. **Warnings:** Some Boards use this as a prescribed text. Check your specification! **Workshop/rehearsal/ideas/notes:** Character work. Very strong, vastly differing characters. Explore the comedy and passion. Stanislavski. Treat audience as part of classes/lecture hall. **Research:** Read *Sex in Mind and in Education* by Henry Maudsley. Look up the history of Girton College. See images.	
	Section or scene(s)	Act 1 Scene 1 with the bicycle, Scene 2 The 4 men. Selected parts of Scene 3, all of Scene 4. Scene 5 MRS WELSH'S monologue. Scene 9 RALPH & TESS. Scene 10 Merits of moral science. Scene 11 An Arrival. Scene 13 An Education. Act 2 Scenes 2, 4, 6 LLOYD'S monologue. Scenes 8, 11 and 12.	

Play 174

	Title & publisher	Our Day Out	Methuen Drama
	Playwright/Date	Willy Russell	1977
	Casting	15M: 7F Very flexible cast. Much reduced with multi-role adult parts	GCSE A range of abilities
	Notes, guidance and considerations for teachers/students	**Description:** Comedy. **Summary:** The story of a school trip for the students of the remedial class: comedy and chaos, full of energy yet haunted by the suggestion that these children have little else to look forward to. **Where:** Liverpool and North Wales. Mainly on a coach between the two, UK. **When:** 1970s. **Themes:** Lack of education and opportunity; respect for authority; poverty and class. **Notes:** A timeless classic, which still has charm and a message. **Design/tech notes:** Fantastic opportunities for set designers. The coach can be as minimal as a set of movable chairs or a slice of a coach. The other scenes – a cafe, the zoo, castle, fairground and a cliff top – can be as challenging as you want. Good LX/FX plots. **Warnings:** Children smoking! **Workshop/rehearsal/ideas/notes:** Hot seating, role on wall, ensemble. Status/pecking order games. **Resources:** Heinemann edition has KS4 notes and study section.	
	Section or scene(s)	Fast moving. Scene 1 LES & CAROL. Scenes 4, 5 and 6. Scenes 14–20, The zoo scenes. Scene 31 Conwy Castle. Scene 32, The beach Scene 35 The cliff top, Final scene. Any combination of scenes to suit your requirements and cast but keep to the sequence! Monologues: Scene 5 BRIGGS *'The boss thought it . . .'* Mrs KAY Scene 31. *'Well I'd suggest'* to *'Factories have closed down'*.	

Play 175

	Title & publisher	Scenes from 68* Years	Methuen Drama
	Playwright/Date	Hannah Khalil	2016
	Casting	16M: 7F	GCE Demanding
	Notes, guidance and considerations for teachers/students	**Description:** Political theatre/black humour. **Summary:** The real human story of the dreams, comedy, sadness and frustrations of daily life in the shadow of the 'separation wall'. **Where:** Palestinian territory. **When:** 1948 to present time. **Themes:** Life under occupation; how the Israeli–Palestinian conflict Impacts upon even the smallest aspects of people's lives. **Notes:** Very busy, fast-paced criss-cross of action/places and characters on a versatile stage. **Design/tech notes:** Minimalist set/props with multiple uses. Good opportunities for design students with projections and SFX. **Warnings:** Strong language in some scenes. Acts of violence and persecution. **Workshop/rehearsal/ideas/notes:** Improvise with ideas and props. **Research:** Gaza strip/war and Palestine. Compare Warsaw ghetto images. A Brechtian approach works with the busy character led scenes.	
	Section or scene(s)	A series of scenes without number. The order must be respected. The opening sequence followed by a selection of scenes chosen according to the skills/needs of the group leading up to the two very final scenes. Monologues: Scene 2016 RULA Page 36 *'Bastana el daw al Akhdar. Waiting . . .'* Scene 2002 page 80. OLD MAN *'Our village stood here . . .'*	

Play 176

	Title & publisher	*Boudica*	NHB
	Playwright/Date	Tristan Bernays	2017
	Casting	18M: 6F	GCSE/GCE Challenging roles
	Notes, guidance and considerations for teachers/students	**Description:** Ancient history play. Feminist theatre. **Summary:** After the death of the King of the Iceni, his widow, Boudica, tried to claim her rightful throne. For defying Rome, the Queen was flogged, her daughters raped, and they were banished from their lands. Boudica has returned looking for revenge and now she has an army! **Where:** Britannia, on the far-flung western borders of the Roman Empire. **When:** 61 CE. **Themes:** Women; history; war; power. **Notes:** This is epic, with battle scenes and a stage awash with Roman blood! However, for the examiner we must consider the beautifully worded dialogues and monologues (some Iambic Pentameter). I saw the fight sequences begin at a slow pace then build both in pace and volume. They worked very well and added to the epic feel of the piece. **Design/tech notes:** Epic but mainly achieved through lighting for exam performance. Good opportunities for props and costume. **Warnings:** Strong language. Carefully choreograph all fight scenes. Weapons training for any used or find another way, for example Slow Mo/lighting/SFX. **Workshop/rehearsal/ideas/notes:** Epic theatre. Choreographed dance/fight. Marc Rees, also Gecko. Ensemble battle sequences. The tension of revenge and war. Brecht.	
	Section or scene(s)	Act 1 Scenes 1, 2, 4. Act 2 Scenes 1, 2, 3 from BOUDICA's entrance. Act 3 Scenes 1, 2 BOUDICA with daughters. Scenes 4, 5. Act 4 Scenes 3, 4, 6 (BLODWYNN & ALONNA) Act 5 Scenes 1, 4, Epilogue. Monologues: Prologue, CLOTHEN Act 2 Scene 3. DRUID Act 3 Scene 1. CATUS Soliloquy Act 4 Scene 2. BLODWYNN Act 4 Scene 6. ALONNA Act 5 Scene 1. BOUDICA then SUETONUS Act 5 Scene 4 Epilogue.	

Play 177

	Title & publisher	*War Horse*	Faber & Faber
	Playwright/Date	Michael Morpurgo Adapted by Nick Stafford	2007
	Casting	28M: 3F (Three or four students will suffice for exam performance in particular)	GCSE/GCE
	Notes, guidance and considerations for teachers/students	**Description:** Stage adaptation of a novel. **Summary:** Young Albert's beloved horse, Joey, is taken by the cavalry and shipped to France at the start of WW1. Albert cannot forget Joey and embarks on a dangerous mission to find him. **Where:** Devon and later the trenches. **When:** WW1. **Themes:** Love; courage; friendship and family; war. **Notes:** For exam purposes I saw this stripped of even the puppet horse. The boy who played Albert spoke to, reacted with and touched a space in front of him and I believed! **Design/tech notes:** No school can compete with the resources of the National Theatre. I have included this play simply because when I saw it performed by a group of four Year 11 boys it reminded me how imaginative students can be and what a beautifully crafted text this is. **Warnings:** Do not try to copy the NT West End phenomenon but do let students experiment with the material. It is well worth it. **Workshop/rehearsal/ideas/notes:** Minimalism, real suspension of disbelief and knowing your students!	
	Section or scene(s)	Scene 2 ALBERT, TED & NED reacting to unseen JOEY. Scene 3 NARRACOTT's farm. Scene 5 including ROSE's monologue. Scene 7 recruitment. Scenes 18, 29 to Black-out.	

Play 178

	Title & publisher	*Dr Faustus*	Methuen Drama
	Playwright/Date	Christopher Marlowe	1529
	Casting	24M: 8F Flexible	GCE/GCSE
	Notes, guidance and considerations for teachers/students	**Description:** Elizabethan tragedy. **Summary:** Doctor Faustus, a scholar, believes he has learned everything he can from the conventional academic disciplines. Dissatisfied, he turns to magic. A Good Angel and an Evil Angel arrive, representing a choice between Christian conscience and damnation. 'Good' advises not to pursue magic, while 'Bad' tempts him. **Where:** Medieval Wittenberg, Germany; Papal palace in Rome; Court and kingdom of Carolus, King of Spain and Holy Roman Emperor. **When:** 16th century. **Themes:** Pride and sin; man's potential and limitations; flesh and spirit; damnation; redemption/salvation and many more! **Notes:** Students usually study the A-text. B-text scenes are included in the appendix. **Design/tech notes:** Marlowe's sets were extravagant in their time, but depending on your chosen interpretation, can be as minimalist as you wish. Levels help, and lighting/projections can be important for location, natural/supernatural. Costume too can be as flamboyant as you wish. Flowing robes of different colours work well. Props can offer some great design challenges, from a fake leg to a horse head or a giant spoon. **Warnings:** Potentially a very large cast. For the exam performance, keep this workable. Some Boards use this as a prescribed text. Check your specification! **Workshop/rehearsal/ideas/notes:** The ensemble should look at the proxemics of status. Developing characters through their physicality. Master/servant games. Music and movement. Berkoff for ensemble/chorus. Lecoq. **Resources:** Firebird Theatre Education through Arts Council England have produced an excellent resource.	
	Section or scene(s)	**Chorus/prologues:** Scene 1 FAUSTUS and the ANGELS. Scene 2. Scene 3. First appearance of MEPHASTOPHILIS. Scene 5 with the ANGELS. Scenes 7, 10, 11, 12, 13. Monologues: FAUSTUS's opening soliloquy Scene 7 *'I cannot repent'* Scene 8 FAUSTUS, and later MEPHASTOPHILIS. Scene 10 the EMPEROR. CHORUS 3. Scene 12 *'Was this the face'...'* Scene 13 FAUSTUS as the watch strikes.	

Play 179

	Title & publisher	*Under Milk Wood*	Samuel French
	Playwright/Date	Dylan Thomas	1954
	Casting	17M: 17F Adaptable/multi-role	GCSE/GCE
	Notes, guidance and considerations for teachers/students	**Description:** Welsh adapted radio play (narrator led). **Summary:** The citizens of a small Welsh town are asleep. The narrator (first voice/second voice) informs the audience that they are witnessing the townspeople's dreams. **Where:** Llareggub, a fictional Welsh town ('Bugger all' reversed!). **When:** 1960s but can be later. **Themes:** Community; village life; time; the sea; relationships; death; secrets; and much more. **Notes:** Described as 'a play for voices'. Pace, pitch, power and pause, not to mention accent, are of heightened importance. **Design/tech notes:** Minimalist with great lighting. **Warnings:** Uses prose, verse and song. **Workshop/rehearsal/ideas/notes:** Very detailed character work. Stanislavski. **Resources:** Visit 'Discover Dylan Thomas education' (https://www.discoverdylanthomas.com/resources/education-2).	
	Section or scene(s)	A good idea is to read through then select characters that appeal to the students. Select scenes/moments with the characters in mind. Monologues: FIRST VOICE, SECOND VOICE.	

Play 180

	Title & publisher	*Fear and Misery of the Third Reich* Methuen Drama
	Playwright/Date	Bertolt Brecht 1935
	Casting	60M: 25F: 3N GCE Multi-role/cross-casting can reduce Or very able GCSE this to six
	Notes, guidance and considerations for teachers/students	**Description:** Brechtian epic theatre. **Summary:** The fear and suspicion of German citizens, in particular Jewish families, in ordinary households during the rise of Hitler and fascism. **Where:** Nazi Germany. **When:** 1930s. **Themes:** Fascism; fear; suspicion; love; politics; defiance. **Notes:** The 24 interconnected playlets can be linked by cast, music, staging and/or narration. **Design/tech notes:** Minimal, white backdrop, projections. Bare stage flooded in bright white light. As few or many props as you need. I suggest a minimalistic approach. **Warnings:** Mild adult themes. **Workshop/rehearsal/ideas/notes:** Brecht. Alienation. Breaking the fourth wall, narration, song. The use of placard and prop. The actor presents the character as a narration. Gestus. Non-naturalism. **Research:** Nazi Germany. The musical *Cabaret*.
	Section or scene(s)	Some scenes work better than others, but these have been used by students with great success. The Jewish Wife (with or without monologue), The Spy. The Black Shoes. The Chalk Cross. Peat Bog Soldiers. Charity Begins at Home. The Sermon on the Mount. Times vary from 2 or 3 minutes to 15. Great opportunities for cross casting and monologues.

Plays with Flexible Casting

Play 181

	Title & publisher	*Adult Child, Dead Child* Methuen Drama
	Playwright/Date	Andy Hamilton and Claire Dowie 1987
	Casting	1: Gender non-specific GCE Can be shared/split Or an able GCSE group
	Notes, guidance and considerations for teachers/students	**Description:** Black comedy/stand-up. **Summary:** The protagonist depicts a life being controlled through excessive discipline and punishment, of hours in a cupboard under the stairs, and a building tension/madness. Their only comfort is an imaginary friend. **Where:** Unspecified, then later in a house in London, UK. **When:** Present covering two years. **Themes:** Mental illness (Schizophrenia); abuse/negligence of children; isolation. **Notes:** Although written as a one-person show, for the purposes of performance it can be sensitively divided. Cast gender is not an issue. **Design/tech notes:** Whatever the script moves you to create. **Warnings:** Disturbing themes. **Workshop/rehearsal/ideas/notes:** Physical theatre. Physicalising feelings/individual words and what they do to the body. Of losing control. **Research:** mental illness (Schizophrenia).
	Section or scene(s)	25 mins read-through and physicalise selected pieces. Powerful dialogue. Respect the order.

Play 182

	Title & publisher	*Mobile Phone Show*	Methuen Drama NT Connections 2013
	Playwright/Date	Jim Cartwright	2013
	Casting	3-100 Flexible casting with no gender specified	GCSE A range of abilities
	Notes, guidance and considerations for teachers/students	**Description:** Youth theatre. **Summary:** Our relationship with the mobile phone and our values. **Where:** Anywhere. **When:** Now. **Themes:** How communication is evolving as the mobile phone evolves; our dependency on them; fitting in and loneliness; instant communication and intelligence. **Notes:** Cartwright really wants a young cast to take ownership of the script and use their imaginations to interpret meaning and movement. An excellent ensemble piece with helpful production notes in the NT Connections copy. **Design/tech notes:** No set at all, or as elaborate as you want! **Technical:** Needs only the mobile but try to involve the latest phone technology. I saw lighting controlled by a phone. Projected live feeds of texting/twitter. Creative use of the phone's torch app. All the performers need is a mobile phone! **Warnings:** Audience participation can get out of hand. Try to have control mechanisms. House lights or projected signs. Phones off/Phones on etc. Do not allow students to share personal numbers with audience. **Workshop/rehearsal/ideas/notes:** Literally anything goes! Use what the students like and experiment with the new. Create as an ensemble but go with ideas! Enjoy!	
	Section or scene(s)	Any, if not all of it. Contains good monologues. Experiment with the chorus and dividing parts. Rap, song, Haiku. 50 mins approx.	

Play 183

	Title & publisher	*Collected Grimm's Tales*	Faber & Faber
	Playwright/Date	Carol Anne Duffy and Tim Supple	2003
	Casting	Varied and flexible according to which tales	GCSE A range of abilities
	Notes, guidance and considerations for teachers/students	**Description:** Stage adaptation. Physical theatre. **Summary:** The tales of the Brothers Grimm. **Where:** Anywhere. **When:** Anytime. **Themes:** Varied, usually carry a moral warning. **Notes:** Some schools choose to present a selection of the ten dramatised stories in the book with small groups of four or five in each. Good when you want to keep the whole class focussed on one theme. Good physical theatre pieces. Great opportunity for shadow puppetry. (Some Boards permit this.) **Design/tech notes:** Minimalist set (works well in the round) and easy to costume. Good work with mask/puppet and eerie backlighting. Musical instruments. **Warnings:** Can be quite horrific. **Workshop/rehearsal/ideas/notes:** The edition used contains two scripts for each tale. Use the uncut Duffy versions as texts for initial reading and rehearsal, then consider the performance texts which resulted from the original work done by Tim Supple. Try for a fusion of both. Emma Rice. Storytelling/Polly Teal, Marianne Elliot. Narration, Physicalisation.	
	Section or scene(s)	15 dramatisations. It is quite possible/desirable to perform two or more stories using the same group of performers. Respect the rhythm and order of the pieces.	

Play 184

	Title & publisher	*Mother Courage and her Children*	Methuen Drama
	Playwright/Date	Bertolt Brecht	1939
	Casting	Large but very flexible M/F cast can be reduced by multi-role	GCE Many varied opportunities
	Notes, guidance and considerations for teachers/students	\multicolumn{2}{l}{Description: Brechtian epic theatre. Summary: A chronicle play of the 30 Years War. MOTHER COURAGE follows the armies selling provisions to the troops with tragic consequences. Where: Various battle sights/camps in Sweden and Northern Europe, Poland. When: 12 years (1624 to 1636), represented in 12 scenes. Themes: Society and class; wealth and warfare; religion; rules, power and corruption. Notes: The use of music/song is essential. Design/tech notes: Minimal, white backdrop, projections. Bare stage flooded in bright white light. A moveable wagon/cart which can double up as a performance/level would be a good tech project. Warnings: Keep to small cast and multi-role. Overcasting will be confusing for an exam performance! Workshop/rehearsal/ideas/notes: Brecht, alienation, breaking the fourth wall, narration, song. The use of placard and prop. The actor presents the character as a narration. Gestus Non-naturalism.}	
	Section or scene(s)	12 scenes. Scene 1 The RECRUITER, MOTHER COURAGE, SERGEANT & ELIF & SWISS CHEESE. Scenes 3, 4, 7, 8, 11, 12 suggested. However, choose scenes according to cast available and numbers. Study the play and select. Respect order.	

Play 185

	Title & publisher	*The Caucasian Chalk Circle*	Methuen Drama
	Playwright/Date	Bertolt Brecht	1944
	Casting	Large but very flexible M/F Cast can be reduced by multi-role	GCSE A range of abilities
	Notes, guidance and considerations for teachers/students	Description: Brechtian epic theatre. Summary: The play is a parable about a peasant girl who rescues a baby and becomes a better mother than its wealthy natural parents. Where: Caucasus mountains, Grusinia, Republic of Georgia. When: Post-WW2. Themes: Justice; law; motherhood; corruption and greed. Notes: The singer acts as stage manager and commentator. Songs can be spoken as a poem if preferred. Design/tech notes: Minimal, white backdrop, projections. Bare stage flooded in bright white light. Warnings: Keep to small cast and multi-role. Overcasting will be confusing for an exam performance! Some Boards use this as a prescribed text. Check your specification! Workshop/rehearsal/ideas/notes: Brecht, alienation, breaking the fourth wall, narration, song, The use of placard and prop. The actor presents the character as a narration. Gestus Non-naturalism. Complicité, Meyerhold.	
	Section or scene(s)	Six scenes. Can concentrate on the play within the play. Read and select with cast. Very flexible. Great opportunities for a range of abilities.	

Play 186

	Title & publisher	*The Resistible Rise of Arturo Ui*	Methuen Drama
	Playwright/Date	Bertolt Brecht	1941
	Casting	Large but very flexible M/F cast can be reduced by multi-role	GCSE or GCE
	Notes, guidance and considerations for teachers/students	**Description:** Satire. **Summary:** Satire in blank verse on the rise of Hitler, set in the grocery business in Chicago and a takeover bid by a small-time gangster. **Where:** Chicago, USA. **When:** Post-WW2 to 1980s. **Themes:** A satirical allegory of the rise of Adolf Hitler and the Nazi Party in Germany prior to WW2; business; crime; deceit; history and corruption. **Notes:** The vast cast can be reduced and scenes omitted but the running order must be respected. **Design/tech notes:** Can be a bare stage with minimal clutter. Large puppets of Hitler, Göring, Goebbels etc., loud and brash as in a circus ring or a fair ground. Noise/light and loud music. Brecht himself wanted performances to have a grand style which if possible reflected elements of the Elizabethan theatre. Proscenium arch stage, curtains etc. Rich with possibilities. **Warnings:** The character of Dogsborough must be strong, powerful and immovable. The gangsters should be as American movie/Al Capone as possible. **Workshop/rehearsal/ideas/notes:** Alienation, breaking the fourth wall, narration, song, The use of placard and prop. The actor presents the character as a narration. Gestus. Non-naturalism, whilst maintaining the stereotypical Chicago gangster. **Research:** Al Capone etc.	
	Section or scene(s)	15 scenes. Announcer (prologue) and epilogue are important. Large monologues/verses. Study/read and select according to students.	

Play 187

	Title & publisher	*The Cheviot, the Stag and the Black, Black Oil*	Methuen Drama
	Playwright/Date	John McGrath	1973
	Casting	Large versatile cast. No protagonists Readers/performers	GCE Able very diverse dramatic styles
	Notes, guidance and considerations for teachers/students	**Description:** Musical/political/historical. **Summary:** The exploitation of the Scottish people. **Where:** A Highland ceilidh, the Highlands of Scotland. **When:** 1700s–1800s land clearance, development of the stag hunts in the 19th century and 1960s–70s North Sea oil boom. **Themes:** Exploitation; nationalism; the role of women; change; the history of the Highlands of Scotland. **Notes:** Performed as a Highland ceilidh, combining live comedy, farce, drama and song, the audience is very much a part of this. Consider your examiner. Could be promenade. **Design/tech notes:** Uses multimedia projections and music. **Warnings:** Adult themes. **Workshop/rehearsal/ideas/notes:** Non-naturalistic, Brechtian, slap and tickle. Symbolism and the Gaelic language. Pay particular attention to the factual readings. Marianne Elliot.	
	Section or scene(s)	The Beginning, (Cheviot) Middle (Stag) End (North Sea oil). Continuous narration and audience address. Study and select according to skills/talents available and passions aroused.	

Play 188

	Title & publisher	*Pool (no water)*	Methuen Drama
	Playwright/Date	Mark Ravenhill	2006
	Casting	Flexible casting	GCE An able imaginative group
	Notes, guidance and considerations for teachers/students	**Description:** Experimental/Physical theatre. **Summary:** An artist invites friends to her home and new pool. A freak accident reveals their very human natures! They come together again for a night of horror and nostalgia. **Where:** Various, house/pool/hospital. **When:** Contemporary. **Themes:** Success and envy; ambition; friendship; art and artists. **Notes:** The lines are not assigned to particular characters or parts. Casting can be very flexible for a group. Works well with 2 male and 2 female, but can be more. **Design/tech notes:** Great set and lighting/projection design opportunities. Set should be fairly uncluttered with easily accessible/visible levels. Needs carefully selected music/song. **Warnings:** Adult themes. The whole piece requires massive energy. **Workshop/rehearsal/ideas/notes:** Artaud/Frantic. Katie Mitchell. Moving imagery, co-existing with the performers' own movement. Carefully consider movement/routines that explore the meaning behind the lines. Use music in rehearsals.	
	Section or scene(s)	How the lines are assigned is part of the process. Some lines are spoken by everyone/shared. Some lines are monologue. Try to highlight the moments of savage/shocking truth as they are exposed, by facial expression, movement, light or music/silence.	

Play 189

	Title & publisher	*Games* and *After Liverpool*	Samuel French
	Playwright/Date	James Saunders	1971
	Casting	Flexible casting (Mainly duologues)	GCE
	Notes, guidance and considerations for teachers/students	**Description:** A suite of pieces. **Summary:** A series of sketches and vignettes. Brief, witty and pointed. *After Liverpool* is not a play, but a suite of pieces. **Where:** Anywhere. **When:** Anytime. **Themes:** Love; the games people play; freedom; responsibility and choice. **Notes:** Published along with *Games*. There is no such thing as the definitive performance. An excellent minimalist tool to get students thinking! **Design/tech notes:** Literally whatever you want. I have stuck to minimalism with my students. **Warnings:** Sexual content and adult language in some sketches. **Workshop/rehearsal/ideas/notes:** I have very successfully used Frantic Assembly with this material but seen it done in many very imaginative ways. Brechtian character work/kitchen sink and mask work. Music works well.	
	Section or scene(s)	There are some shared themes and it is possible to follow a pattern, with each leading to another. Variations and order changes are encouraged. Monologues: W in *After Liverpool*. *Games* part VII.	

Play 190

📖	Title & publisher	*The Mysteries*	Faber & Faber
✏️	Playwright/Date	Tony Harrison	1985
👥	Casting	Flexible casting	GCE Able group
📋	Notes, guidance and considerations for teachers/students	**Description:** Communal mystery plays/ensemble (can be promenade). **Summary:** Creation, the Nativity, the Passion and Doomsday are the Wakefield, York, Chester and Coventry cycles of the Mystery plays. **Where:** Various biblical locations. **When:** From creation to last judgement. Biblical/Medieval. **Themes:** Biblical/Medieval interpretations of the Creation, the Nativity, the Passion and Doomsday. **Notes:** Three cycles in verse. Uses music and song/dance extensively. **Design/tech notes:** Set should be very moveable, with members of the cast responsible for the constant changes. Often done as a piece of promenade theatre. **Warnings:** Pay particular attention to accent and the meter/alliteration of verse. The dialect is part of the heritage of the piece. An example is the 'Whose Tups are these?' song which is sung by the Shepherds in the Nativity. **Workshop/rehearsal/ideas/notes:** Allow students to experiment with the original promenade ideas of moving a piece of theatre through a village. Works well with good ensemble, physical theatre, Berkoff, for example. Strong characters. **Research:** YouTube has most of the original Mysteries at the Cottesloe theatre.	
🎬	Section or scene(s)	*Nativity*. The creation from fanfare to ADAM & EVE & SATAN. CAIN & ABEL. NOAH. ABRAHAM & ISAAC. 3 SHEPHERDS. HEROD & DEATH. *Passion*. JESUS & BLIND MAN. *The Last Supper*. Remorse of JUDAS. JESUS & MINER. *Doomsday*. MARY & JESUS, THE SOULS & DEVILS.	

The Ten Shakespeare Plays

Play 191

📖	Title & publisher	*Twelfth Night* Or *What You Will*	Arden Shakespeare (Performance edition)
✏️	Playwright/Date	William Shakespeare	1601/2
👥	Casting	10M: 3F Plus courtiers and musicians	GCSE/GCE
📋	Notes, guidance and considerations for teachers/students	**Description:** Elizabethan romantic comedy. **Summary:** Twin brother and sister are shipwrecked and separated on the shores of Illyria. They both find their way into love and through mistaken identity and disguise they navigate sub-plots and foolery to a happy ending. **Where:** Fictional land of Illyria. **When:** Can be any time but lends itself to the historical. **Themes:** Love in all its forms; disguise; deception; gender and sexual identity; madness and class. **Notes:** Musical instruments played live are of great significance, if you have the talents in the cast use them! All the main characters in the play are in love at one or more moments in the play. **Design/tech notes:** The costumes you choose are important as a method of disguise and gender identification. However, they can be as sumptuous as the Elizabethan era or as minimalist as you wish. Set and props should be considered carefully. Do not overcomplicate performance space. Lighting and sound opportunities abound. **Warnings:** The complicated plot should not be lost. Take care when selecting scenes. Character led. Some Boards use this as a prescribed performance text. Check your specification! **Workshop/rehearsal/ideas/notes:** Explore the many forms of love. Look at Petrarchan love, sexual identity. Match the action to the words. Character maps. Making meaning. Objective and super objective. Identify mood changes within soliloquy. **Resources:** RSC.	
🎬	Section or scene(s)	Notable soliloquy and monologues: ORSINO'S Act 1 Scene 1. OLIVIA Act 2 Scene 2. MALVOLIO Act 2 Scene 5. Duologues: all meetings between OLIVIA & ORSINO, VIOLA & ORSINO, VIOLA & OLIVIA. FESTE & VIOLA Act 3 Scene 3 the drunken scene in OLIVIA's house. Act 2 Scene 4, Act 4 Scene 2.	

Play 192

🎭	Title & publisher	*King Lear*	Arden Shakespeare (Performance edition)
✏️	Playwright/Date	William Shakespeare	1605
👥	Casting	11M: 3F Plus various servants, soldiers and attendants	GCSE/GCE
📋	Notes, guidance and considerations for teachers/students	**Description:** Tragedy. **Summary:** The story of a king who bequeaths his kingdom to two of his three daughters after they declare their love for him, through fawning love and pandering to his ego. His youngest daughter, however, has other ideas. **Where:** Middle England. **When:** Pre-Christian England. **Themes:** Good vs. evil; law and authority/natural order; old age; madness; love; insight and blindness. **Notes:** Excellent performance opportunities with Lear's madness/schizophrenic spirituality. **Design/tech notes:** Lear's costume should reflect his status (as later he divests himself of this finery). **Warnings:** Complex plot. **Workshop/rehearsal/ideas/notes:** Character study (Stanislavski). Declan Donnellan. Cheek by Jowl. Motivations. Physicality/status games, role on wall. **Resources:** RSC.	
🎬	Section or scene(s)	Act 1 Scene 1. EDMUND'S deception of GLOUCESTER Scene 2. Act 2 Scene 2, Act 3 Scene 4, Act 4 Scene 3, Act 5 Scenes 1, 3. Act 1 Scene 1 CORDELIA *'Unhappy that I am'*. Act 1 Scene 2 EDMUND *'Thou nature art my Goddess'*. Act 2 Scene 4 LEAR *'Oh reason not the need'*. Act 3 Scene 2 LEAR *'Blow winds and crack your cheeks'*.	

Play 193

🎭	Title & publisher	*The Tempest*	Arden Shakespeare (Performance edition)
✏️	Playwright/Date	William Shakespeare	1611
👥	Casting	12+ M 2+ F Flexibility with gender and numbers	GCSE A mixed ability group
📋	Notes, guidance and considerations for teachers/students	**Description:** Comedy (Romantic). **Summary:** Prospero uses his magic to create a storm and torments the shipwreck's survivors, who include his own treacherous brother and the King of Naples. The king's son Ferdinand (who they believe to be dead) falls in love with Prospero's daughter, Miranda. **Where:** An island off the coast of Italy. **When:** 1600s, but works at any moment you want. **Themes:** Magic; betrayal; corruption; forgiveness and love. **Notes:** Casting can be very flexible with gender (note, e.g., Helen Mirren's Prospera!) **Design/tech notes:** Some of the best design work I've ever seen has been in this play! The set, levels and colour/light and SFX, costume and makeup, Caliban, Ariel. **Warnings:** Not all parts need to be filled for exam performance. Some Boards use this as a prescribed text. Check your specification! **Workshop/rehearsal/ideas/notes:** Freeze and step out of the action to focus on specific moments. Character work. Forum Theatre. Let the action match the words! Early rehearsals using costume, mask and SFX. **Research:** Li Tre Satiri, A commedia dell'arte piece. Forbidden Planet and many more. **Resources:** RSC.	
🎬	Section or scene(s)	Act 1 Scenes 2 and 3, Act 2 Scenes 2 and 3, Act 3 Scenes 2 and 3, Act 4 Scene 1, Act 5. Keep cast small and respect order of the play. Selection of scenes should also consider design students' opportunities. Monologues: Act 1 Scene 2 MIRANDA *'If by your art, my dearest father'*. Act 3 Scene 1 FERDINAND *'There be some sports are painful'*. Act 3 Scene 3 ARIEL *'You are three men of sin'*. Act 4 Scene 1 PROSPERO *'Our revels now are ended'*.	

Play 194

	Title & publisher	*A Midsummer Night's Dream*	Arden Shakespeare (Performance edition)
	Playwright/Date	William Shakespeare	1595
	Casting	12M: 4F: 7N Flexible cast	GCSE A range of abilities
	Notes, guidance and considerations for teachers/ students	**Description:** Comedy. **Summary:** Events surrounding the marriage of Theseus, the Duke of Athens, to Hippolyta. The play includes the adventures of four young Athenian lovers and a group of six amateur actors (the Mechanicals) who are manipulated by the fairies who inhabit the forest. A play within a play (Pyramus and Thisbe) is also performed. **Where:** Athens and a forest outside of Athens, Greece. **When:** 12th century, or any time! **Themes:** Love; plays within plays; relationships; ambition and control; the supernatural and dreams. **Notes:** One of Shakespeare's most performed comedies, it is enjoyed by performers, audiences and examiners alike! Many opportunities for high-calibre multi-role. (Theseus and Oberon etc.). Many opportunities for comedy, soliloquy, fighting, dancing and so much more. Music can be important! Try to contrast the city and its formality with the magical/fantasy of the forest. **Design/tech notes:** Works as minimalist with great lighting and tech, or with a lavish set and SFX. **Warnings:** Some Boards use this as a prescribed performance text. Check your specification! A confusing storyline. **Workshop/rehearsal/ideas/notes:** Cicely Berry, resistance exercises. Stanislavski for character. Ways into text page to stage. Match the actions to the words. Cheek by Jowl. **Resources:** RSC.	
	Section or scene(s)	PYRAMUS & THISBE (the play within the play) performed by the Mechanicals is often performed as a piece and can be cross cast. 14–15 mins. OBERON & TITANIA's quarrel, the lovers' fights in the forest and anything involving the Mechanicals. . . . . . Takes as long as you need. Monologues: Act 1 Scene 1 EGEUS '*Full of vexation come I*'. Act 2 Scene 1 TITANIA '*These are the forgeries of jealousy*'. Act 2 Scene 1 PUCK '*I am that merry wanderer of the night*'. Act 2 Scene 1 OBERON '*I know a bank where the wild Thyme blows*' and many more.	

Play 195

	Title & publisher	*The Winter's Tale*	Arden Shakespeare (Performance edition)
	Playwright/Date	William Shakespeare	1609
	Casting	12M: 6F and assorted servants, soldiers and attendants	GCSE A range of abilities
	Notes, guidance and considerations for teachers/ students	**Description:** Comedy (also considered one of Shakespeare's late romances). **Summary:** King Leontes in a fit of jealousy accuses his wife of infidelity. She hides and the king exiles his new-born daughter Perdita to be raised by shepherds. After 16 years she returns and falls in love with Leontes' friend. A statue of Hermione, her mother, comes to life as she returns to her home. **Where:** First part in the Sicilian court of the king and the second in the Bohemian countryside. **When:** Firstly, in a cold winter, and later, in midsummer. **Themes:** Loyalty; fidelity and honesty; suffering and tyranny; forgiveness and resurrection. **Notes:** Dance, music and physical theatre work very well in this piece. **Design/tech notes:** As it contains two different settings and times, costume (winter/summer) and lighting should not be overlooked by design students. Alison Chitty. **Warnings:** Note changes in season. **Workshop/rehearsal/ideas/notes:** Do not be afraid to include the songs/music from the play or step it up with modern pieces. I have seen it done beautifully to U2. Character study, love and jealousy, proxemics. Declan Donnellan/Cheek by Jowl. Character work. Target/motive within the scene. **Research:** *Pandosto* by Robert Greene. The Royal Ballet production and English National Opera for ideas. **Resources:** RSC. See also Cheek by Jowl production.	
	Section or scene(s)	Act 1 Scenes 1, 2 to LEONTES '*Is whispering nothing?*', Act 2 Scenes 1 and 3. Act 3 Scenes 2, 3. Act 4 Scene 1 Time/chorus 16 years passing. Act 5, Scenes 2 and 3. Allow students to experiment with the more physical scenes, using music. Monologues: Act 1 Scene 2 CAMILLO '*My gracious lord, I may be negligent, foolish and fearful*'. Act 3 Scene 2 HERMIONE '*Sir, spare your threats*'. Act 4 Scene 6 PERDITA '*You'd be so lean, that blasts of January*'.	

Play 196

	Title & publisher	*Romeo and Juliet*	Arden Shakespeare (Performance edition)
	Playwright/Date	William Shakespeare	1595
	Casting	16M: 4F	GCSE/GCE
	Notes, guidance and considerations for teachers/students	**Description:** Tragedy. **Summary:** Two star-crossed lovers in (forbidden) love, in spite of an ancient family feud, marry with tragic consequences. **Where:** Verona Italy, but could be anywhere. **When:** The 1300s, but could be any time. **Themes:** Forms of love; love at first sight and its power; fate, marriage and death; violence; conflict between the individual and society/parents. **Notes:** As with any Shakespeare piece, it is vital that performers know the meaning of each word/sentence they utter onstage. Pruning of the text should be done with great care. There are good examples available. Concentrate on characters and how they relate. **Design/tech notes:** As lavish or minimalist as you want! I concentrate on the actions on stage with colour and material highlighting the conflict. Simple stage and lighting. Music/song, live or recorded, works so well with this piece. Try not to be too obvious. **Warnings:** Take care with fight scenes. As with any stage combat, it should be taught and choreographed/managed properly by experts or represented another way. Audiences have massive expectations of certain scenes. Avoid being too cheesy! Some Boards use this as a prescribed performance text. Check your specification! **Workshop/rehearsal/ideas/notes:** Cicely Berry, resistance exercises, Stanislavski for character. Ways into text page to stage. Match the actions to the words. **Resources:** RSC.	
	Section or scene(s)	The opening scene with the Capulets and the Montagues. Looks and sounds great when carefully choreographed. Scenes with the NURSE and ROMEO or JULIET for comedic value. Their first meeting! The fateful comedy leading up to the death of MERCUTIO. Great monologues: FRIAR LAWRENCE. LORD CAPULET and JULIET. ROMEO.	

Play 197

	Title & publisher	*Hamlet*	Arden Shakespeare (Performance edition)
	Playwright/Date	William Shakespeare	1601
	Casting	22M: 2F Flexible with numbers	GCE An able group
	Notes, guidance and considerations for teachers/students	**Description:** Tragedy. **Summary:** Prince Hamlet seeks revenge against his uncle, Claudius, who has murdered Hamlet's father in order to seize his throne and marry Hamlet's mother. **Where:** A castle and grounds, Denmark. **When:** 13th century, but may be any time. **Themes:** Madness; mortality; revenge; love; religion and deceit. **Notes:** A massive play of huge importance. Much quoted and misquoted. There is so much that can be done with this eternal piece of theatre. The fight scenes are very popular with students, as are the many deaths and soliloquies. **Design/tech notes:** Swords, skulls and everything in between! With the set, for me it's minimalism every time, but if you have ambitious design students the opportunities are rich – from castle ramparts, great halls to graveyards and lakes. **Warnings:** The whole play, unabridged, can last over four hours and contains over 4000 lines! **Workshop/rehearsal/ideas/notes:** Literally anything you like. I entered my students in the Shakespeare Schools Festival with a very frantic, 20-minute version which was loved by cast and audiences alike. For exams, choose scenes that are not too overcrowded. Characterisation work is vital. Cheek by Jowl. Declan Donnellan. **Resources:** RSC.	
	Section or scene(s)	Littered with soliloquies/monologues: HAMLET's meeting with his Father's ghost. HAMLET, GERTRUDE & CLAUDIUS Act 1 Scene 2, Act 4 Scene 5, Act 5 Scene 1 in the churchyard, Act 5 Scene 2 everyone dies ... and much more!	

Play 198

	Title & publisher	*As You Like It*	Arden Shakespeare (Performance edition)
	Playwright/Date	William Shakespeare	1600
	Casting	20+M: 5F Flexible and easily reduced	GCSE/GCE
	Notes, guidance and considerations for teachers/students	**Description:** Comedy (pastoral). **Summary:** Forced into exile, lovers Orlando and Rosalind become entangled in love, lust and mistaken identity. **Where:** The French Royal court and then the fictional Forest of Arden, France. **When:** 16th century. **Themes:** The delight of love; the human condition and how malleable humans are; city life vs. country life. **Notes:** As with *A Midsummer Night's Dream*, look to highlight the magic/fantasy and liberation of the forest. **Design/tech notes:** A set which adheres to the pastoral tradition is always very pleasing. Lighting plays an important role. I once saw it work very well on a traverse stage. **Warnings:** As with any play with a large cast, for exams it is best to keep things simple, with good characters and not overcrowding of the space. If done well, the character Jaques is very challenging. **Workshop/rehearsal/ideas/notes:** The pastoral theme lends itself to some great physical/dance/movement work. DV8. Character work. Pay attention to the body language found within the lines of the lovers' exchange.	
	Section or scene(s)	Act 1 Scenes 2 and 3, Act 2 Scenes 1, 2 and 4, Act 3 Scenes 3, 4 and 5, Act 4 Scenes 1 and 3, Act 5 Scenes 1, 2 and 4. Notable duologues: between BEATRICE & BENEDICK. Monologues: Act 2 Scenes 5 and 7 JAQUES. ROSALIND's Epilogue. Also OLIVER, TOUCHSTONE, ORLANDO & PHEBE have numerous great speeches.	

Play 199

	Title & publisher	*Macbeth*	Arden Shakespeare (Performance edition)
	Playwright/Date	William Shakespeare	1606
	Casting	20M: 8F Can be reduced to 5M: 4F main characters	GCSE A range of abilities
	Notes, guidance and considerations for teachers/students	**Description:** Tragedy. **Summary:** The story of an ambitious man who takes some poor advice, resulting in multiple murders and the eventual death of him and his wife. **Where:** Scotland, on a heath and in a castle. Brief scene in England. **When:** 11th century. **Themes:** The corrupting power of ambition; the power of prophesy; masculinity; kingship; fate and free will; appearance and reality. **Notes:** A very busy stage. Don't overcast. Remember the examiner! **Design/tech notes:** Don't let the sets or costumes detract from performances! Vocal quality and physicalisation can bring the witches to stark reality more than the classic witch costume. A red silk cloth held at each corner can be the table for the banquet and have multiple uses throughout. Alison Chitty. **Warnings:** Murder and hauntings. Battle scenes can be epic but for exam performances concentrate on the character work. Witches can be male! **Workshop/rehearsal/ideas/notes:** Join your students in looking for clues in the language. Explore the main themes. Look at the physical effects on a man/woman, of guilt/fear/ambition/ruthlessness. Cheek by Jowl. Physical theatre. Encourage students to make interpretative ensemble choices. Should we see the dagger or the ghost? **Resources:** RSC.	
	Section or scene(s)	The WITCHES upon the heath. MACBETH/BANQUO and later MACBETH alone. MACBETH & LADY MACBETH, any scene post- or pre-DUNCAN. BANQUO and MACBETH. The Banquet. Monologues: Act 1 Scenes 1, 5 LADY MACBETH 'The raven himself is hoarse'. Act 1 Scene 7 'He has almost supped'. Act 5 Scene 5 'Oh life! Disease hath spread to my whole self'. Act 1 Scene 7 MACBETH 'If it were done when 'tis done, then 'twere well'. Act 2 Scene, 1 'Is this a dagger?'. Act 5 Scene 5 'She should have died hereafter'. Look for the thoughts and changes in monologues/soliloquy.	

Play 200

	Title & publisher	*Julius Caesar*	Arden Shakespeare (Performance edition)
	Playwright/Date	William Shakespeare	1599
	Casting	26M: 2F Flexible and easily reduced	GCE An able group
	Notes, guidance and considerations for teachers/students	\multicolumn{2}{l}{**Description:** Tragedy (History). **Summary:** Caesar returns from the war, all-conquering, but mutiny is rumbling through the corridors of power. An epic political tragedy, as the race to claim the empire spirals out of control. **Where:** Rome, Italy. **When:** 42–44 BCE. **Themes:** Ambition; politics; fate vs. free will; interpretation and misinterpretation; public self and private self. **Notes:** As is often the case with Shakespeare, the play has very few female characters. However, scenes for exams can be reduced to 5 or 6 and feature Calpurnia and Portia. **Design/tech notes:** If you only have performers, keep it simple. However, costume is very rewarding and a simple yet effective working set can be a real challenge. **Warnings:** Do not overcast for the exam. Use the basic main characters. Some bloody moments. **Workshop/rehearsal/ideas/notes:** Explore the proxemics of power. Status games. Cicely Berry, resistance exercises. Stanislavski for character. Look for ways from text page to stage. Match the actions to the words. **Resources:** RSC.}	
	Section or scene(s)	\multicolumn{2}{l}{MURELLUS & FLAVIUS Act 1 Scene 1. CASSIUS & BRUTUS Scene 2. Act 2 Scenes 1 and 2, Act 3 Scenes 1 and 2, Act 4 Scene 3. Act 5 Scenes 1, 2, 3 and 5. Monologues: too many to mention, but the best belong to ANTHONY, CASSIUS, CASCA, PORTIA, CALPURNIA, MARULLUS.}	

INDEX OF PLAYS

4.48 Psychosis 51, (play 50)
100 50, 55, 57, (play 75)

A Doll's House 51, 56, 57, 58, 59, (play 101)
A Memory of Lizzie 37, 50, (play 3)
A Midsummer Night's Dream 9, 10, 37, 40, 43, 44, 54, 56, (play 194)
A Taste of Honey 55, (play 80)
A View from the Bridge 56, 59, (play 143)
Abigail's Party 12, 51, 58, (play 72)
Accidental Death of an Anarchist 59, (play 95)
Adrian Mole 13 3/4 7, 37, (play 165)
Adult Child, Dead Child (play 181)
Advice for The Young at Heart 55, (play 54)
After Liverpool and Games 57, (play 189)
Agnes of God 56, (play 4)
An Inspector Calls 49, 51, (play 105)
Andorra 54, (play 151)
Animal Farm 7, (play 110)
Antigone 12, 54, 55, (play 73)
As You Like it 37, (play 198)
At the Black Pig's Dyke 36, 55, (play 139)

Barber Shop Chronicles (play 40)
Bazaar and Rummage (play 14)
Be My Baby (play 13)
Beautiful Burnout 57, 58, (play 118)
Bedroom Farce 18, (play 119)
Beside Herself 10, (play 81)
Billy Liar 54, 55, (play 111)
Biloxi Blues (play 114)
Black Comedy 58, (play 71)
Black Harvest (play 148)

Black Watch 55, 56, (play 39)
Blackout 58, (play 22)
Blood 57, (play 43)
Blood Brothers 15, 36, 50, 56, 59, (play 117)
Blood Wedding (play 149)
Blue/Orange (play 29)
Blue Remembered Hills 10, (play 102)
Blue Stockings (play 173)
Boudica 56, 57, (play 176)
Bouncers 10, 12, 15, 19, 25, 36, 55, 59, (play 31)
Britannia Waves the Rules 59, (play 79)
Bruised 52, 55, (play 92)
Bully Boy 55, (play 28)
Burning Bridges 57, (play 69)
Butcher Butcher Burning Bright (play 121)

Cagebirds (play 17)
Chatroom 19, (play 86)
Children of Killers (play 107)
Christmas is Miles Away (play 49)
Circles (play 52)
Cloud 9 (play 163)
Colder Than Here (play 51)
Confusions 'Mother figure' (play 48)
Cuttin' it (play 2)

Daisy Pulls it off (play 18)
Dancing at Lughnasa 36, 56, (play 113)
Dealer's Choice 52, (play 35)
Death and Dancing 36, 55, 57, (play 44)

INDEX OF PLAYS

Death and the Maiden 25, 36, (play 47)
Di and Viv and Rose (play 5)
Disco Pigs 56, 57, (play 45)
DNA 19, (play 137)
Dr Faustus 49, (play 178)
Dreamjobs (play 12)

Entertaining Mr Sloane 49, (play 53)
Equus 36, 54, 55, (play 112)

Family Planning (play 103)
Fear and Misery of the Third Reich 52, 58, (play 180)
Female Transport 37, 58, (play 134)
Fences (play 106)
Find Me 37, 50, 54, 55, (play 123)
Five Kinds of Silence (play 108)
Four Nights in Knaresborough 19, (play 94)

Ghetto 54, (play 155)
Girls (play 6)
Girls Like That (play 15)
Gone too Far (play 131)
Grimm's Tales 10, 17, 22, 28, 55, 56, (play 183)
Groping for Words 50, (play 62)
Gut Girls (play 96)

Hamlet 43, 44, 50, 51, 55, 57, 58, 59, (play 197)
Hannah and Hanna (play 1)
Hard to Swallow (play 115)
Holloway Jones (play 84)
Hymns 57, 58, (play 33)

Jane Eyre 36, 57, (play 167)
Jerusalem 55, (play 162)
Journey's End (play 38)
Joyriders (play 66)
Julius Caesar 12, 37, 54, 56, 59, (play 200)
Jumpy (play 125)

Kinder Transport 57, (play 85)
King Lear 43, 54, 55, (play 192)
Kvetch 19, 29, 52, 54, 55, 58, 59, (play 78)

La Chunga 54, 57, (play 98)
Language Roulette (play 93)
Leaves (play 70)
Like a Virgin (play 65)
Living with Lady Macbeth (play 153)
Look Back in Anger 55, 59, (play 77)
Lord of the Flies 56, (play 37)
Lovesong 57, 58, (play 57)

Macbeth 10, 37, 40, 41, 42, 43, 44, 50, 54, 55, 57, 59, (play 199)
Metamorphsis 53, 54, 55, 58, (play 76)
Mobile Phone Show (play 182)
Monsters 54, 59, (play 55)
Mother Courage and her Children 19, 37, 58, (play 184)
My Mother Said I Never Should 15, 51, (play 10)

Neville's Island (play 32)
Notes to Future Self (play 8)

Observe the Sons of Ulster 56, (play 36)
Oedipus the King (play 145)
Of Mice and Men 54, 56, (play 138)
Once a Catholic 49, (play 160)
Our Country's Good 7, 22, 56, (play 132)
Our Day Out (play 174)
Oxford Street (play 109)

Paper Flowers 11, 54, 57, (play 42)
People, Places and Things 49, (play 136)
Pigeon English (play 159)
Pink Mist 58, (play 89)
Playhouse Creatures 55, (play 11)
Pool (no water) 54, 55, (play 188)
Private Peaceful (play 23)
Pronoun (play 144)
Punk Rock (play 129)

Refugee Boy (play 158)
Risk (play 83)
Road (play 161)
Romeo and Juliet 43, 44, 49, 50, 54, 58, (play 196)

INDEX OF PLAYS

Rosencrantz and Guildenstern are Dead 3, 56, 57, (play **120**)

Scenes from 68* Years (play **175**)
School Play 36, 58, (play **56**)
Scratching the Surface (play **97**)
Shades 55, (play **90**)
Shakers Re-stirred 12, 55, (play **9**)
Sink the Belgrano 54, 55, 58, (play **82**)
Sparkleshark (play **130**)
Stags and Hens 12, (play **152**)
Stones in His Pockets (play **27**)

Tartuffe (play **133**)
Teechers 7, 12, 53, 55, (play **46**)
That Face 36, 49, 58, (play **63**)
The 39 Steps 19, 52, 54, (play **64**)
The Beauty Manifesto 17, 55, (play **124**)
The Birthday Party 18, 50, 58, (play **100**)
The Caretaker 53, (play **30**)
The Caucasian Chalk Circle 55, 56, (play **185**)
The Cheviot, the Stag and the Black, Black Oil 36, 55, (play **187**)
The Crucible 35, 49, 56, 59, (play **172**)
The Curious Incident of The Dog in the Night-Time 10, 56, (play **140**)
The Duck Variations (play **24**)
The Dumb Waiter (play **25**)
The Exam (play **146**)
The Glass Menagerie 25, (play **59**)
The Government Inspector 37, 55 (play **166**)
The Guffin 57, (play **122**)
The History Boys 58, (play **157**)
The Homecoming (play **99**)
The House of Bernarda Alba (play **20**)
The Importance of Being Earnest 54, 58, (play **127**)
The Long Road (play **74**)
The Madness of Esme and Shaz 57, (play **16**)
The Magdalen Whitewash (play **171**)

The Maids 56, (play **7**)
The Memory of Water 58, (play **91**)
The Mysteries 36, 56, 58, (play **190**)
The Persians 54, 55, (play **67**)
The Pillowman 54, (play **116**)
The Playboy of the Western World (play **150**)
The Resistable Rise of Arturo Ui 35, 59, (play **186**)
The Rover 50, (play **169**)
The Servant of Two Masters 58, (play **128**)
The Static 56, (play **58**)
The Suicide (play **164**)
The Tempest 26, (play **193**)
The Train Driver (play **26**)
The Usual Auntijis 57, (play **68**)
The Winter's Tale 54, 55, (play **195**)
Things I Know to be True 57, (play **87**)
Those Legs (play **88**)
Tomorrow I'll be Happy (play **126**)
Tonypandemonium 55, (play **104**)
Too Fast (play **154**)
Too Much Punch for Judy 55, 57, 59, (play **135**)
Top Girls 55, 56, 57, 59, (play **19**)
Translations (play **141**)
True Brits 57, (play **21**)
Twelfth Night 10, 22, 40, 51, (play **191**)
Two 7, 50, (play **41**)

Under Milk Wood 53, (play **179**)

Virgins 56, 58, (play **61**)
Volpone (play **156**)

Waiting for Godot 51, 57, (play **34**)
Walking with Shadows 22, (play **170**)
War Horse (play **177**)
What are they Like? 52, (play **147**)
Who's Afraid of Virginia Woolf? (play **60**)
Womberang (play **142**)
Woyzeck 51, 54, (play **168**)

INDEX OF PLAYWRIGHTS

Note: Playwrights are referenced by play number.

Addai, Levi David 109
Aeschylus 67
Agbaje, Bola 131
Albee, Edward 60
Almond, Suzy 56
Anderson, Davey 22, 58
Anouilh, Jean 73
Ayckbourn, Alan 48, 119

Bano, Alia 90
Barlow, Patrick 64
Barlow, Steve 167
Beckett, Samuel 34
Behn, Aphra 169
Bennett, Alan 157
Berkoff, Steven 76, 78, 82
Bernays, Tristan 176
Bovell, Andrew 87
Brecht, Bertolt 180, 184, 185, 186
Brenton, Howard 122
Bronte, Charlotte 167
Bucham, Patrick 64
Büchner, Georg 168
Bullmore, Amelia 5
Burke, Gregory 39
Butterworth, Jez 162

Caldwell, Lucy 8, 70
Campton, David 17
Cartwright, Jim 41, 161, 182
Carville, Daragh 93
Churchill, Caryl 19, 163
Clarke, Noel 88
Coxon, Lucinda 147

Daniels, Sarah 16, 81, 96
de Angelis, April 11, 125

Deegan, Denise 18
De-lahay, Rachel 52
Delaney, Shelagh 80
Dorfman, Ariel 47
Dowie, Claire 44, 181
Duffy, Carol Anne 183

El-Bushra, Suhayla 164
Ellams, Inua 40
Erdman, Nikolai 164

Farr, Gareth 79
Firth, Tim 32
Fo, Dario 95
Foxton, David 3
Frantic Assembly 57, 87, 118
Friel, Brian 113, 141
Frisch, Max 151
Fugard, Athol 26

Genet, Jean 7
Godber, John 9, 31, 46
Gogol, Nikolai 166
Golding, William 37
Goldini, Carlo 128
Gooch, Steve 134
Goodwin, Valerie 171
Gray, Nigel 148

Haddon, Mark 140
Hall, Katori 107
Hall, Lee 128
Hall, Willis 111
Hamilton, Andy 181, 146
Harrison, Tony 190
Harvey, Johnathan 126
Heimann, Christoper 75
Hussain, Emteaz 43

INDEX OF PLAYWRIGHTS

Ibsen, Henrik 101
Ikoko, Theresa 6

James, Charlene 2
John, Rob 153
Jones, Graham 12
Jones, Marie 27
Jonson, Ben 156

Kafka, Franz 76
Kane, Sarah 50
Keatley, Charlotte 10
Kelly, Dennis 137
Kelman, Stephen 159
Khalil, Hannah 175

Lavery, Bryony 118
Leigh, Mike 72
Leyshon, Nell 124
Lorca, Federico García 20, 149

McDonagh, Martin 116
McGrath, John 187
McGuiness, Frank 36
Macmillan, Duncan 136
Mamet, David 24
Marber, Patrick 35
Marlowe, Christopher 178
Maxwell, Douglas 154
Miller, Arthur 143, 172
Moliere, Jean-Baptiste 133
Monaghan, Neil 75
Morgan, Abi 57
Morpourgo, Michael 23, 177
Moss, Chloe 49
Myers, Ben 170

Obisesan, Gbolahan 159
O'Connell, Chris 33
O'Malley, Mary 160
Orton, Joe 53
Orwell, George 110
Osborne, John 77

Patel, Vinay 21
Penhall, Joe 29
Petterle, Diene 75
Pielmeier, John 4
Pinter, Harold 25, 30, 99, 100

Placey, Evan 15, 84, 144
Potter, Dennis 102
Priestley, John Boynton 105

Rådström, Niklas 55
Ravenhill, Mark 188
Reade, Simon 23
Reid, Christina 66
Retallack, John 1, 61, 83
Ridley, Philip 130
Russell, Willy 117, 152, 174

Samuels, Diane 85
Saunders, James 189
Schindler, Amy 69
Shaffer, Peter 71, 112
Shakespeare, William 191, 192, 193,
    194, 195, 196, 197, 198, 199, 200
Sheers, Owen 89
Sherriff, Robert Cedric 38
Simon, Neil 114
Sissay, Lemn 158
Skidmore, Steve 167
Sobol, Joshua 155
Sophocles 73, 145
Stafford, Nick 177
Steele, Gordon 65
Stenham, Polly 63
Stephens, Simon 129, 140
Stephenson, Shelagh 74, 91, 108
Stoppard, Tom 120
Supple, Tim 183
Swale, Jessica 173
Synge, John Millington 150

Thomas, Dylan 179
Thornton, Jane 9
Toksvig, Sandi 28
Townsend, Sue 14, 62, 142, 165
Trevannion, Matthew 92
Trezise, Rachel 104

Vickery, Frank 103
Virk, Paven 68

Wade, Laura 51
Walsh, Enda 45, 86
Waterhouse, Keith 111
Webb, Paul 94

INDEX OF PLAYWRIGHTS

Wertenbaker, Timberlake 132
Wheeller, Mark 97, 115, 121, 135
Whittington, Amanda 13
Wilde, Oscar 127
Williams, Nigel 37
Williams, Roy 54
Williams, Tennessee 59

Wilson, August 106
Wolff, Egon 42
Woods, Vincent 139
Wooldridge, Ian 110
Wymark, Olwen 123

Zephaniah, Benjamin 158

www.ingramcontent.com/pod-product-compliance
Lightning Source LLC
Chambersburg PA
CBHW050816160426
43192CB00010B/1781